REVIEW OF RESEARCH IN EDUCATION, 28

REVIEW OF RESEARCH

CONTRIBUTORS

AWO KORANTEMAA ATANDA
PATRICIA GÁNDARA
EUGENE GARCIA
JENNIFER JELLISON HOLME
MARVIN LYNN
RACHEL MORAN
LAURENCE PARKER
ANITA TIJERINA REVILLA
DANIEL G. SOLÓRZANO
WILLIAM F. TATE IV
LINDA C. TILLMAN
AMY STUART WELLS
TARA J. YOSSO

IN EDUCATION
28
2004

ROBERT E. FLODEN
Editor
Michigan State University

PUBLISHED BY THE
AMERICAN EDUCATIONAL RESEARCH ASSOCIATION
1230 Seventeenth Street, NW
Washington, DC 20036-3078

Contents

Introduction: *Brown*'s Influence on Education and Education Research: ix
Critical Insights, Uneven Implementation, and Unanticipated
Consequences

1. From Jim Crow to Affirmative Action and Back Again: 1
   A Critical Race Discussion of Racialized Rationales
   and Access to Higher Education

   Authors: *Tara J. Yosso, Laurence Parker,*
   Daniel G. Solórzano, and Marvin Lynn
   Consulting Editors: *William F. Tate IV and Gloria Ladson-Billings*

2. Legacy of *Brown*: *Lau* and Language Policy in the United States   27

   Authors: *Patricia Gándara, Rachel Moran, and Eugene Garcia*
   Consulting Editors: *Robert Linquanti and Russell Rumberger*

3. How Society Failed School Desegregation Policy: 47
   Looking Past the Schools to Understand Them

   Authors: *Amy Stuart Wells, Jennifer Jellison Holme,*
   Anita Tijerina Revilla, and Awo Korantemaa Atanda
   Consulting Editors: *Jomills Braddock and Vanessa Siddle Walker*

4. African American Principals and the Legacy of *Brown*   101

   Author: *Linda C. Tillman*
   Consulting Editors: *Kofi Lomotey and Rodney T. Ogawa*

5. *Brown*, Political Economy, and the Scientific Education   147
   of African Americans

   Author: *William F. Tate IV*
   Consulting Editors: *William Clune and Frances P. Lawrenz*

Introduction: *Brown*'s Influence on Education and Education Research: Critical Insights, Uneven Implementation, and Unanticipated Consequences

ROBERT E. FLODEN
Michigan State University

In recognition of the 50th anniversary of the Supreme Court's decision in *Brown v. Board of Education* (1954), this volume of *Review of Research in Education* looks at education research linked to issues addressed in that decision. In the *Brown* case, the court asserted the central importance of the government's role in education:

> Today, education is perhaps the most important function of state and local governments. Compulsory school attendance laws and the great expenditures for education both demonstrate our recognition of the importance of education to our democratic society. . . . It is the very foundation of good citizenship. Today it is a principal instrument in awakening the child to cultural values, in preparing him for later professional training, and in helping him to adjust normally to his environment. In these days, it is doubtful that any child may reasonably be expected to succeed in life if he is denied the opportunity of an education.

The court reversed the previous legal doctrine that had permitted "separate but equal" schools for Black and White children, setting the stage for court-ordered school desegregation in the decades to follow. The chapters in this volume recognize the tremendous significance of the *Brown* decision and the subsequent "Brown II" decision (1955), in which the court laid out principles for the manner and timing of compliance with the order for the elimination of segregated schools. But these chapters also discuss research that has looked at both the limits on the effects of the decision and the ways in which the decision had unintended consequences that undercut the quality of education for children from minority groups.

The *Brown* decisions also set precedents for the use of social science evidence in U.S. legal processes. Kenneth Clark's (1950) psychological research on the effects of racial discrimination on children's self-concept was among the work cited by the Supreme Court to support the claim that segregation affected motivation and educational development. Chapters in this volume examine connections between social science (including education research) and education policy, looking at the ways in which issues of race are addressed by research and shape the topics and methods of research.

In outlawing segregated schools, the *Brown* decision was intended to address the harmful consequences of racial discrimination and prejudice. Yosso, Parker, Solórzano, and Lynn, in their chapter in this volume, consider research that describes changes in racial discrimination, arguing that Brown brought important changes but that discrimination has continued, often in forms that are more subtle but still damaging. Their chapter's central concept is "critical race theory," a framework that originated in legal scholarship but has been widely applied within education research. Since the ideas of critical race theory were introduced into education research a decade ago, these ideas have been used to provide new perspectives on education policies and practices. In contrast or contradiction to the views of mainstream academia, critical race theory introduces "counterstories" that offer different interpretations. The chapter brings the discussion back to the Supreme Court with a consideration of the recent decisions around affirmative action in admission to higher education.

The 50th anniversary of *Brown* was also the 30th anniversary of another landmark education decision handed down by the Supreme Court. In the *Lau v. Nichols* (1974) decision, the court established the right of children from language minority groups to have equal educational opportunities. As with the *Brown* decision, the general principle supported equal educational opportunity for children from minority groups, but the implementation of the decision has proved to be complicated. In their chapter, Gándara, Moran, and Garcia review research on the historical development of policies following *Lau*, with attention to the role that education research has played in policy debates. In the wake of *Lau*, competing models for educating English language learners have been developed, debated, and studied, with results that have often been further debated. The authors argue that legislative and judicial decisions have undercut the gains that *Lau* seemed to promise.

The *Brown* decision was based in part on social science findings regarding the damaging consequences school segregation had for the education of Black children. Subsequent social science studies, starting with Coleman's national survey (Coleman et al., 1966), attempted to describe the connections between student achievement and a broad range of school characteristics. In their chapter, Wells, Holme, Revilla, and Atanda examine several lines of research on the connections between student achievement and school characteristics, noting both contributions and limitations of each line of work. Their central criticism of past research is that it typically focused little attention on the ways in which broader political and social contexts shape the effectiveness of schools. Thus, the literature yielded inconsistent results, with pendulum swings from characterizations of schools as impotent to views of them as solely responsible for improving student achievement. An examination of the literature on the effects of school desegregation shows a similar pattern, with individual studies yielding information about particular aspects of the effects of desegregation but most studies limited by important omissions, whether insufficient attention to broad contexts, neglect of the particular ways in which desegregation was carried out, or use of only self-reported attitudinal data. The authors conclude with some initial results from their own study of six desegregated high schools that addressed the major design weaknesses of prior research. Their work shows that school desegregation made important contributions to fostering equal educational opportunity but fell short of the hopes many had for the *Brown* decision. Moreover, their findings reveal how the local political and social contexts of these schools influenced the particular ways in which desegregation had its effects.

The *Brown* decision affected both students and those who educated them. Tillman argues that insufficient attention has been paid to *Brown*'s effects on African American school administrators. Although the system of separate, segregated schools comprised many African American schools with inadequate resources, that system also included African American segregated schools that had committed administrators and teachers achieving remarkable results. The *Brown* decision altered the roles played by African American school leaders both by creating new positions in the desegregated schools and by decreasing the centrality of schools within the African American community. Tillman draws on the literature on Black school administrators, including many case studies of outstanding school principals, to sketch ideas about a different model of effective school leadership. Echoing the earlier chapter on critical race theory, Tillman presents counternarratives that offer alternative views of effective school leadership, including a greater emphasis on the educational development of Black pupils, resistance to repressive ideologies, cultural congruence, and caring as leadership qualities.

In this volume's final chapter, Tate explores post-*Brown* interconnections between scientific knowledge and African American education. He looks at scientific knowledge as a domain of student achievement, as a content area within the U.S. curriculum, and as a tool for affecting education policy. He argues that science, broadly construed to include mathematics, has a particularly important status among the domains of knowledge, controlling access to further educational opportunities and to preparation for high-status, high-income occupations. Thus, research on African American students' science achievement deserves special attention. The importance of an understanding of science has gained additional significance as science has begun to influence political and legal matters. Both this chapter and earlier chapters stress that the *Brown* decision broke new ground in judicial attention to scientific results.

The chapters in this volume show how research on a variety of topics repeats the theme that the *Brown* decision was instrumental in school desegregation but that the consequences of the decision include some unanticipated losses in addition to the gains for minority groups. African American schools before *Brown* lacked material resources but often drew on community resources to make good use of what they had. The connections to these resources have sometimes been weakened or broken in the redistribution of students and educators across schools. In the case of *Brown*, as well as in the *Lau* decision regarding students from language minority groups, some of the anticipated gains have been lost in implementation. The legal system has a greater ability to change overt practices than to change attitudes. As a result, some forms of discrimination have shifted from overt to subtle. Likewise, some school desegregation implementations were minimally compliant, reducing the chances for noticeable improvements in education.

The *Brown* decision was also significant in regard to its use of social science evidence. In the subsequent decades, social science, including education research, has maintained some visibility in policy debates. With hindsight, we can see limitations of the most visible research, as well as the often loose links between research and policy. Education remains one of the most important functions of state and local governments. Since the time of the *Brown* decision, education has become a more important function of the federal government as well. The current emphasis on evidence-based policy offers new opportunities for a fruitful conjunction between research and policy, making it all the more important to address the weaknesses of earlier studies.

REFERENCES

Brown v. Board of Education, 347 U.S. 483 (1954).

Brown v. Board of Education, 349 U.S. 294 (1955).

Clark, K. B. (1950). *The effects of prejudice and discrimination on personality development.* Washington, DC: Federal Security Agency.

Coleman, J. S., Campbell, E. Q., Hobson, C. J., McPartland, J., Mood, A. M., Weinfeld, F. D., & York, R. L. (1966). *Equality of educational opportunity.* Washington, DC: U.S. Government Printing Office.

Lau v. Nichols, 414 U.S. 563 (1974).

Chapter 1

From Jim Crow to Affirmative Action and Back Again: A Critical Race Discussion of Racialized Rationales and Access to Higher Education

TARA J. YOSSO
University of California, Santa Barbara
LAURENCE PARKER
University of Illinois at Urbana-Champaign
DANIEL G. SOLÓRZANO
University of California, Los Angeles
MARVIN LYNN
University of Maryland at College Park

In order to get beyond racism, we must first take account of race. (Blackmun, 1978, cited in *Bakke v. Regents of the University of California*, 438 U.S. 265, 407)

Without Affirmative Action it's segregation all over again. What's next, a Jim Crow Law? (African American female high school student, in letter to Judge Friedman, February 9, 2001)[1]

As part of his 1978 opinion in the *Bakke v. Regents of the University of California* case, Justice Blackmun's quotation speaks to the persistence of "problem of the color line" that W. E. B. DuBois identified in 1903. In a letter to Judge Friedman of the U.S. 6th District Court in Detroit, Michigan, the African American high school student's remarks express her worry that the courts will eliminate the single policy in education that aims to account for race. Her comments refer to the University of Michigan's race-conscious admission policy, challenged at the undergraduate and law school levels by White female candidates denied admission to the selective campus (see *Gratz v. Bollinger*, 2003; *Grutter v. Bollinger*, 2003). Taken together, these quotations reveal the "color-line problem" that undergirds affirmative action debates in higher education.

Indeed, U.S. schools continue to limit equal educational access and opportunity based on race (Kozol, 1991; Lewis, 2003). Students of color remain severely underrepresented in historically White colleges and universities, and the few granted access to these institutions often suffer racial discrimination on and around campus (Lawrence & Matsuda, 1997; Smith, Altbach, & Lomotey, 2002; Solórzano, Ceja, & Yosso, 2000). Insidiously usurping civil rights language and ignoring the historical and contemporary realities of communities of color, opponents of affirmative

1

action claim that accounting for race in higher education discriminates against Whites. This ahistorical reversal of civil rights progress injures students of color under the guise of a color-blind, race-neutral meritocracy. Fifty-one years have passed since the Supreme Court declared that educational opportunity "is a right which must be made available to all on equal terms" (*Brown v. Board of Education*, 1954, p. 493), yet, as noted by Derrick Bell (1987), "we are not saved."

In this chapter, we outline critical race theory (CRT) as an analytical framework that originated in schools of law to examine and challenge the continuing significance of race and racism in U.S. society. We then describe the CRT framework within the field of education. CRT scholarship offers an explanatory structure that accounts for the role of race and racism in education and works toward identifying and challenging racism as part of a larger goal of identifying and challenging other forms of subordination. Next, with the historical backdrop of *Brown v. Board of Education* (1954), we address the debates over affirmative action in higher education evidenced in *Bakke v. Regents of the University of California* (1978) and *Grutter v. Bollinger* (2003).

BRIEF INTRODUCTION TO CRITICAL RACE THEORY

CRT draws from and extends a broad literature base of critical theory in law, sociology, history, ethnic studies, and women's studies. In the late 1980s, various legal scholars felt limited by work that separated critical theory from conversations about race and racism. These scholars sought "both a critical space in which race was foregrounded and a race space where critical themes were central" (Crenshaw, 2002, p. 19). Mari Matsuda (1991) defined that CRT space as "the work of progressive legal scholars of color who are attempting to develop a jurisprudence that accounts for the role of racism in American law and that [works] toward the elimination of racism as part of a larger goal of eliminating all forms of subordination" (p. 1331).

CRT emerged from criticisms of the critical legal studies (CLS) movement. CLS scholars questioned the role of the traditional legal system in legitimizing oppressive social structures. With this insightful analysis, CLS scholarship emphasized critique of the liberal legal tradition as opposed to offering strategies for change. Some scholars asserted that the CLS approach failed because it did not account for race and racism, and this failure restricted strategies for social transformation (Delgado, 1995a; Ladson-Billings, 1998). They argued that CLS scholarship did not take into account the lived experiences and histories of those oppressed by institutionalized racism. Critical race theorists began to pull away from CLS because the critical legal framework restricted their ability to analyze racial injustice (Crenshaw, 2002; Crenshaw, Gotanda, Peller, & Thomas, 1995; Delgado, 1989; Delgado & Stefancic, 2000a).

Initially, CRT scholars focused their critique on the slow pace and unrealized promise of civil rights legislation and articulated their critiques of ongoing societal racism in Black and White terms. Women and people of color asserted that many of their gendered, classed, sexual, immigrant, and language experiences and histories could not be fully understood by the Black/White binary (Williams, 1991). They noted that a two-dimensional discourse limits understandings of the multiple ways African Americans, Native Americans, Asian/Pacific Islanders, Chicana/os, and Latina/os continue to experience, respond to, and resist racism and other forms of oppression (see Delgado & Stefancic, 1993, 1995; Harris, 1993).

For example, women of color challenged CRT to address feminist critiques of racism and classism through FemCrit theory (see Caldwell, 1995; Wing, 1997, 2000). Latina/o critical race (LatCrit) scholars highlighted layers of racialized subordination based on immigration status, sexuality, culture, language, phenotype, accent, and surname (see Arriola, 1997, 1998; Johnson, 1999; Montoya, 1994; Stefancic, 1998; Valdes, 1997, 1998). Over the years, the CRT family tree expanded to incorporate the racialized experiences of women, Latina/os, Native Americans, and Asian Americans. Branches of CRT such as LatCrit, TribalCrit, and AsianCrit evidence an ongoing search in Chicana/o, Latina/o, Native American, and Asian American communities for a framework that addresses racism and its accompanying oppressions (see Brayboy, 2001, 2002; Chang, 1993, 1998; Chon, 1995; Delgado, 1998; Espinoza, 1998; Espinoza & Harris, 1998; Gee, 1997, 1999; Ikemoto, 1992; Perea, 1998; R. Williams, 1997). In addition, White scholars expanded CRT with WhiteCrit, by "looking behind the mirror" to expose White privilege and challenge racism (see Delgado & Stefancic, 1997).

Rooted in the scholar-activist traditions found in ethnic and women's studies and informed by theoretical models such as Marxism, internal colonialism, feminisms, and cultural nationalism, today's CRT offers a dynamic and evolving analytical framework. Scholarship originating from CRT's roots and branches recognizes the limits of social justice struggles that omit or silence the multiple experiences of people of color.

OUTLINING CRITICAL RACE THEORY IN EDUCATION

In 1995, Gloria Ladson-Billings and William Tate (1995) introduced CRT to the field of education. Since then other scholars in education, social sciences, and humanities have informed the critical race movement in this area (see Aguirre, 2000; Dixson & Rousseau, 2005; Lopez & Parker, 2003; Lynn & Adams, 2002; Lynn, Yosso, Solórzano, & Parker, 2002; Parker, Deyhle, Villenas, & Crossland, 1998; Solórzano, 1997, 1998; Solórzano & Delgado Bernal, 2001; Solórzano & Villalpando, 1998; Tate, 1994, 1997).[2] For at least the past decade, CRT scholars in education have theorized, examined, and challenged the ways in which race and racism shape schooling structures, practices, and discourses.[3] These scholars and practitioners place special emphasis on understanding how communities of color experience and respond to racism as it intersects with other forms of subordination in the U.S. educational system. Daniel Solórzano (1997, 1998) identified five tenets of CRT in education, as follows

1. *Intercentricity of race and racism with other forms of subordination:* CRT starts from the premise that race and racism are central, endemic, permanent, and a

fundamental part of defining and explaining how U.S. society functions (Bell, 1992; Russell, 1992). CRT acknowledges the inextricable layers of racialized subordination based on gender, class, immigration status, surname, phenotype, accent, and sexuality (Collins, 1986; Crenshaw, 1991, 1993; Valdes, McCristal-Culp, & Harris, 2002).

2. *Challenge to dominant ideology:* CRT challenges White privilege and refutes the claims that educational institutions make toward objectivity, meritocracy, color-blindness, race neutrality, and equal opportunity. CRT argues that traditional claims of "objectivity" and "neutrality" camouflage the self-interest, power, and privilege of dominant groups in U.S. society (Bell, 1987; Calmore, 1992; Delgado, 2003a; Solórzano, 1997).

3. *Commitment to social justice:* CRT's social and racial justice research agenda exposes the "interest convergence" of civil rights gains in education (Bell, 1987; Taylor, 2000) and works toward the elimination of racism, sexism, and poverty, as well as the empowerment of people of color and other subordinated groups (Freire, 1970, 1973; Lawson, 1995; Solórzano & Delgado Bernal, 2001).

4. *Centrality of experiential knowledge:* CRT recognizes the experiential knowledge of people of color as legitimate, appropriate, and critical to understanding, analyzing, and teaching about racial subordination (Delgado Bernal, 2002). CRT draws explicitly on the lived experiences of people of color by including such methods as storytelling, family histories, biographies, scenarios, parables, *cuentos*, *testimonios*, chronicles, and narratives (Bell, 1987, 1992, 1996; Carrasco, 1996; Delgado, 1989, 1993, 1995a, 1995b, 1996; Delgado Bernal & Villalpando, 2002; Espinoza, 1990; Love, 2004; Montoya, 1994; Olivas, 1990; Solórzano & Delgado Bernal, 2001; Solórzano & Yosso, 2000, 2001a, 2002b; Villalpando, 2003; Yosso, 2005).

5. *Transdisciplinary perspective:* CRT extends beyond disciplinary boundaries to analyze race and racism within both historical and contemporary contexts (Calmore, 1997; Delgado & Stefancic, 2000b; Gotanda, 1991; Gutiérrez-Jones, 2001; A. Harris, 1994; Olivas, 1990).

We conceive of CRT as a social justice project that works toward realizing the liberatory potential of schooling (Freire, 1970, 1973; hooks, 1994; Lawrence, 1992). Many in the academy and in community organizing, activism, and service who look to challenge social inequality will most likely recognize the tenets of CRT as part of what, why, and how they do the work they do. Indeed, these five themes are not new, but collectively they challenge the existing modes of scholarship in education. Guided by these tenets, we define CRT in education as an analytical framework that examines and challenges the effects of race and racism on educational structures, practices, and discourses.

Each of the scholarly and activist traditions included in Figure 1—ethnic studies, women's studies, multicultural education, and critical pedagogy—inform our

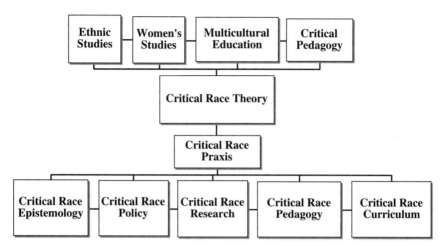

FIGURE 1   Genealogy of Critical Race Theory in Education

CRT framework in education. CRT draws on the strengths these traditions bring to the study of race and racism both in and out of schools. CRT also learns from the blind spots of some of these academic traditions (e.g., the tendency to decenter race and racism in multicultural education and critical pedagogy; see Sleeter & Delgado Bernal, 2002). As Figure 1 indicates (see Yosso, 2005), we acknowledge the scholarly and activist traditions in education and in ethnic and women's studies found in the roots and branches of CRT in the legal field. With the power of historical hindsight and the strength of multiple intellectual and community traditions, we engage CRT as a framework that shapes our praxis (our theoretically informed practice).

Figure 1 also shows epistemology, policy, research, pedagogy, and curriculum as five branches of education informed by CRT. For example, scholars such as Dolores Delgado Bernal (1998, 2002) and Gloria Ladson-Billings (2000, 2003) look to the work of Black and Chicana feminist theorists to examine how race and gender shape knowledge and to conceptualize a critical race epistemology. Similarly, critical race scholars interrogate racism within "race-neutral" schooling policies to examine how educational administrators might engage critical race policy and leadership in secondary and postsecondary education (e.g., Lopez, 2003; Villalpando & Parker, in press).

Over the past decade, most CRT discussions in education publications have focused on critical race research. In particular, scholars have engaged the tenets of CRT to conduct qualitative research designed to identify and challenge the subtle as well as overt forms of racism experienced by students of color (DeCuir & Dixson,

2004; Duncan, 2002a, 2002b, 2005; Fernandez, 2002; Solórzano, Ceja, & Yosso, 2000). They have also questioned the racialized stereotypes embedded in teaching practices (Solórzano, 1997; Solórzano & Yosso, 2001b). Drawing on Paulo Freire's critical pedagogy, they have asserted that a critical race pedagogy can empower marginalized students and teachers of color and help prepare future teachers to engage in education as a liberatory project (e.g., Iseke-Barnes, 2000; Ladson-Billings & Tate, 1995; Lynn, 1999, 2002; Solórzano & Yosso, 2001c). Moreover, extending on ethnic and women's studies traditions, critical race scholars have exposed the ways in which curriculum structures, practices, and discourses tend to omit and distort the histories of people of color and restrict students of color from accessing higher education. They suggest the need to transform schools with a critical race curriculum (e.g., Jay, 2003; Yosso, 2002).

Alongside a growing number of scholars across the country, critical race scholars are asking at least four questions about race and education:

- How do racism, sexism, classism, and other forms of subordination shape institutions of education?
- How do educational structures, practices, and discourses maintain race-, gender-, and class-based discrimination?
- How do students and faculty of color respond to and resist racism, sexism, classism, and other forms of subordination in education?
- How can education become a tool to help end racism, sexism, classism, and other forms of subordination (Montoya, 2002)?

In the remainder of this chapter, we discuss the first two questions in relation to debates over affirmative action in higher education.

CHALLENGING RACISM IN TRADITIONAL ACADEMIC STORYTELLING

At least three legal rationales—color-blind, diversity, and remedial—attempt to explain the need to eliminate or maintain affirmative action. Conservatives challenge affirmative action based on a color-blind rationale, insisting that race-neutral admission policies ensure meritocratic, fair access to higher education. Liberals defend affirmative action policies based on a diversity rationale, arguing that bringing underrepresented minority students into historically White institutions enriches the learning environment for White students. The third or remedial rationale asserts that universities must take affirmative action and grant members of historically underrepresented racial minority groups access to institutions of higher learning as a partial remedy for past and current discrimination against communities of color in general and students of color in particular.

Race, racism, and White privilege shape each of these rationales. Ian Haney Lopez (1996) and other critical race scholars (Harris, 1993; Higginbotham, 1992) define race as a socially constructed category created to differentiate groups primarily on the basis of skin color, phenotype, ethnicity, and culture for the purpose of showing the superiority or dominance of one group over another. The social meanings applied to race are based on and justified by an ideology of racism. We define racism as (a) a false belief in White supremacy that handicaps society, (b) a system that upholds Whites as superior to all other groups, and (c) the structural subordination of multiple racial and ethnic groups (see Lorde, 1992; Marable, 1992; Pierce, 1995). With its macro and micro, interpersonal and institutional, and overt and subtle forms, racism is about institutional power, and communities of color in the United States have never possessed this form of power.

The systemic oppression of communities of color privileges Whites. We define White privilege as a system of advantage resulting from a legacy of racism and benefiting individuals and groups on the basis of notions of whiteness (Leonardo, 2004; McIntosh, 1989; Tatum, 1997). Legal White privilege can also be viewed from a CRT perspective as a form of property right that supersedes the rights of persons of color in terms of the federal courts' failure to consistently provide remedy for past government-sanctioned discrimination in the form of slavery (with African Americans) and violation of treaty rights in regard to land acquisition (with Tribal Nation Indians; see Harris, 1993). Whiteness intersects with forms of privilege based on gender, class, phenotype, accent, language, sexuality, immigrant status, and surname (Carbado, 2002).

Color-Blind Rationale

As a system of advantage, White privilege supports the construction of "color-blind" stories about race in higher education. CRT scholars refer to stories that uphold White privilege as "majoritarian stories" (Delgado, 1993). Majoritarian stories claim to be race neutral and objective, yet they implicitly make race-based assumptions and form race-based conclusions. For example, majoritarian stories of affirmative action claim that "unqualified" students of color receive "racial preferences" at the expense of "qualified" White students. In this story, all students in the United States compete for university admission on a level playing field, and as a result of raced-based preferences White students are denied admission to universities because underqualified Black or Latina/o students "take" their rightful spot.

The majoritarian storyteller recalls history selectively, minimizing past and current racism against communities of color, disregarding obviously unequal K–12 schooling conditions that lead to minimal college access, and dismissing the hostile campus racial climates that many students of color endure at the college level. Majoritarian storytellers advocate for "color-blind" or "race-neutral" admission policies.

Diversity Rationale

Well-intentioned affirmative action diversity advocates inadvertently support majoritarian stories because they do not acknowledge the historical and ongoing racism that shapes the experiences of students of color. Advocates of the diversity rationale urge universities to engage in affirmative action to ensure a diverse learning environment at historically White institutions. In this scenario, admitting qualified students of color and White female students adds to the diversity of the college learning environment. Admissions officers then consider race and gender as "plus" factors in deciding between multiple highly qualified candidates.

Advocates argue that the diversity rationale involves at least three benefits: (a) cross-racial understanding that challenges and erodes racial stereotypes, (b) more dynamic classroom discussions, and (c) better preparation for participating in a diverse workforce (see *Grutter v. Bollinger*, 2003). Because of the resistance to enrolling students of color in historically White institutions, the diversity rationale articulates these benefits in relation to White students. The unquestioned majoritarian story within this rationale is that students of color are admitted so that they can help White students become more racially tolerant, liven up class dialogue, and prepare White students for getting a job in a multicultural, global economy. How this scenario enriches the education of students of color remains unclear. Seemingly, students of color benefit from merely being present at a predominantly White institution and attending college with White students. The university "adds" their presence so that students of color in turn will "add" diversity to the campus.

Remedial and Community Service Rationale

In the remedial rationale, race-based affirmative action is used as a *remedy to compensate* for past and current racial discrimination against students of color. Extending this argument, the community service rationale asserts that universities include race in their admissions policies to (a) improve the delivery of social services to underserved minority communities in the areas of health care, legal services, education, business, government, and political representation; (b) develop a leadership pool in the minority community; and (c) provide role models for minorities in these communities. Many civil rights activists of the 1960s and 1970s unapologetically asserted these remedial and service rationales as the grounds for race-based affirmative action. Where did these two diverging rationales (i.e., diversity and remedial) come from? Do they link to an earlier time in civil rights history? In attempting to find the connection to the past, we look to the 1954 *Brown v. Board of Education* Supreme Court case.

Brown v. Board of Education

In the 1954 *Brown* case, the Supreme Court unanimously ruled that separate educational facilities were inherently unequal and ruled this arrangement unconstitutional but did not offer a timetable for school districts to desegregate their schools. In 1955, in *Brown II*, the Supreme Court provided its answer and directed schools to desegregate "with all deliberate speed." These four words gave school districts in both the North and the South the mandate to focus their desegregation efforts on the word "deliberate," thus slowing desegregation to a crawl.

Grounded in an integration rationale, this ruling emphasized that Black students should be allowed to attend school with White students. In *Brown*, integrated or desegregated education took precedence over equal education. In other words, the integration rationale prioritized Black students attending school with White students and seemingly presumed that this desegregation would translate into equal education for Black students. With this historical backdrop, we move forward 24 years to the 1978 *Bakke v. Regents of the University of California* case to ascertain whether and how rationales for equal educational opportunity have changed.

Bakke v. Regents of the University of California

With Title VI of the 1968 Civil Rights Act, the federal government granted colleges and universities the authority to take affirmative action in setting goals and timetables to remedy the racial discrimination found in U.S. society. Less than 10 years later, as the numbers of students of color and women admitted to universities began to increase, the University of California at Davis Medical School denied admission to a White male applicant, Allen Bakke.

In line with affirmative action guidelines, and in an effort to begin to desegregate its medical school, UC Davis had set aside 16 of its 100 slots for underrepresented minority students. Bakke believed his denial to medical school occurred because of this racially conscious admission policy. Lawyers for Bakke argued that setting aside those 16 slots violated their client's 14th Amendment right to equal protection. Subsequently, Bakke filed a class action lawsuit arguing that UC Davis' use of race in its admissions racially discriminated against Whites. In the *Bakke* (1978) case, the Supreme Court issued two rulings. In the first, 5–4 decision, the court ruled that preferential racial quotas in the form of 16 admission slots set aside for Blacks, Latinos, and Native Americans violated the Civil Rights Act of 1964, which prohibited discrimination based on race, color, or national origin. In a second de facto majority decision referred to as the Powell Compromise, five justices ruled that race could be used as one factor in setting up affirmative action admission programs.

However, in a series of dissents, four Supreme Court justices (Brennan, White, Marshall, and Blackmun) challenged the first majority opinion (i.e., eliminating quotas) and asserted a remedial rationale: "Where there is a need to overcome the effects of past racially discriminatory or exclusionary practices engaged in by a federally funded institution, race-conscious action is not only permitted but required to accomplish the *remedial* objectives of Title VI" (*Bakke v. Regents of the University of California*, 1978, italics added). Although challenged in both federal and state courts, the Bakke majority and Justice Powell's compromise have remained the affirmative action law of the land since 1978. In 2003, the U.S. Supreme Court upheld the *Bakke* diversity opinion with the *Grutter v. Bollinger* University of Michigan Law School affirmative action case.

Grutter v. Bollinger

Three parties were involved in the *Grutter* litigation: (a) the plaintiff, Barbara Grutter, a White female applicant placed on the wait list and ultimately denied admission to the University of Michigan Law School; (b) the defendant, Lee Bollinger, the past president of the University of Michigan and former dean of the university's law school; and (c) the "student intervenors," a group that included 41 Black, Chicano/a, Latino/a, Asian American, and other students (high school, college, and University of Michigan law students). The plaintiffs claimed that the University of Michigan's race-conscious admission policy discriminated against "more qualified" White applicants such as Grutter. The university defended its use of race in admissions, arguing that the policy of considering race furthered its goal of realizing the benefits of a diverse student body. The student intervenors—representing a third party rarely included in affirmative action cases—defended the use of race in admissions as a policy necessary to maintain the limited presence of students of color in higher education and to remedy past and current racial and gender discrimination at the University of Michigan. In the end, the Supreme Court, in a 5–4 decision, ruled that the University of Michigan Law School's race-based admissions program was constitutional on the basis of the diversity rationale.

Critical Race Counterstories in Higher Education

Critical race counterstories recount the experiences of socially and racially marginalized people. Counterstories challenge discourse that omits and distorts the experiences of communities of color. While legal remedies avoid taking them into consideration, we assert that critical race counterstories centered on the voices and knowledge of communities of color should be taken into account in higher education policy and practice. Indeed, counterstories can expose, analyze, and challenge the traditional stories of racial privilege often repeated in the halls of academia. Counterstories relating the histories and lived experiences of students of color can help strengthen traditions of social, political, and cultural survival and resistance.

Community histories documented by scholars such as Monica White (2002) and Jerome Morris (2004) function as critical race counterstories outlining the failings of *Brown*. This research shows how the integration rationale led to the closing of multiple all-Black schools in the South and to the displacement of many Black students, teachers, and principals. Instead of desegregation heralding in opportunities for equal education, these scholars explained that many Black communities experienced desegregation as a disruptive and often violent process. White and Morris concluded that desegregation became a long-term detriment to many Black communities.

Indeed, W. E. B. DuBois forewarned, 19 years before the *Brown* decision, the importance of equal schooling versus unequal, integrated schooling:

There is no magic, either in mixed schools or in segregated schools. A mixed school with poor and unsympathetic teachers with hostile public opinion, and no teaching of truth concerning black folk, is bad. A segregated school with ignorant placeholders, inadequate equipment, poor salaries, and wretched housing, is equally bad. (1935, p. 335)

Many activists, while supporting the *Brown* case, supported the notion outlined by DuBois, and many argued for equal educational opportunity for Black students as a remedy as opposed to integration with White students (Bell, 2004; Carter, 1980). Specifically, they believed that the Supreme Court should ensure students of color equal educational opportunities by mandating quality schools, quality teachers, and equal funding in communities of color. The *Brown* case did not mandate these remedies (Bell, 2004; Carter, 1980).

Robert Carter, one of the lead architects of the NAACP legal strategy in the *Brown* case, also believed that the focus on integration as the primary remedy represented a lost opportunity for an equal education remedy: "In the short run, we have to concentrate on finding ways of improving the quality of education in these schools [Black schools], even if it means or results in less effort being expended on school integration" (1980, p. 26). Carter went on to state:

If I had to prepare for Brown today, instead of looking principally to the social scientists to demonstrate the adverse consequences of segregation, I would seek to recruit educators to formulate a concrete definition of the meaning of equality in education, and I would seek to persuade the Court that equal education in its constitutional dimensions must, at the very least, conform to the contours of equal education as defined by the educators. (p. 27)

In *Silent Covenants: Brown v. Board of Education and the Unfulfilled Hopes for Racial Reform*, Derrick Bell (2004) indicated his agreement with Carter and laid out a plan. He argued that the *Brown* decision achieved neither equal educational opportunity nor integrated education. In fact, Bell (1987, 2004) noted that, were he a Supreme Court justice, he would have not ruled in the majority in the *Brown* case. Instead of supporting the integration argument, he would have called for an equal education opportunity remedy. Bell explained that, as a Supreme Court justice, he would have ordered relief for the Black plaintiffs in three phases: equalization (all schools within the district must be equalized in terms of physical facilities, teacher training, experience, and salary with the goal of each district, as a whole, measuring up to national norms within 3 years), representation (school boards and other policy-making bodies must be immediately restructured to ensure that those formally excluded from representation have individuals selected by them in accordance with the percentage of their children in the school system), and access (any child seeking courses or instruction not provided in the school in which he or she is assigned may transfer without regard to race to a school where the course or instruction is provided).

Unfortunately, the *Brown* decision did not emphasize the educational equity envisioned by DuBois, Carter, or Bell. *Brown* intended to "integrate," not necessarily "equally educate," students of color. Bell's arguments draw on the lived histories of Black communities that, 50 years after *Brown*, are still struggling for access to an equal education. Without listening to these lived histories, the Supreme Court could not foresee that the onus of eliminating racism in schools would subsequently be placed on those who experienced its subordination (see Love, 2004). Even in voluntary desegregation programs today, students of color bear the burden of busing and integration.

A few consistent patterns surface in analyses of the Supreme Court's rationales addressing the ongoing "problem" of race in education. For example, the integration rationale in *Brown*, while well intended and a victory devastating to Jim Crow segregation, focused on integrating White schools with students of color. Indeed, it was one-way desegregation, with students of color being bused into previously all-White schools. This connects with the diversity rationale laid out by both the University of Michigan defense in the *Grutter* case and the UC Davis defense in the *Bakke* case. Both of these universities focus on diversifying White universities with students of color. Similarly, the color-blind rationale links the complaints of the White plaintiffs and the split court opinions in both the *Bakke* and *Grutter* cases. However, *Grutter v. Bollinger* differs significantly from *Bakke* and other affirmative action cases because student intervenors were allowed as a third party to the case. A major part of the student intervenors' argument echoed the four dissenting justices' remedial rationale in the *Bakke* case. Both the *Bakke* and the *Grutter* cases raise issues about traditional notions of access and equity in higher education.

The community histories of Morris (2004) and White (2002) document some of the counterstories never considered by the Supreme Court in *Brown* (see Love, 2004). The student intervenors in the *Grutter* case likewise presented numerous counterstories of ongoing racial discrimination both on and off university campuses, stories that the court chose to ignore (see Allen & Solórzano, 2001; Solórzano, Allen, & Carroll, 2002; Solórzano et al., 2000). Yet, the majoritarian story about race and the legacy of racism in education remains without legal remedy.

Because the courts in these cases rarely listen to the experiences of communities of color or address the effects of racial discrimination, their legal rationale and, thus, their remedy to educational inequality rely on the majoritarian story. In cases of affirmative action, the majoritarian story informs a diversity rationale generated from Justice Powell's "compromise" opinion in the *Bakke* (1978) case. Powell argued: "The diversity that furthers a compelling state interest encompasses a far broader array of qualifications and characteristics of which racial or ethnic origin is but a single though important element" (cited in *Bakke v. Regents of the University of California*, 1978).

Advocates of affirmative action since the *Bakke* case tend to begin with Powell's broad definition of diversity in developing policies intended to build and maintain a diverse student population. For example, in the following passage of *Grutter v. Bollinger* (2003), the Supreme Court invoked a diversity rationale to affirm the use of race in university admissions: "More important, for reasons set out below, today we endorse Justice Powell's view that a *student body diversity* is a compelling state interest that can justify the use of race in university *admissions*" (italics added).

In reflecting on the "color-blind" rationale against affirmative action, CRT scholars ask (a) Whose experiences inform this rationale? and (b) Whose experiences are silenced? Lisa Ikemoto (1992) asserted that "the standard legal story does not expressly speak to race and class" (p. 487). However, majoritarian stories imbue racism and White privilege in a "race-neutral," "color-blind" discourse. Opponents of affirmative action are not against special treatment based on race, as long as the beneficiaries of such policies are White. Indeed, Thurgood Marshall's dissenting opinion in the 1978 *Bakke* case reminds us that the U.S. Supreme Court was consistently unwilling to forbid differential racial treatment. He noted that in the 1896 *Plessy v. Ferguson* case, when the Supreme Court required railroad companies to offer "separate but equal" accommodations for Black and White passengers: "The majority of the Court rejected the principle of color blindness, and for the next 60 years, from *Plessy* to *Brown v. Board of Education*, ours was a Nation where, *by law*, an individual could be given 'special' treatment based on the color of his skin."

Justice Marshall's note about "special" treatment based on skin color referred to the daily institutionalized privileges afforded to Whites according to Jim Crow statutes that maintained racial segregation. He went on to explain that the race-conscious approach to university admissions and employment had gone into effect only 10 years before the 1978 anti–affirmative action *Bakke* case. In examining the color-blind rationale through a CRT lens, we listen carefully to Justice Marshall's comments outlining the elusive quest for racial equality in the United States. The majoritarian story outlined in *Bakke* fails to account for the historical realities of racism. Twenty-three years later, the African American female student whose letter opens this chapter seemed to echo Justice Marshall's concluding remarks in the *Bakke* case. She wondered whether the end of affirmative action would lead back to racial segregation and Jim Crow laws. Similarly, in 1978, Justice Marshall wrote in his *Bakke* dissent:

I fear that today we have come full circle. After the Civil War our Government started several "affirmative action" programs. This Court in the *Civil Rights Cases* and *Plessy v. Ferguson* destroyed the movement toward complete equality. For almost a century no action was taken, and this nonaction was with the tacit approval of the courts. Then we had *Brown v. Board of Education* and the Civil Rights Acts of Congress, followed by numerous affirmative-action programs. Now, we have this Court again stepping in, this time to stop affirmative-action programs of the type used by the University of California. (438 U.S. 265, 402)

In 2005, we share Justice Marshall's fear. Indeed, the color-blind rationale advocated by the forces primed against affirmative action silences the history of racism in the United States and dismisses the contemporary experiences of people of color.

In reflecting on the diversity rationale supporting affirmative action, CRT scholars again ask whose experiences inform this rationale and whose experiences are silenced. According to Richard Delgado and Jean Stefancic (1993), majoritarian stories stem from the "bundle of presuppositions, perceived wisdoms, and shared cultural understandings persons in the dominant race bring to the discussion of race" (p. 462). We assert that majoritarian stories also recount gender, class, language, and other forms of privilege. In other words, a majoritarian story privileges the experiences of upper/middle-class Whites, men, and heterosexuals by naming them as natural or normative points of reference.

The unquestioned "standard" or "normative" point of reference reveals the basis for the diversity rationale. By their presence, students of color diversify otherwise White, homogeneous university campuses. This rationale centers White students as the standard or normative students. By default, students of color fulfill the role of enriching the learning environment for White students. The goal is not necessarily to provide access and equal opportunities for students of color but to provide access to diverse groups so that White students can learn in a diverse context.

CRT further challenges us to ask why the *Grutter* case did not address either the remedial or community service rationale. The Federal District Court in Detroit, Michigan; the Sixth Circuit Court of Appeals; and the Supreme Court ignored the student intervenors' case. In silencing these students, the courts failed to acknowledge the value of the critical race counterstory. Specifically, Justice Rehnquist, writing for the majority in the companion undergraduate case (*Gratz v. Bollinger*, 2003), reaffirmed the district court's decision to dismiss the intervenors' claims, and the University of Michigan's silence about its own institutionalized racism bolstered the Supreme Court's dismissal. In the words of Justice Rehnquist (*Gratz v. Bollinger*, 2003):

The [District] court explained that respondent-intervenors "failed to present any evidence that the discrimination alleged by them, or the continuing effects of such discrimination, was the real justification for the [law school's] race-conscious admissions programs" *(Id.,* at 795). We agree, and to the extent respondent-intervenors reassert this justification, a justification the University has *never* asserted throughout the course of this litigation, we affirm the District Court's disposition of the issue. (539 U.S. 244, 257)

Because the University of Michigan did not listen to the student intervenors, the university's case in *Grutter* did not address racism and White privilege. Instead, the university maintained the diversity rationale, and the majoritarian story remained unchallenged. Ironically, the court's ruling upholding affirmative action confirmed that such diverse experiences are a compelling state interest to include in higher education but chose not to address these experiences through the student intervenors' case.

In *Grutter*, the White female plaintiff failed to mention that White women have benefited from affirmative action more than any other group. Instead, the argument of the plaintiff's lawyers was based on an assumption that society provides a level educational playing field for all students to compete for law school admission. This position also assumes that racism no longer matters and cannot explain contemporary social inequality.

The student intervenors asserted that racism continues to exist in both its overt and covert forms and that, as long as it remains, policies and practices need to be in place to compensate for the barriers that racism erects in higher education settings. For example, expert witness reports filed on behalf of the student intervenors showed that many undergraduate and law school students confronted a hostile campus racial climate marked by daily incidents of discrimination (see Allen & Solórzano, 2001; Solórzano et al., 2002). Students at three major U.S. universities reported experiencing episodes of racial aggression in academic and social campus spaces. These subtle verbal and nonverbal insults target people of color often automatically or unconsciously (Pierce, 1970, 1974, 1995; Solórzano, 1998; Solórzano et al., 2000). Such layered racial put-downs assume inferiority based on race, gender, class, sexuality, language, immigration status, phenotype, accent, or surname. Accumulation of these incessant episodes of racial aggression causes unnecessary stress to students of color while privileging Whites (see Carroll, 1998; Davis, 1989; Smith, Yosso, & Solórzano, in press).

Students also indicated feeling that their university gives lip service to issues of diversity while maintaining an unwelcoming, exclusionary atmosphere in which students of color are viewed as unintelligent and as taking the place of "more academically qualified" Whites. They described a campus climate wherein Whites enjoy a sense of entitlement and members of racial minority groups are viewed as unqualified, unworthy, and unwelcome (Bonilla-Silva & Forman, 2000). As a result of this negative campus racial climate, students of color internalized feelings of self-doubt, alienation, and discouragement, which led to their dropping classes, changing majors, and even changing schools. The majority of the court in *Grutter* dismissed this position.

The four dissenting justices in the Supreme Court's *Bakke* (1978) decision did make the remedial argument. Yet, without Justice Powell, they were one vote short of that position being the law of the land. In her dissent in the undergraduate *Gratz v. Bollinger* (2003) case, Supreme Court Justice Ruth Bader Ginsberg raised aspects of the remedial argument but failed to garner the five votes needed to carry this argument for race-based affirmative action. A CRT framework insists that we listen and respond creatively to the words, stories, and silences of the courts, social science, and academia by acknowledging and validating students of color as "holders and creators of knowledge" (Delgado Bernal, 2002, p. 106).

DISCUSSION: BATTLING THE PUSH BACK TOWARD JIM CROW IN HIGHER EDUCATION

To fully understand the ways in which race and racism shape educational institutions and maintain various forms of discrimination, we must look to the lived experiences of students of color both in and out of schools as valid, appropriate, and necessary forms of data. Taking DuBois's insight from 1935, along with Bell and Carter's assessments in *Brown*, much work remains to finally achieve equal educational opportunities for students of color. Revisiting the *Grutter v. Bollinger* case from the perspective of these insights, clearly the goal of affirmative action in higher education cannot merely be diversifying the university and classroom. Heeding these insights, activists such as the student intervenors—while guardedly pleased with the diversity victory—continue to fight for the remedial and community service arguments as the underlying purpose of affirmative action programs. Such programs were initially developed to ameliorate the harmful effects of past and current discrimination and to train professionals of color to work and serve as role models in underserved communities of color.

We assert the need to extend the legacy of *Grutter* to provide equal educational opportunity in higher education admissions as well as in retention, financial aid, and faculty hiring programs. Specifically, we refer to the lack of equal educational opportunity in higher education resulting from past and current discriminatory policies and practices. We are reminded that the remedial and community service justifications for race-based affirmative action dominated the civil rights community discussion before the 1978 *Bakke* case. We believe that these arguments still hold true today, and our research and discourse should reflect that fact.

Although the Supreme Court upheld the need to consider race as one of the factors in university admissions, Delgado (2003b) warned that "a law reform strategy must not rest content with a seeming victory, but remain ever-vigilant for the inevitable backlash" (p. 150). Indeed, an analysis of the *Brown* aftermath shows that certain states and local communities immediately and continuously fought against integrated schools. In fact, some districts closed their public schools for many years in lieu of allowing Black students to enroll under a *Brown* mandate (Bell, 2004). Rather than allow universities to continue with race-conscious admissions policies, as per the *Grutter* case decision, the backlash against affirmative action of any kind has already begun. For instance, the former chair of the University of California Board of Regents, John Moores, made the following statement (and was subsequently criticized for using race as a pretext for his own political agenda by former University of California at Berkeley admissions official Bob Laird):

How did the university get away with discriminating so blatantly against Asians? Through an admissions policy with the vague term *"comprehensive review."* The policy includes factors like disabilities, low family income, first generation to attend college, need to work, disadvantaged social and educational environment, [and] difficult personal and family situations. This means that a student from a poor background whose parents didn't go to college is given preference over a kid raised by middle-class, educated parents—all other things being equal. (Laird, 2005, pp. 221–224)

The Supreme Court's rulings in *Grutter* and *Gratz*, Moores's comments, and Justice Scalia's anti–affirmative action dissent in *Grutter* all indicate impending strategies of the anti–affirmative action forces. To detract attention from policies that unfairly advantage White students (e.g., legacy admissions, advanced placement and honors credits, residential preferences), opponents of affirmative action will probably use the language of the color-blind rationale to engage in the following strategies:

- *Contest the concept of "critical mass":* The critical mass concept asserts that because students of color add to the diversity of a campus and enrich the education of White students, universities should commit to enriching the education of students of color by ensuring that they are not isolated and marginalized, that is, by admitting, retaining, and graduating a "critical mass" of underrepresented students. Affirmative action opponents claim that such efforts to enhance the education of students of color are too similar to the idea of "quotas," which a narrow minority deemed unconstitutional in the 1978 *Bakke* decision.

- *Oppose comprehensive admissions:* Comprehensive admissions aim to diminish the current overreliance on grade point average (GPA) and SAT/Law School Admission Test/Graduate Record Examination scores by considering an applicant's potential in more holistic terms. These efforts acknowledge some of the inequalities built into standardized exams and GPAs weighted according to advanced placement and honors courses completed (Solórzano & Ornelas, 2002, 2004). Applicants are asked to develop a more robust profile that might include an essay about their community service activities, a letter of reference about their ability to overcome personal and economic hardships, or other background information. Opponents of affirmative action charge that comprehensive admission policies disguise racial preferences for students of color. They ignore the racial preferences for Whites hidden in weighted GPAs and standardized tests.

- *Challenge outreach programs:* Outreach programs seek to increase the numbers of underrepresented students at colleges and universities by offering tutoring, summer courses, information seminars, mentoring, and skill-building workshops. Many of the most successful outreach programs, such as Upward Bound and Migrant Education, originated with President Johnson's "War on Poverty" and the civil rights legislation of the mid-1960s. These programs serve historically underrepresented racial minority groups as well as low-income Whites and first-generation students. Opponents of affirmative action again charge that supporting access to college for communities of color discriminates against Whites.

- *Focus on racial disparities in SAT scores and GPAs of admitted students:* Research shows that the SAT is not a useful indicator of a student's college or career potential (Oseguera, 2004). Rather than acknowledging this research or eliminating the additional grade points awarded to students in advanced placement and honors high school courses, proponents of the color-blind rationale are likely to spotlight the supposed superiority of White students and some Asian groups over Black and Chicana/o students.

- *Challenge campus retention programs:* Retention programs work to ensure that students make the transition from high school and community college to 4-year institutions successfully. Such programs often offer tutoring, academic counseling, peer counseling, and other types of support to facilitate retention and graduation of underrepresented students, first-generation students, and low-income students. While many university-funded athletic programs and university-sponsored Greek fraternity organizations offer similar support networks privileging athletes and White middle/upper-class students, only retention programs that target underrepresented students are questioned as discriminatory.

• *Pit Asian Americans against Black, Latina/o, and Native American students:* While arguing that White students are racially discriminated against by policies that are race conscious, the color-blind rationale also creates a false sense of resentment and animosity between groups of color. Moores's earlier comments demonstrate this strategy of diverting attention away from the actual ways universities discriminate against students of color.

CRT offers a proactive framework that can be used in the ongoing battle to provide equal educational access and opportunity to historically underrepresented students. We need to build on the work outlined in Jean Stefancic and Richard Delgado's (1996) *No Mercy: How Conservative Think Tanks and Foundations Changed America's Social Agenda* and Lee Cokorinos's (2003) The *Assault on Diversity: An Organized Challenge to Racial and Gender Justice* to examine the economic and intellectual roots of anti–affirmative action forces. Subsequently, as outlined briefly earlier, we need to anticipate upcoming attacks on affirmative action. Finally, we need to engage in proactive research efforts to extend arguments for affirmative action. This would mean restating and expanding the *Grutter* decision to read as follows: Student body diversity, compensation for past and current racial discrimination, and improving the delivery of social services to underserved minority communities are compelling state interests that can justify the use of race in university *admissions, outreach, retention programs, financial aid, and faculty recruitment, hiring, and retention.*

If the Supreme Court acknowledges the importance of the diversity rationale, then we must recognize that outreach, retention, financial aid, and faculty recruitment, hiring, and retention programs are the pillars for implementing diversity in higher education. Our research must focus on the goal of racial justice, including addressing the racist barriers that exist before a student applies to college (e.g., access to gifted and talented education programs and advanced placement courses), during the admission process itself (e.g., weighted GPAs and standardized tests), during college (e.g., campus racial and gender climate), and as students apply to graduate and professional school (e.g., graduate examinations).

We must continue to go on the offensive and challenge those admissions criteria that privilege wealth or position and encumber those without it. Indeed, Laurence Parker and David Stovall (2004) asserted that CRT is a "call to work." As critical race educators, we commit ourselves to the remedial and community service rationales by (a) documenting the past and continuing significance of race and racism in the educational lives of students of color and (b) emphasizing the importance of providing professionals of color to serve communities of color.

We must challenge the presence of racism in policies intended to remedy racism. We need to remember that, originally, affirmative action sought to ameliorate the harmful effects of past and current discrimination and provide service and role models to underserved communities. Delgado (2003b) encouraged critical race scholars to "consider that race is not merely a matter for abstract analysis, but for struggle. It should expressly address the personal dimensions of that struggle and what they mean for intellectuals" (p. 151). These struggles should be at the forefront of a critical race analysis of postsecondary education.

NOTES

Thanks to Heidi Oliver-O'Gilvie and Tommy Totten for editorial assistance on early versions of this chapter.

[1] Although this student signed her letter to the judge, we keep her name confidential.

[2] For discussions of WhiteCrit in education, see the special issue of the *International Journal of Qualitative Studies in Education* edited by Marx (2003).

[3] For instance, William Tate's 1994 autobiographical article in the journal *Urban Education*, "From Inner City to Ivory Tower: Does My Voice Matter in the Academy?" represents the first use of CRT principles in education. A year later, Gloria Ladson-Billings and Tate wrote an article titled "Toward a Critical Race Theory of Education" in *Teachers College Record*. Two years later, Daniel Solórzano's 1997 *Teacher Education Quarterly* essay, "Images and Words That Wound: Critical Race Theory, Racial Stereotyping, and Teacher Education," applied CRT to a specific subfield of teacher education. Also in 1997, William Tate's "Critical Race Theory and Education: History, Theory, and Implications," published in *Review of Research in Education*, furthered our understanding of the history of CRT in education. The 1998 special issue on critical race theory in education in the *International Journal of Qualitative Studies in Education* significantly expanded the field (and became the edited book *Race Is . . . Race Isn't: Critical Race Theory and Qualitative Studies in Education*; see Parker, Deyhle, & Villenas, 1999). Individual scholars also presented papers on CRT at professional conferences across the country and subsequently published their work in various academic journals such as *Urban Education*, the *Journal of Negro Education*, *Educational Researcher*, and the *Journal of Latinos in Education*. In 2002, the journals *Qualitative Inquiry* and *Equity and Excellence in Education* each dedicated a special issue to CRT in education. In 2004, the American Educational Research Association conference symposium "And We Are Still Not Saved: Critical Race Theory in Education Ten Years Later" acknowledged the 10-year anniversary of Tate's 1994 article officially introducing CRT to education. This symposium led to *Race, Ethnicity, and Education* dedicating a 2005 special issue to CRT. *Educational Administration Quarterly* will soon publish a special issue on CRT and educational leadership (see Villalpando & Parker, in press). Finally, Tara Yosso's (in press) *Critical Race Counterstories Along the Chicana/Chicano Educational Pipeline* marks the first sole-authored book on CRT in education.

REFERENCES

Aguirre, A. (2000). Academic storytelling: A critical race theory story of affirmative action. *Sociological Perspectives, 43,* 319–339.

Allen, W., & Solórzano, D. (2001). Affirmative action, educational equity, and campus racial climate: A case study of the University of Michigan Law School. *Berkeley La Raza Law Journal, 12,* 237–363.

Arriola, E. (1997). LatCrit theory, international human rights, popular culture, and the faces of despair in ins raids. *Inter-American Law Review, 28,* 245–262.

Arriola, E. (Ed.). (1998). Difference, solidarity and law: Building Latina/o communities through LatCrit theory [special issue]. *Chicano-Latino Law Review, 19*(1).

Bakke v. Regents of the University of California, 438 U.S. 265 (1978).

Bell, D. (1987). Neither separate schools nor mixed schools: The chronicle of the sacrificed Black schoolchildren. In D. Bell (Ed.), *And we are not saved: The elusive quest for racial justice* (pp. 102–122). New York: Basic Books.

Bell, D. (1992). *Faces at the bottom of the well: The permanence of racism.* New York: Basic Books.

Bell, D. (1996). *Gospel choirs: Psalms of survival for an alien land called home.* New York: Basic Books.

Bell, D. (2004). *Silent covenants: Brown v. Board of Education and the unfulfilled hopes for racial reform.* New York: Oxford University Press.

Bonilla-Silva, E., & Forman, T. (2000). 'I'm not a racist but . . .': Mapping White college students' racial ideology in the U.S.A. *Discourse and Society, 11,* 51–86.

Brayboy, B. (2001, November). *Toward a tribal critical theory in higher education.* Paper presented at the annual meeting of the Association for the Study of Higher Education, Richmond, VA.

Brayboy, B. (2002, April). *Tribal critical race theory in education.* Paper presented at the annual meeting of the American Educational Research Association, New Orleans, LA.

Brown v. Board of Education, 347 U.S. 483 (1954).

Caldwell, P. (1995). A hair piece: Perspectives on the intersection of race and gender. In R. Delgado (Ed.), *Critical race theory: The cutting edge* (pp. 267–277). Philadelphia: Temple University Press.

Calmore, J. (1992). Critical race theory, Archie Shepp, and fire music: Securing an authentic intellectual life in a multicultural world. *Southern California Law Review, 65,* 2129–2231.

Calmore, J. (1997). Exploring Michael Omi's 'messy' real world of race: An essay for 'naked people longing to swim free.' *Law and Inequality, 15,* 25–82.

Carbado, D. W. (2002). Straight out of the closet: Race, gender, and sexual orientation. In F. Valdes, J. McCristal Culp, & A.P. Harris (Eds.), *Crossroads, directions, and a new critical race theory* (pp. 221–242). Philadelphia: Temple University Press.

Carrasco, E. (1996). Collective recognition as a communitarian device: Or, of course we want to be role models! *La Raza Law Journal, 9,* 81–101.

Carroll, G. (1998). *Environmental stress and African Americans: The other side of the moon.* Westport, CT: Praeger.

Carter, R. (1980). A reassessment of Brown v. Board. In D. Bell (Ed.), *Shades of brown: New perspectives on school desegregation* (pp. 21–28). New York: Teachers College Press.

Chang, R. (1993). Toward an Asian American legal scholarship: Critical race theory, poststructuralism, and narrative space. *California Law Review, 81,* 1243.

Chang, R. (1998). Who's afraid of Tiger Woods? *Chicano-Latino Law Review, 19,* 223.

Chon, M. (1995). On the need for Asian American narratives in law: Ethnic specimens, native informants, storytelling and silences. *Asian Pacific American Law Journal, 3,* 4–32.

Cokorinos, L. (2003). *The assault on diversity: An organized challenge to racial and gender justice.* Lanham, MD: Rowman & Littlefield.

Collins, P. H. (1986). Learning from the outsider within: The sociological significance of Black feminist thought. *Social Problems, 33,* S14–S32.

Crenshaw, K. (1989). Demarginalizing the intersection of race and sex: A Black feminist critique of antidiscrimination doctrine, feminist theory and antiracist politics. In *University of Chicago Legal Forum* (pp. 139–167). Chicago: University of Chicago.

Crenshaw, K. (1991). Mapping the margins: Intersectionality, identity politics, and the violence against women of color. *Stanford Law Review, 43,* 1241–1299.

Crenshaw, K. (2002). The first decade: Critical reflections, or 'a foot in the closing door.' In F. Valdes, J. McCristal Culp, & A. Harris (Eds.), *Crossroads, directions, and a new critical race theory* (pp. 9–31). Philadelphia: Temple University Press.

Crenshaw, K., Gotanda, N., Peller, G., & Thomas, K. (Eds.). (1995). *Critical race theory: The key writings that formed the movement.* New York: New Press.

Davis, P. (1989). Law as microaggression. *Yale Law Journal, 98,* 1559–1577.

DeCuir, J. T., & Dixon, A. D. (2004). "So when it comes out, they aren't that surprised that it is there": Using critical race theory as a tool of analysis of race and racism in education. *Educational Researcher, 33*(5), 26–31.

Delgado, R. (1989). Storytelling for oppositionists and others: A plea for narrative. *Michigan Law Review, 87,* 2411–2441.

Delgado, R. (1993). On telling stories in school: A reply to Farber and Sherry. *Vanderbilt Law Review, 46,* 665–676.

Delgado, R. (1995a). *The Rodrigo chronicles: Conversations about America and race.* New York: New York University Press.

Delgado, R. (Ed.). (1995b). *Critical race theory: The cutting edge.* Philadelphia: Temple University Press.

Delgado, R. (1996). *The coming race war?: And other apocalyptic tales of America after affirmative action and welfare.* New York: New York University Press.

Delgado, R. (1999). *When equality ends: Stories about race and resistance.* Boulder, CO: Westview Press.

Delgado, R. (2003a). *Justice at war: Civil liberties and civil rights during times of crisis.* New York: New York University Press.

Delgado, R. (2003b). Crossroads and blind alleys: A critical examination of recent writing about race. *Texas Law Review, 82,* 121–152.

Delgado, R., & Stefancic, J. (1993). Critical race theory: An annotated bibliography. *Virginia Law Review, 79,* 461–516.

Delgado, R., & Stefancic, J. (1995). Critical race theory: An annotated bibliography 1993, a year of transition. *University of Colorado Law Review, 66,* 159–193.

Delgado, R., & Stefancic, J. (Eds.). (1997). *Critical White studies: Looking behind the mirror.* Philadelphia: Temple University Press.

Delgado, R., & Stefancic, J. (2000a). *Critical race theory: The cutting edge* (2nd ed.). Philadelphia: Temple University Press.

Delgado, R., & Stefancic, J. (2000b). California's racial history and constitutional rationales for race-conscious decision making in higher education. *UCLA Law Review, 47,* 1521–1614.

Delgado, R., & Stefancic, J. (2001). *Critical race theory: An introduction.* New York: New York University Press.

Delgado Bernal, D. (1998). Using a Chicana feminist epistemology in educational research. *Harvard Educational Review, 68,* 555–582.

Delgado Bernal, D. (2002). Critical race theory, LatCrit theory, and critical raced-gendered epistemologies: Recognizing students of color as holders and creators of knowledge. *Qualitative Inquiry, 8,* 105–126.

Delgado Bernal, D., & Villalpando, O. (2002). An apartheid of knowledge in academia: The struggle over the "legitimate" knowledge of faculty of color. *Equity and Excellence in Education, 35,* 169–180.

Dixson, A. D., & Rousseau, C. K. (Eds.). (2005). Critical race theory in education [special issue]. *Race, Ethnicity, and Education, 8*(1).

DuBois, W. E. B. (1935). Does the Negro need separate schools? *Journal of Negro Education, 4,* 328–335.

Duncan, G. (2002a). Beyond love: A critical race ethnography of the schooling of adolescent Black males. *Equity and Excellence in Education, 35,* 131–143.

Duncan, G. (2002b). Critical race theory and method: Rendering race in urban ethnographic research. *Qualitative Inquiry, 8,* 85–104.

Duncan, G. (2005). Critical race ethnography in education: Narrative, inequality and the problem of epistemology. *Race, Ethnicity, and Education, 8,* 93–114.

Espinoza, L. (1990). Masks and other disguises: Exposing legal academia. *Harvard Law Review, 103,* 1878–1886.

Espinoza, L. (1998). Latino/a identity and multi-identity: Community and culture. In R. Delgado & J. Stefancic (Eds.), *The Latino/a condition: A critical reader* (pp. 17–23). New York: New York University Press.

Espinoza, L., & Harris, A. (1998). Embracing the tar-baby: LatCrit theory and the sticky mess of race. *La Raza Law Journal, 10,* 499–559.

Fernandez, L. (2002). Telling stories about school: Using critical race and Latino critical theories to document Latina/Latino education and resistance. *Qualitative Inquiry, 8,* 45–65.

Freire, P. (1970). *Education for critical consciousness.* New York: Continuum.

Freire, P. (1973). *Pedagogy of the oppressed.* New York: Seabury Press.

Gee, H. (1997). Changing landscapes: The need for Asian Americans to be included in the affirmative action debate. *Gonzaga Law Review, 32,* 621–658.

Gee, H. (1999). Beyond Black and White: Selected writings by Asian Americans within the critical race theory movement. *St. Mary's Law Journal, 30,* 759–799.

Gotanda, N. (1991). A critique of 'our constitution is color-blind.' *Stanford Law Review, 44,* 1–68.

Gratz v. Bollinger, 539 U.S. 244, 306 (2003).

Gutiérrez-Jones, C. (2001). *Critical race narratives: A study of race, rhetoric, and injury.* New York: New York University Press.

Haney Lopez, I. F. (1996). *White by law: The legal construction of race.* New York: New York University Press.

Harris, A. (1994). Forward: The jurisprudence of reconstruction. *California Law Review, 82,* 741–785.

Harris, C. I. (1993). Whiteness as property. *Harvard Law Review, 106,* 1707–1791.

Higginbotham, L. (1992). An open letter to Justice Clarence Thomas from a federal judicial colleague. In T. Morrison (Ed.), *Race-ing justice, en-gendering power: Essays on Anita Hill, Clarence Thomas, and the construction of social reality* (pp. 3–39). New York: Random House.

hooks, b. (1994). *Teaching to transgress: Education as the practice of freedom.* New York: Routledge.

Ikemoto, L. (1992). Furthering the inquiry: Race, class, and culture in the forced medical treatment of pregnant women. *Tennessee Law Review, 59,* 487–519.

Iseke-Barnes, J. M. (2000). Ethnomathematics and language in decolonizing mathematics. *Race, Gender and Class in Education, 7,* 133–149.

Jay, M. (2003). Critical race theory, multicultural education, and the hidden curriculum of hegemony. *Multicultural Perspectives, 5,* 3–10.

Johnson, K. R. (1999). How did you get to be Mexican? *A White/Brown man's search for identity.* Philadelphia: Temple University Press.

Kozol, J. (1991). *Savage inequalities: Children in America's schools.* St. Helen, OR: Perennial Press.

Ladson-Billings, G. (1998). Preparing teachers for diverse student populations: A critical race theory perspective. In A. Iran-Nejad & P. D. Pearson (Eds.), *Review of research in education* (Vol. 24, pp. 211–247). Washington, DC: American Educational Research Association.

Ladson-Billings, G. (2000). Racialized discourses and ethnic epistemologies. In N. Denzin & Y. Lincoln (Eds.), *Handbook of qualitative research* (2nd ed., pp. 257–277). Thousand Oaks, CA: Sage.

Ladson-Billings, G. (Ed.). (2003). *Critical race theory perspectives on social studies: The profession, policies and curriculum.* Greenwich, CT: Information Age.

Ladson-Billings, G., & Tate, W. (1995). Toward a critical race theory of education. *Teachers College Record, 97,* 47–68.

Laird, B. (2005). *The case for affirmative action in university admissions.* Berkeley, CA: Bay Tree.

Lawrence, C. (1992). The word and the river: Pedagogy as scholarship as struggle. *Southern California Law Review, 65,* 2231–2298.

Lawrence, C., & Matsuda, M. (1997). *We won't go back: Making the case for affirmative action.* Boston: Houghton Mifflin.

Lawson, R. (1995). Critical race theory as praxis: A view from outside to the outside. *Howard Law Journal, 38,* 353–370.

Leonardo, Z. (2004). The color of supremacy: Beyond the discourse of 'White privilege.' *Educational Philosophy and Theory, 36,* 138–152.

Lewis, A. E. (2003). *Race in the schoolyard: Negotiating the color line in classrooms and communities.* New Brunswick, NJ: Rutgers University Press.

Lopez, G. (2003). Parental involvement as racialized performance. In G. Lopez & L. Parker (Eds.), *Interrogating racism in qualitative research methodology* (pp. 71–95). New York: Peter Lang.

Lopez, G., & Parker, L. (Eds.). (2003). *Interrogating racism in qualitative research methodology.* New York: Peter Lang.

Lorde, A. (1992). Age, race, class, and sex: Women redefining difference. In M. Anderson & P. H. Collins (Eds.), *Race, class, and gender: An anthology* (pp. 495–502). Belmont, CA: Wadsworth.

Love, B. J. (2004). *Brown* plus 50 counter-storytelling: A critical race theory analysis of the "majoritarian achievement gap" story. *Equity and Excellence in Education, 37,* 227–246.

Lynn, M. (1999). Toward a critical race pedagogy: A research note. *Urban Education, 33,* 606–626.

Lynn, M. (2002). Critical race theory and the perspectives of Black men teachers in the Los Angeles public schools. *Equity and Excellence in Education, 35,* 119–130.

Lynn, M., & Adams, M. (Eds.). (2002). Critical race theory in education [special issue]. *Equity and Excellence in Education, 35*(2).

Lynn, M., Yosso, T., Solórzano, D., & Parker, L. (Eds.). (2002). Critical race and qualitative research [special issue]. *Qualitative Inquiry, 8*(1).

Marable, M. (1992). *Black America.* Westfield, NJ: Open Media.

Marx, S. (Ed.). (2003). Critical White studies in education [special issue]. *International Journal of Qualitative Studies in Education, 16*(1).

Matsuda, M. (1991). Voices of America: Accents, antidiscrimination and a jurisprudence for the last reconstruction. *Yale Law Journal, 100,* 1329–1407.

McIntosh, P. (1989, July/August). White privilege: Unpacking the invisible knapsack. *Peace and Freedom,* pp. 10–12.

Montoya, M. (1994). *Mascaras, trenzas, y grenas:* Un/masking the self while un/braiding Latina stories and legal discourse. *Chicano-Latino Law Review, 15,* 1–37.

Montoya, M. (2002). Celebrating racialized legal narratives. In F. Valdes, J. McCristal-Culp, & A. Harris (Eds.), *Crossroads, directions, and a new critical race theory* (pp. 243–250). Philadelphia: Temple University Press.

Morris, J. (2004). Can anything good come from Nazareth? Race, class, and African American schooling and community in the urban South and Midwest. *American Educational Research Journal, 41,* 69–112.

Olivas, M. (1990). The chronicles, my grandfather's stories, and immigration law: The slave traders chronicle as racial history. *Saint Louis University Law Journal, 34,* 425–441.

Oseguera, L. (2004). *Individual and institutional influences on the baccalaureate degree attainment of African American, Asian American, Caucasian, and Mexican American undergraduates.* Unpublished doctoral dissertation, University of California, Los Angeles.

Parker, L., Deyhle, D., & Villenas, S. (Eds.). (1999). *Race is . . . race isn't: Critical race theory and qualitative studies in education.* Boulder, CO: Westview Press.

Parker, L., Deyhle, D., Villenas, S., & Crossland, K. (Eds.). (1998). Critical race theory and education [special issue]. *International Journal of Qualitative Studies in Education, 11*(1).

Parker, L., & Stovall, D. O. (2004). Actions following words: Critical race theory connects to critical pedagogy. *Journal of Educational Philosophy and Theory, 36,* 167–183.

Perea, J. F. (1998). The Black/White binary paradigm of race: The 'normal science' of American racial thought. *La Raza Law Review, 10,* 127–172.

Pierce, C. (1970). Offensive mechanisms. In F. B. Barbour (Ed.), *The Black 70's* (pp. 265–282). Boston: Porter Sargent.

Pierce, C. (1974). Psychiatric problems of the Black minority. In S. Arieti (Ed.), *American handbook of psychiatry* (pp. 512–523). New York: Basic Books.

Pierce, C. (1995). Stress analogs of racism and sexism: Terrorism, torture, and disaster. In C. Willie, P. Rieker, B. Kramer, & B. Brown (Eds.), *Mental health, racism, and sexism* (pp. 277–293). Pittsburgh, PA: University of Pittsburgh Press.

Russell, M. (1992). Entering great America: Reflections on race and the convergence of progressive legal theory and practice. *Hastings Law Journal, 43,* 749–767.

Sleeter, C. E., & Delgado Bernal, D. (2002). Critical pedagogy, critical race theory, and antiracist education: Implications for multicultural education. In J. A. Banks & C. A. Banks (Eds.), *Handbook of research on multicultural education* (2nd ed., pp. 240–258). San Francisco: Jossey-Bass.

Smith, W. A., Altbach, P. G., & Lomotey, K. (Eds.). (2002). *The racial crisis in American higher education: Continuing challenges to the twenty-first century.* Albany: State University of New York Press.

Smith, W. A., Yosso, T., & Solórzano, D. (in press). Challenging racial battle fatigue on historically White campuses: A critical race examination of race-related stress. In C. A. Stanley (Ed.), *Faculty of color teaching in predominantly White institutions.* Bolton, MA: Anker.

Solórzano, D. (1997). Images and words that wound: Critical race theory, racial stereotyping, and teacher education. *Teacher Education Quarterly, 24,* 5–19.

Solórzano, D. (1998). Critical race theory, racial and gender microaggressions, and the experiences of Chicana and Chicano scholars. *International Journal of Qualitative Studies in Education, 11,* 121–136.

Solórzano, D., Allen, W., & Carroll, G. (2002). A case study of racial microaggressions and campus racial climate at the University of California-Berkeley. *UCLA Chicano/Latino Law Review, 23,* 15–111.

Solórzano, D., Ceja, M., & Yosso, T. (2000). Critical race theory, racial microaggressions, and campus racial climate: The experiences of African American college students. *Journal of Negro Education, 69,* 60–73.

Solórzano, D., & Delgado Bernal, D. (2001). Examining transformational resistance through a critical race and LatCrit theory framework: Chicana and Chicano students in an urban context. *Urban Education, 36,* 308–342.

Solórzano, D., & Ornelas, A. (2002). A critical race analysis of advanced placement classes: A case of educational inequality. *Journal of Latinos in Education, 1,* 215–229.

Solórzano, D., & Ornelas, A. (2004, February/March). A critical race analysis of Latina/o and African American advanced placement enrollment in public high schools. *High School Journal,* pp. 15–26.

Solórzano, D., & Villalpando, O. (1998). Critical race theory, marginality, and the experience of minority students in higher education. In C. Torres & T. Mitchell (Eds.), *Emerging issues in the sociology of education: Comparative perspectives* (pp. 211–224). New York: State University of New York Press.

Solórzano, D., & Yosso, T. (2000). Toward a critical race theory of Chicana and Chicano education. In C. Tejeda, C. Martinez, Z. Leonardo, & P. McLaren (Eds.), *Charting new terrains of Chicana(o)/Latina(o) education* (pp. 35–65). Cresskill, NJ: Hampton Press.

Solórzano, D., & Yosso, T. (2001a). Critical race and LatCrit theory and method: Counter-storytelling Chicana and Chicano graduate school experiences. *International Journal of Qualitative Studies in Education, 14,* 471–495.

Solórzano, D., & Yosso, T. (2001b). From racial stereotyping toward a critical race theory in teacher education. *Multicultural Education, 9,* 2–8.

Solórzano, D., & Yosso, T. (2001c). Maintaining social justice hopes within academic realities: A Freirean approach to critical race/LatCrit pedagogy. *Denver Law Review, 78,* 595–621.

Solórzano, D., & Yosso, T. (2002). A critical race counter-story of race, racism, and affirmative action. *Equity and Excellence in Education, 35,* 155–168.

Stefancic, J. (1998). Latino and Latina critical theory: An annotated bibliography. *La Raza Law Journal, 10,* 423–498.

Stefancic, J., & Delgado, R. (1996). *No mercy: How conservative think tanks and foundations changed America's social agenda.* Philadelphia: Temple University Press.

Tate, W. (1994). From inner city to ivory tower: Does my voice matter in the academy? *Urban Education, 29,* 245–269.

Tate, W. (1997). Critical race theory and education: History, theory, and implications. In M. Apple (Ed.), *Review of research in education* (Vol. 22, pp. 195–247). Washington, DC: American Educational Research Association.

Tatum, B. D. (1997). *Why are all the Black kids sitting together in the cafeteria?: And other conversations about race.* New York: Basic Books.

Taylor, E. (2000). Critical race theory and interest convergence in the backlash against affirmative action: Washington State and Initiative 200. *Teachers College Record, 102,* 539–561.

Valdes, F. (Ed.). (1997). LatCrit theory: Naming and launching a new direction of critical legal scholarship [special issue]. *Harvard Latino Law Review, 2*(2).

Valdes, F. (Eds.). (1998, Spring). LatCrit: Latinas/os and the law [special issue]. *La Raza Law Journal, 10.*

Valdes, F., McCristal-Culp, J., & Harris, A. (Eds.). (2002). *Crossroads, directions, and a new critical race theory.* Philadelphia: Temple University Press.

Villalpando, O. (2003). Self-segregation or self-preservation? A critical race theory and Latina/o critical theory analysis of findings from a longitudinal study of Chicana/o college students. *International Journal of Qualitative Studies in Education, 16,* 619–646.

Villalpando, O., & Parker, L. (Eds.). (in press). Critical race theory and educational leadership [special issue]. *Educational Administration Quarterly.*

White, M. A. (2002, Spring). Paradise lost? Teachers' perspectives on the use of cultural capital in the segregated schools of New Orleans, Louisiana. *Journal of African American History,* pp. 269–281.

Williams, P. (1991). *The alchemy of race and rights: Diary of a law professor.* Cambridge, MA: Harvard University Press.

Williams, R. (1997). Vampires anonymous and critical race practice. *Michigan Law Review, 95,* 741–765.

Wing, A. K. (Ed.). (1997). *Critical race feminism: A reader.* New York: New York University Press.

Wing, A. K. (Ed.). (2000). *Global critical race feminism: An international reader.* New York: New York University Press.

Yosso, T. J. (2002). Toward a critical race curriculum. *Equity and Excellence in Education, 35,* 93–107.

Yosso, T. J. (2005). Whose culture has capital? A critical race theory discussion of community cultural wealth. *Race Ethnicity and Education, 8,* (1), 69-91

Yosso, T. J. (in press). *Critical race counterstories along the Chicana/Chicano educational pipeline.* New York: Routledge.

Chapter 2

Legacy of *Brown*: *Lau* and Language Policy in the United States

PATRICIA GÁNDARA
University of California, Davis
RACHEL MORAN
University of California, Berkeley
EUGENE GARCIA
Arizona State University

The 50th anniversary of *Brown v. Board of Education* in 1954 also recalls the anniversary of *Lau v. Nichols*, decided exactly 20 years later in 1974. The two decisions were monumental in the history of civil rights and, interestingly, have shared similarities in the ways in which they have been reinterpreted since they were first decided several decades ago. The history of both of these decisions reminds us that the struggle for civil rights in the United States is not over. The great promise of this democracy is an equal opportunity to affect the decisions and the laws that rule our lives. The great challenge is to make good on that promise. *Brown v. Board of Education* and *Lau v. Nichols* are both morality tales about the inherent difficulty of sustaining minority rights in the face of majority interests. In this chapter, we argue that the two cases have been intertwined in interesting ways and that three types of strategies have been used to undermine both decisions: legal, regulatory, and public relations. In concert, these strategies have been at least moderately effective in undoing the promise of equity that each decision represented.

BROWN AND *LAU*: THE LEGACY

On May 17, 1954, the United States Supreme Court, in the case of *Brown v. Board of Education*, ruled that racial segregation in public schools was unconstitutional. Relying on the 14th Amendment, the court held that "separate educational facilities are inherently unequal." The *Brown* decision initiated the process of ending legal segregation and altered the course of race relations in this country. This decision, however, did not stand alone. The struggle for civil rights in this country is a multicolored history of marginalized groups seeking access to the promise of equal treatment through the Constitution. *Brown* was preceded by important historic events that had primed the nation for the end of racial segregation, and it has left a legacy of legal decisions that continue to this day. Certainly, one critical legacy was the *Lau v. Nichols* decision, which would affirm the right of non-English-speaking students to an education equal to that of their English-speaking peers.

Eight years before *Brown*, a U.S. district court ruled that schools in Orange County, California, had violated the 14th Amendment by assigning Mexican-origin children to separate schools from their European American peers. The decision was upheld on appeal, and the county was ordered to begin the process of dismantling segregation in the fall of 1948. Because California officials accepted the circuit court decision, the case never went to the Supreme Court, and thus a national decision had to wait until 1954. However, *Méndez v. Westminster*, as it came to be known, led to successful challenges in Arizona and Texas and was followed closely by the architects of the *Brown* case. Thurgood Marshall and Robert L. Carter filed amicus curiae briefs for the *Méndez* case during the appeals process. According to Carter, the briefs were a "dry run for the future," and they contained all of the key arguments that would later be used in *Brown* (González, 1999). Thus, Mexican-origin students were involved in the roots of *Brown* as well as in its legacies.

The importance of *Brown v. Board of Education* extends far beyond its direct impact on the case against the Topeka schools and on racial segregation. Its legacy reaches to all forms of racial, ethnic, and linguistic inequalities. *Brown* opened the door for federal involvement in the protection of equal access to educational opportunities for a number of previously marginalized groups—a radical departure from the interpretation of the Constitution that had accepted southern discrimination. However, after a decade of foot dragging by schools in the South, it became clear that the decision would be difficult to enforce in the absence of a larger foundation of legal rights. Congress passed the Civil Rights Act in 1964, which forbade discrimination on the grounds of race, religion, or national origin by any institution receiving federal funds. This broadened the scope of *Brown* and ultimately extended it to include members of language minority groups under the national origin provision. With the addition of Title VII of the Elementary and Secondary Education Act (ESEA), the stage was set for the Supreme Court's decision in *Lau v. Nichols* in 1974.

The *Lau* case was a suit brought on behalf of 1,856 Chinese-speaking students in the San Francisco schools who claimed that the schools made no effort to accommodate their needs and that they were therefore denied equal access to an education. The lower federal court had rejected the students' claim, and the Ninth Circuit Court of Appeals, in refusing to intervene on the students' behalf, concluded that children had arrived at school with "different advantages and disadvantages caused in part by social, economic and cultural background, created and continued completely apart from any contribution by the school system." In the Ninth Circuit's view, schools were not required to rectify these differences and disadvantages. The Supreme Court reversed the ruling but did not find a violation of the 14th Amendment as it had in *Brown*; rather, it found that the district had violated Title VI of the Civil Rights Act, relying heavily on the view of the Office for Civil Rights (OCR) that language discrimination was a form of national-origin discrimination. Moreover, language policies that effectively excluded children from an educational program could amount to impermissible discrimination. In adopting OCR's interpretation, the court did not order any specific remedy. Instead, the justices urged the school district to apply its expertise to devise appropriate accommodations for the Chinese-speaking students and supported OCR's authority to regulate in this area. Because there was no finding that the district's actions were motivated by animus, the court remained optimistic that school officials would act in good faith to redress the problem.

Thus, the court, as it has been wont to do in cases involving educational remedies, asked the education experts in the schools and federal court officials to find a solution to providing access to the core curriculum for limited English speakers.[1] For many, but not for all, this implied bilingual education, and the interpretation of the *Lau* decision became a lightning rod for divided views about the appropriate education of students who were not proficient in English. Hence, the U.S. Department of Education was prevailed upon by state agencies to clarify state responsibilities under the *Lau* decision. The *Lau* remedies, promulgated by the Department of Education in 1975, advised schools to provide bilingual instruction, when feasible, for elementary school children who did not speak English. The default program was transitional bilingual education (TBE), which would normally mainstream English learners within 2 to 4 years (Crawford, 2004a). English-as-a-second-language (ESL) programs were proposed in the case of older students and those with some understanding of English, although the door was left open for other approaches as well. The guidelines did not, however, settle the issue or reduce the controversy. As with *Brown*, neither a Supreme Court decision nor federal regulations would be sufficient to convince the many skeptics that such policies were good for children or the schools that educated them.

BROWN AND *LAU*: PARALLEL HISTORIES

The history of *Lau* has followed a path similar to that of *Brown*. While the court's decision in each case broke new legal ground, both decisions suffered numerous challenges in implementation. Critics of social policies that would desegregate the schools (the goal of *Brown*) and provide access to the curriculum for English learners (the goal of *Lau*) via primary language instruction were plentiful. While the *Brown* decision had relied heavily on social science evidence that Black children were made to feel inferior by being segregated from their White peers, research on the effects of desegregation had yet to be conducted. Likewise, although the *Lau* decision was based on a finding of clear discrimination against children who, through no fault of their own, could not avail themselves of instruction in English, research on the effectiveness of bilingual and other educational strategies to meet these students' needs had not been undertaken.

Thus, the moral authority that these decisions were able to summon relied heavily on social justice interpretations of social and educational conditions. Was it morally defensible to support policies that encouraged Black children to dislike their blackness? Or to foreclose meaningful instruction from non–English speakers until the point at which they spoke English? How much weight should be given to the perceived costs of desegregation and bilingual education to majority students and to schools? As research was generated attempting to answer social science questions— for example, were desegregation and bilingual education effective in raising minority achievement (without lowering majority students' achievement)?—findings were interpreted through the same majority/minority prism. The fact that both decisions were initially implemented with naive optimism and inadequate remedies also stacked the deck against their success. As Kenneth Clark, the Black sociologist upon whose work the *Brown* decision in part relied, noted in 1996 as he surveyed the state of resegregation: "I didn't realize how deep racism was in America, and I suppose the court didn't realize it either" (cited in Kunen, 1996, p. 40).

THE FRAMING OF THE LANGUAGE "PROBLEM"

In January 1968, President Lyndon B. Johnson signed into law the Bilingual Education Act, or Title VII of the ESEA, marking the federal government's first involvement in the education of English learners. In an era of civil rights, the act enjoyed widespread political support, although it skirted the issue of the intent of "bilingual" education: whether it was to in fact encourage the development of languages other than English or simply help students make the transition to English as quickly as possible. Crawford (2004a) noted that Senator Yarborough of Texas, the measure's prime sponsor, "did nothing to clarify this issue." Thus, the *Lau* remedies gave clear preference to bilingual education as the primary means for meeting the needs of children who had no command of English, specifically ruling out ESL as a sole method of instruction for these children unless districts could demonstrate that it was equally as effective as bilingual programs (Crawford, 1992); however, the ambiguity of *Lau*'s goals, while probably key to its approval, had also sown the seeds of controversy as programs were implemented in the states.

Legislation was passed in many states in the 1970s and 1980s regulating program implementation. In 1976, on the heels of *Lau*, the California legislature passed the Chacon-Moscone Bilingual-Bicultural Education Act. While the act authorized bilingual education as the default program for English learners, it also declared that "the primary goal of all programs under this article is as effectively and efficiently as possible to develop in each child fluency in English" (California Education Code, 1976, Section 52161). Seemingly progressive at the time, the California law had framed the challenge facing English learners—and their teachers—as primarily a *language problem*, and it had framed the solution to this "problem" as TBE: acquisition of English as rapidly as possible, notwithstanding students' need to learn subjects other than English as well. Several programmatic models, in addition to TBE, have been developed to teach students who are not proficient in English. Table 1 displays the most prevalent models.

While there are clearly many pathways to English acquisition and to successful academic achievement among English learners, framing of the primary language as a

TABLE 1   Major Program Models for English Learners

Program	Description
English immersion ("sheltered English")	Use of English-only strategies; English as a second language; specially designed academic instruction in English; usually lasts 1–3 years
Transitional bilingual education/early exit	Instruction using some primary language for transitional support; may teach early reading in primary language but normally makes transition to English only within 2–3 years; goal is literacy in English
Developmental bilingual/late exit	Emphasis on developing competence in two languages; students may receive instruction in primary and second language for many years; goal is literacy in two languages
Two-way immersion ("dual immersion")	English speakers and English learners taught together with focus on two languages; emphasis on strengthening minority language; goal is biliteracy; usually lasts 6 years or more

problem that must be remediated leads to a pedagogy that is not necessarily in the best interests of many students and to a policy framework that severely limits both cognitive and linguistic options for second-language learners. Ruiz (1984) asserted that there are three ways in which the linguistic challenges facing students of limited English proficiency can be framed: *language as problem*, which focuses on replacing the "problem language" with English; *language as right*, which focuses on the social justice aspects of language and promotes policies that support primary language development; and *language as resource*, which views one's primary language as an important tool in learning. The latter two orientations toward language result in policies that value native languages and their role in teaching and learning, while the first takes a much more limiting view of the language non–English speakers bring to school with them.

No amount of evidence of the effectiveness of bilingual instructional methods designed to develop and sustain primary languages will convince believers in English only as state policy. However, a considerable body of research does exist to show that such instructional methods can produce high levels of achievement (Hakuta, 1986; Slavin & Cheung, 2003) that in some cases are superior to the outcomes seen for English immersion strategies (Greene, 1998; Willig, 1985) and that, at a minimum, produce results among these students no worse than those produced by English-only methods (Baker & de Kanter, 1983). Moreover, they have the added benefit of conferring competence in two languages and promoting certain cognitive (Bialystok, 2001) and intercultural (Genesee & Gándara, 1999) advantages. In this light, the narrow construction of non-English languages as a problem must be viewed, if not harmful to English learners, at least as educationally limiting for them.

THE UNDOING OF *BROWN* AND *LAU*: THE COURTS

The optimism with which the court delivered the *Lau* decision is an echo of the hopefulness expressed by Chief Justice Earl Warren, author of the *Brown* decision, when he wrote: "In my entire public career I have never seen a group of men more conscious of the seriousness of a situation, more intent upon resolving it with as little disruption as possible, or with a greater desire for unanimity" (cited in Orfield, 1996, p. 29). In 1971, the court ruled in *Swann v. Charlotte-Mecklenburg Board of Education* that desegregation must be achieved in each of a district's schools (not just in the district as a whole), and it approved busing as a means of achieving that goal. Shortly thereafter, the *Keyes v. Denver School District No. 1* (1973) decision extended desegregation orders into northern and western states and recognized the right of desegregation for Latino students as well.

Although many districts across the South, such as Charlotte-Mecklenburg, enjoyed notable success in their desegregation plans, by the mid-1970s a strong movement had begun to return to neighborhood schools, citing the "obvious failure" of busing (Morantz, 1996). This perception of failure was based on the continued strife in many areas over reassignment policies, claims that parent involvement had been undermined by the demise of "neighborhood schools," and the movement of some White families from the cities to the suburbs. The fact that many urban and suburban parents continued to put their children on buses to attend elite (segregated) schools did not sway the courts. Nor did the fact that the majority of students who actually rode the bus for desegregation purposes were African American, and their parents were not complaining. An increasingly conservative Supreme Court, with four of its nine justices recently appointed by President Nixon, began to dismantle desegregation efforts with the *Milliken v. Bradley* case in 1974. Increasing segregation of minority groups in inner cities and suburbanization of the White population had led to desegregation plans that crossed district boundaries to achieve racial balance. *Milliken v. Bradley*, however, prohibited such plans, making it virtually impossible to create racially balanced schools in racially isolated urban areas. Contrary to the claims of those who fought reassignment plans, the evidence suggests that the end of busing resulted in neither enhanced achievement nor increased parent involvement in neighborhood schools (Eaton, 1996; Morantz, 1996).

In 1954, when the court ordered the end of racial segregation in U.S. public schools, few people in this country had thought through exactly what this would mean, how it could be achieved peacefully, and what kinds of measures would have to be enacted to change hundreds of years of social behaviors. The schools and society were ill equipped for the challenge. As a result, *Brown* initially met with resistance, followed by obfuscation through internal segregation within "desegregated" schools and then curriculum tracking ostensibly based on unbiased measures that, in practice, correlated highly with race. Ultimately, more and more courts simply retreated from desegregation efforts in frustration by finding school districts unitary (desegregated) in spite of considerable evidence to the contrary. As one court observer noted, "We [the court] still agree with the goal of school desegregation, but it's too hard, and we're tired of it, and we give up" (Hansen, cited in Kunen, 1996, p. 39). Today, the nation's schools are more segregated than they were in the early 1970s (Orfield & Lee, 2004).

There are several key elements of the Supreme Court's decision in *Lau*. First, by enforcing Title VI of the Civil Rights Act of 1964, *Lau* accepted the view that Congress has the power to ban harmful practices that do not amount to constitutional violations. The Constitution prohibits intentional racial discrimination, but, in the court's view, it does not extend to actions that merely have a racially unequal impact. Even so, the justices found that, under Section 5 of the 14th Amendment, Congress can enforce a norm of racial equality by recognizing claims of disparate impact, for example due to exclusionary language policies. Second, the court found that Congress exercised these powers when enacting Title VI of the Civil Rights Act; that is, the statute pertained not just to intentional discrimination but also to acts involving adverse effects. This approach enabled the federal government to police possible wrongdoing even when a discriminatory purpose was difficult to prove.

Third, the court deferred to the OCR in matters of interpretation. Because Congress had delegated civil rights enforcement responsibilities to the OCR, the agency could issue interpretations indicating that Title VI extended to language policies. Fourth, the court assumed that private individuals such as the Chinese-speaking students in San Francisco could sue to ensure Title VI's mandates were met. These private rights of action supplemented federal enforcement actions and were seen as critically important given the limited resources of agencies such as the OCR. Finally, given this legal foundation rooted in congressional power and agency interpretation, the school district's exclusive reliance on English-language instruction could be deemed as wrongfully excluding non-English-speaking children from access to the curriculum in violation of Title VI.

THE FATE OF THE *LAU* DECISION: UNDONE BY LAW

Since *Lau* was handed down in 1974, its legal underpinnings have been under siege in the federal courts as well as in the Department of Education. Little by little, the case is being undone, and its fate grows increasingly uncertain. In recent years, the Supreme Court has expressed significant doubts about the scope of congressional power and the discretion accorded to civil rights enforcement agencies under Title VI. The justices have also eliminated private rights of action for disparate impact claims under the statute, leaving enforcement almost entirely in the hands of executive branch officials.

The first judicial retreat involved *Lau*'s assumption that Title VI addresses both intentional discrimination and disparate impact—that is, discrimination—whether or not it is intended. In *Guardians Association v. Civil Service Commission*, the court found that Title VI authorized compensatory relief only for purposeful wrongs, not actions involving adverse effects. The justices hastened to add that *Lau* technically remained "good law" because it was predicated not only on the statute but on the OCR's interpretation. Although *Guardians Association* produced a fragmented and somewhat confusing set of opinions, the court's position was subsequently clarified in *Alexander v. Choate*. There, the court indicated that while Title VI itself did not support a disparate impact claim, agency regulations could rely on this theory of liability.

Lau suffered another blow in 2001 when the court decided *Alexander v. Sandoval*. There, the justices held that there is no private right of action under Title VI disparate impact regulations. As a result, private plaintiffs can sue only for intentional discrimination. In *Sandoval*, the justices noted that if federal agencies interpreted Title VI as extending to actions with adverse effects, it was up to those agencies to file legal actions based on this theory. In the court's view, Congress had not used clear and unambiguous language to establish a private right to sue on the basis of disparate impact regulations.

Some legal commentators believe that plaintiffs can still sue under Section 1983 of Title VI for disparate impact, because it provides that a person who, under color of state law, is deprived of "any rights, privileges, or immunities secured by the Constitution and laws" can bring a private right of action in federal court. However, the court has been increasingly cautious in allowing these actions when a private lawsuit cannot be brought under the statute itself. Because Title VI no longer permits a person to sue on the basis of a disparate impact regulation, the court might very well conclude that there is no right to be free of such adverse effects under Section 1983. As a result, if federal civil rights agencies are too overburdened to file an action, children will be left without recourse under Title VI unless they can establish discriminatory intent, which is extremely difficult to prove.

In summary, then, *Lau*'s foundational elements are on increasingly shaky ground and are particularly vulnerable to the political whims of any administration in power. The court has held that the language of Title VI itself does not extend to adverse effects but instead applies only to purposeful discrimination. Moreover, the justices have hinted that Congress may lack the power to define discrimination broadly to include intentional wrongs and disparate impact. In addition, the court has concluded that individuals cannot bring a private right of action under Title VI to challenge policies and practices that have adverse racial effects but must instead allege racial animus. After all of these judicial incursions, only the central finding of fact in *Lau* remains uncontested; that is, an English-only curriculum can be exclusionary whether or not school officials act with an intent to harm non-English-speaking students. Of course, as with *Brown*'s finding that separate educational facilities were inherently unequal, this fact unfortunately does not guarantee that the law can be effectively implemented if the courts do not press enforcement.

ALTERNATIVES TO TITLE VI: DOES *LAU'S* UNDOING MATTER?

Lau is not the only source of federal legal protection for English-language learn-ers. If alternative provisions offer ample protection, *Lau's* undoing would not jeop-ardize students' rights. The Equal Educational Opportunities Act (EEOA), the First Amendment guarantee of free speech, and the English Language Acquisition, Language Enhancement, and Academic Achievement Act ("English Language Acquisition Act") are the most promising possibilities for replacing *Lau's* Title VI protections. Yet, none of these options afford a perfect substitute for the anti-discrimination protections in *Lau*.

The best of these alternative sources of protection is the EEOA. Enacted by Con-gress to codify the *Lau* decision, the statute explicitly adopts an effects rather than an intent test in defining wrongful discrimination. Moreover, the EEOA includes an express private right of action enabling individuals to file suit if federal agencies fail to enforce the law. These features of the EEOA clearly have been critical in keeping *Lau's* legacy alive despite recent judicial incursions on Title VI. Although no educational remedies are specified, the EEOA empowers students and their par-ents to rely on disparate impact when challenging instructional practices in federal court. Yet, because the statute addresses only those actions that exclude children from access to instruction, it does not cover some of the educational policies that would be covered by Title VI. For instance, in *GI Forum v. Texas Education Agency*, limited-English-proficient students challenged high-stakes testing that dispropor-tionately barred them from obtaining a high school diploma. The federal district court judge, however, held that they had no cause of action under the EEOA because the testing process was an evaluative procedure rather than part of the instructional program.

A far less promising source of legal protection is the First Amendment, which pro-tects students' and teachers' free speech rights; however, these rights have been sup-ported much more strongly in higher education contexts than in elementary and secondary schools. First Amendment arguments have enjoyed some limited success in litigation challenging official English laws as an undue burden on individual speech rights. However, in the public school setting, rights of expression are circumscribed to permit the learning process to take place. Although students do not relinquish their First Amendment protections at the schoolhouse gate, the Supreme Court has shown an increasing willingness to allow school officials to regulate student expression if restrictions are reasonably related to pedagogical goals. In fact, the court's deferential stance has permitted a great deal of censorship to take place in the name of preserving civility. Under these circumstances, a federal court would be unlikely to find that mandating English-language instruction violates a student's right to speak a language other than English, especially if the goal is to promote Eng-lish acquisition. Even if the instruction has some exclusionary effects, these effects would have to be so severe that the policy would no longer be reasonably related to pedagogical aims.

Teachers, as employees charged with educating pupils in particular subjects, also must curb their speech on school grounds to promote the learning process. After the passage of Proposition 227, which mandates intensive English instruction for all students with limited English proficiency unless they are able to obtain a waiver from this provision,[2] teachers challenged a provision that subjected them to lawsuits if they delivered instruction that was not "overwhelmingly" or "nearly all" in English. The teachers contended that the threat of a lawsuit had a chilling effect on their First Amendment speech rights, particularly given the vagueness of terms such as "overwhelmingly" and "nearly all."

In *California Teachers Association v. State Board of Education*, the Ninth Circuit Court of Appeals noted that teachers enjoy limited rights of expression in the classroom. The court reviewed three competing First Amendment standards in this area: (a) Teachers have no free speech rights in the classroom; (b) teachers have no protection unless they are speaking on a matter of public concern; and (c) regulation of teachers' speech must be reasonably related to legitimate pedagogical concerns. Without deciding which standard was appropriate, the court of appeals concluded that plaintiffs had no viable cause of action under any of the tests, including the last and most generous one. According to the Ninth Circuit, Proposition 227's terms were not so vague that they would significantly limit legitimate speech in the classroom. Moreover, the court held that the state's pedagogical interests outweighed teachers' free speech rights. As explained in the decision:

Because any speech potentially chilled by Proposition 227 enjoys only minimal First Amendment protection, assuming it enjoys any protection at all, and because it is the state's pedagogical interests that are paramount in this context, any vagueness contained in Proposition 227 is even less likely to jeopardize First Amendment values.

Finally, the English Language Acquisition Act (the successor to the Bilingual Education Act) is an unpromising substitute for *Lau*'s enforcement provisions as well. This act is not an anti-discrimination statute but instead is a grant-in-aid program designed to support research, development, innovation, and service delivery in the area of bilingual education and intensive English instruction. The law does not confer enforceable rights on students, and it certainly does not trigger a private right to sue. Instead, it establishes administrative performance and accountability requirements. With respect to civil rights, the act merely states that it should not be interpreted in a manner inconsistent with other protections. Because the act represents "spending" legislation, Congress must put grant recipients on clear notice that acceptance of funds will leave them open to private lawsuits. Yet, there is no provision that would seem to satisfy this requirement.

In summary, then, the EEOA, the First Amendment, and the English Language Acquisition Act fail to offer a strong substitute for *Lau*'s Title VI enforcement provisions. The EEOA continues to provide substantial protection in gaining access to the curriculum, and litigants can look to state courts and state laws to challenge other facets of language policy and practice. Yet, plaintiffs can no longer depend on Title VI's comprehensive, national anti-discrimination provisions. When language barriers stand in the way of access to noninstructional resources and activities (e.g., meeting high-stakes diploma requirements or receiving ancillary school services), *Lau*'s undoing has real consequences for English learners, who increasingly find the federal courthouse doors closed to them. While these students theoretically can turn to the political process for a remedy, in fact neither they nor their parents are apt to have the kind of clout they would have had in the civil rights era of the 1960s to demand responsive policy-making. In fact, these families are increasingly losing one of their greatest sources of leverage in dealing with state and local officials: the threat of litigation.

A case in point is the reluctance of immigrant advocates to sue districts that do not honor parents' legal right to choose the type of educational program they deem most appropriate for their children. While California's Proposition 227 explicitly offers parents the right to seek a waiver from the prohibition on bilingual education for their children, there is accumulating evidence that some districts simply "lose" the waiver applications rather than respond to parents' petitions; others fail to provide information to parents about the availability of a waiver, and still others simply deny the option (Gándara, 2000). Yet, the series of setbacks experienced by lawyers seeking to reconcile the mandate of *Lau* and First Amendment rights with the language of Proposition 227 have made legal advocates extremely cautious about taking such cases to court. Although the Ninth Circuit may contend that Proposition 227 has not "chilled" teachers' right to free speech in the classroom, it certainly has chilled legal advocates' appetite for seeking redress for violation of parents' rights to make choices about their children's education. One hears echoes of frustrated lawyers who have attempted to press the courts on desegregation cases: "We still agree with the goal . . . but it's too hard, and we're tired of it, and we give up."

UNDOING BY REGULATION

The courts have been a more active site in the dismantling of desegregation than have regulatory bodies, probably because the methods specified—reassignment of students and redrawing of school boundaries—were more clearly defined by the courts than the method for creating access to the curriculum for English learners, which was intentionally vague. Less discretion was left to regulatory bodies in the decisions following *Brown* than in those that followed *Lau*. Moreover, desegregation has remained the purview of the federal courts, while state and federal regulations governing programmatic options for English learners have played a more significant role in the history of *Lau*'s implementation.

From the moment that *Lau* became the law, opponents of bilingual education, immigrant rights, and even immigration began a campaign to dismantle any semblance of primary language instruction. Conservative politicians complained about the heavy-handedness of the *Lau* regulations mandating primary language use, and Senator S. I. Hayakawa of California introduced Senate Joint Resolution 72 in 1981, which would have made English the official language of the United States, barring the official use of any other language. The bill did not pass, but Education Secretary Terrell Bell, responding to the tenor of the times, withdrew the *Lau* reg ulations the same year, placing in question the role of primary language instruction among English learners. The pressure was on bilingual programs to demonstrate their superiority as an instructional method or lose their status as a viable instructional option.

Newly minted bilingual programs, with limited resources and few teachers prepared by their colleges to meet the challenge, scrambled to find qualified teachers and appropriate materials and curricula. Most schools were no more prepared to provide high-quality bilingual programs overnight than they had been to desegregate their student body 20 years earlier. And yet social scientists began testing students after they had been involved in bilingual programs for a few months to measure whether achievement gaps had closed. When it was discovered that English learners—often immigrants and among the poorest of children in the schools—had not caught up to their English-speaking, middle-class peers, the "experiment" was deemed a failure.

Not surprisingly, given the huge diversity of programs that labored under the flag of "bilingual education," an American Institutes for Research (AIR) study conducted in the mid-1970s revealed no evidence of the "effectiveness" of bilingual education (Danoff, Coles, McLaughlin, & Reynolds, 1978). Of course, even in its nascent state and with a study rife with methodological flaws (e.g., programs categorized as "bilingual" or "English immersion" often did not differ in appreciable ways), bilingual education fared no worse than other programs assessed in the AIR investigation. Yet, the presumption of critics of bilingual education was that it had to be shown to be superior—not just equal—in producing academic achievement outcomes to be considered an appropriate instructional option for limited-English-proficient students. No such presumption was applied to English-only models. And so the "evidence" was being compiled to begin the discrediting of bilingual instruction virtually from its inception.

At the level of regulation, the *Lau* remedies were constantly under attack for promoting foreign languages at government expense as well as for being formulated and enforced without going through the formal rule-making procedures (Crawford, 1998). The debates continued until Secretary Bell withdrew the regulations in 1981, with the suggestion that states develop their own rules (Crawford, 2004a). Meanwhile, the Bilingual Education Act, which was established to provide funding for programs that assisted English learners through competitive grants for bilingual programs, continued to do so until 1984 when it came up for reauthorization and was modified to be more "flexible." The new iteration of the act allowed special alternative instructional programs that did not require native languages to be used in order to be funded. Each subsequent reauthorization further eroded funding for programs that used primary languages in instruction. In 1988, the Bilingual Education Act, as reauthorized, gave more discretion to local school districts to determine the kind of instructional program they would provide for English learners with their federal funds (Crawford, 2004b). As a result, districts could opt for English-only instruction as a more politically palatable alternative to primary language instruction.

In the mid-1990s, during the Clinton administration, efforts were made to bolster support for bilingual instruction, but such changes were short lived. In the 2001 reauthorization of the ESEA, Congress completely reversed the reauthorization from 1994. Table 2 provides a summary of key differences in how the 1994 and 2001 reauthorizations of the ESEA addressed the education of English learners.

Whereas the 1994 version of the Bilingual Education Act included among its goals "developing the English skills and to the extent possible . . . the native-language skills" of English learners, the new law focused only on attainment of "English proficiency." In fact, the word *bilingual* had been completely eliminated from the law and from any government office affiliated with the law. A new federal office was created to replace the Office of Bilingual Education and Minority Language Affairs and oversee the provisions of the new law (this is now the Office of English Language Acquisition, Language Enhancement, and Academic Achievement for Limited-English-Proficient Students, commonly referred to as OELA). What was formerly known as the National Clearinghouse for Bilingual Education—a repository for research on the instruction of English learners—became the National Clearinghouse for English Language Acquisition and Language Instruction Educational Programs.

As a result of Title III of the No Child Left Behind Act of 2002, federal funds designated to assisting English learners are no longer federally administered via competitive grants designed to ensure equity or promote the quality programs that served as models for the nation's schools. Instead, resources are allocated primarily through a state formula program for language instruction educational programs grounded in "scientifically based research." In these programs, English learners are placed in instructional courses for the purpose of developing English proficiency while meeting challenging state and academic content and academic achievement standards. The programs may make use of both English and a child's native language to enable the child to develop English proficiency.

Formula grants are distributed to each state according to its enrollment of English learners and immigrant students. Each state must then allocate 95% of the funds to individual local education agencies. The argument for the formula grants is that the previous system of competitive grants benefited only a small percentage of English learners in relatively few schools. In fact, resources are now spread more thinly than before—among more states, more programs, and more students. Title VII competitive grants designated for instructional programs previously served approximately 500,000 "eligible" English learners out of an estimated 3.5 million nationwide (Wiese & Garcia, 2001). Under the new law, districts automatically receive funding on the basis of enrollments of English learners and immigrant students. However, the impact of federal dollars is reduced. In 2002, for example, about $360 was spent per student in Title VII–supported instructional programs (Crawford, 2004b). By 2004, despite the overall increase in appropriations, Title III provided less than $135 per student (Crawford, 2004b). Funding for all other purposes—including teacher

TABLE 2 Significant Differences in the 1994 and 2001 Reauthorizations of the ESEA

Issue	1994 Title VII: Bilingual Education Act	2001 Title III: Language Instruction, Limited-English-Proficient and Immigrant Students
Eligible populations	Limited-English-proficient students Recent immigrants who "have not been attending one or more schools in any one or more States for more than three full years" (§7501(7)) Native Americans, Native Alaskans, Native Hawaiians, Native American Pacific Islanders	Limited-English-proficient students Immigrant children and youth (3–21 years of age), not born in any state, who "have not been attending one or more schools in any one or more states for more than 3 full academic years" (§3301(6)) Native Americans, Native Alaskans, Native Hawaiians, Native American Pacific Islanders
Purpose	"(A) To help such children and youth develop proficiency in English, and to the extent possible, their native language; and (B) meet the same challenging State content standards and challenging State student performance standards expected of all children" (§7111(2)) "The use of a child or youth's native language and culture in classroom instruction can . . . promote self-esteem and contribute to academic achievement and learning English by limited English proficient children and youth" (§7102(14)) "Unique status of Native American languages" and language enhancement.	"To help ensure that children who are limited English proficient, including immigrant children and youth, attain English proficiency, develop high levels of academic attainment in English, and meet the same challenging State academic content and student academic achievement standards as all children are expected to meet" (§3102(1)) Programs for Native Americans "develop English proficiency and, to the extent possible, proficiency in their native language" (§3211(2))

40

Programs	Competitive grants to local education agencies (schools, districts); state education agencies approve the grant application before submission but play no official role in the grant's implementation "Quality bilingual education programs enable children and youth to learn English and meet high academic standards including proficiency in more than one language" (§7102(9)) Priority is given to programs which "provide for development of bilingual proficiency both in English and another language for all participating students" (§7116 (i)(1))	"To streamline language instruction educational programs into a program carried out through formula grants to State educational agencies and local educational agencies" (§3102(7)) "To implement language instruction educational programs, based on scientifically-based research on teaching limited English proficient children" (§3102.(9))
Allocation of funds	Cap of 25% of funds for special alternative instructional programs; can be lifted if an applicant has demonstrated that developing and implementing a bilingual education program is not feasible	95% of funds must be used for grants at the local level to teach limited-English-proficient children; each state must spend this percentage to award formula subgrants to districts
Accountability and assessment	Local education agency (LEA) has control and is granted flexibility on how to best serve students; LEA sets its own goals and ways of assessing them	Holding various educational agencies accountable for "increases in English proficiency and core academic content knowledge . . . by requiring . . . . (A) demonstrated improvements in the English proficiency of limited English proficient students each fiscal year; and (B) adequate yearly progress" (§3102(8))

training, research, and support services—is restricted to 6.5% of the total budget. Total funding amounted to approximately $43 million in 2004. By contrast, $100 million was spent on professional development alone in 2002 to address the critical shortage of teachers qualified to meet the needs of English learners (Saracho & Spodek, 2004).

Federal regulation has shifted to emphasize the teaching and learning of English with little regard for the development of academic or bilingual competency among students coming to school speaking a language other than English. The elimination of "bilingual" from federal language is nearly complete, and expenditures for English learners are on the decline even as they begin to compose a larger and larger portion of the total school-aged population in the United States—now approaching 10% (Development Associates, 2003; Kindler, 2002). With the public relations battles lost and both the state and federal governments refashioning regulations for services for English learners, only the courts are left to protect these students' language rights that, in the words of *Lau*, require equal access to an education:

Under these state-imposed standards there is no equality of treatment merely by providing students with the same facilities, textbooks, teachers, and curriculum; for students who do not understand English are effectively foreclosed from any meaningful education. Basic English skills are at the very core of what these public schools teach. Imposition of a requirement that, before a child can effectively participate in the educational program, he must already have acquired those basic skills is to make a mockery of public education. We know that those who do not understand English are certain to find their classroom experiences wholly incomprehensible and in no way meaningful.

Unfortunately, as we have noted, in recent times the courts have not provided much support for either a *language as a right* or a *language as a resource* orientation to the education of English learners.

THE PUBLIC RELATIONS ASSAULT ON DESEGREGATION AND BILINGUAL EDUCATION

The public relations assault on both desegregation and bilingual education came from many quarters. Social science evidence was used to demonstrate that "White flight" had resulted in de facto segregation, that busing to desegregate schools had resulted in hardships for many students and families, that neither Black nor White students were performing any better in desegregated schools, and that desegregation was "enormously costly" (Armor, 1996). Evidence to the contrary—that Black students were, in fact, performing better in desegregated settings (Coleman et al., 1966; Mahard & Crain, 1983)—was often dismissed by politicians anxious to quell restive White voters. Likewise, bilingual education has been described as divisive (Schlesinger, 1991), ineffective (Baker & de Kanter, 1983), a "full employment program" for Latino teachers (Unz, 2000, as cited on PBS's *Uncommon Knowledge*), costly and "wasteful" (Unz & Tuchman, 1997), and even harmful to English learners, leading to "high dropout rates and low English literacy" (Unz & Tuchman, 1997).

Importantly, claims regarding the failure of bilingual education have always been based on program evaluation studies (e.g., the AIR study), while the basis for bilingual education as a pedagogical tool is research on second-language acquisition—research that is, in fact, relatively noncontroversial. This body of work, which has been based largely on learning theory and has focused on the ways in which people learn second languages, has shown that (a) children's degree of native language proficiency is a strong predictor of their English language development (August & Hakuta, 1997); (b) children can learn to read a second language more efficiently if they have already acquired decoding skills in their first language (National Research Council, 1998); and (c) teaching concepts in a language that has been mastered is more efficient than teaching them in a language that is still being acquired (Bialystok & Hakuta, 1994; Krashen, 1996).

These findings form the basis of support for teaching in a first language—when possible—while also teaching English. However, the public relations strategy has been to ignore these commonsense findings in favor of a reliance on program evaluation studies, which are fundamentally incapable of concluding anything more than that well-implemented programs (of any kind) produce better results than poorly implemented programs (of any kind). Which programs will produce better results depends greatly on the individual students, their backgrounds and contexts, and the skills and abilities of the teachers to whom they are assigned. All else being equal, however, the case for the use of primary language instruction is a strong one, notwithstanding the public relations campaigns that have been launched against bilingual education by individuals with political agendas.

Although claims regarding the failure of bilingual education have lacked rigorous research support, the media love a good controversy and were only too happy to provide a forum for such claims. Thus, as with desegregation, the critics pulled out their "scientific evidence" on program evaluations to argue against what psycholinguists held as the most theoretically sound and research-based approach to educating English learners. For example, in a now-infamous *New York Times* article that appeared in the months before Arizonans were to go to the polls to vote on banning bilingual education in that state, Jacques Steinberg (2000) wrote:

Two years after Californians voted to end bilingual education and force a million Spanish-speaking students to immerse themselves in English as if it were a cold bath, those students are improving in reading and other subjects at often striking rates, according to standardized test scores released this week.

Unfortunately, Steinberg took his information from one of Ron Unz's (the author of California's Proposition 227, which severely restricted bilingual education) daily faxes to the press without thoroughly checking the facts. Shortly thereafter, it was found that the data on which the story was based were flawed, and the recalculated scores painted a very different picture, one in which some of the remaining bilingually educated students actually outperformed those in English-only classes. A retraction was never run by the *New York Times*.

CONCLUSION

As both *Lau* and *Brown* are undone by law, the question arises: What remains of the legacy? Both named identifiable wrongs; that is, separate educational facilities are inherently unequal, and an English-only curriculum can effectively exclude public school students who do not yet speak the language. In addition, both *Brown* and *Lau* recognized a legal right to be free of such wrongs. Despite recent incursions, the heart of both cases survives, particularly the naming of segregation and linguistic exclusion as discrimination harming children in profound ways. Even so, enforcement of *Brown* rests with the endurance and creativity of courts overseeing school desegregation, while *Lau* rests its future on the vestiges of administrative authority under Title VI and the individual lawsuits that can be brought under the EEOA. As long as a commitment to equal educational opportunity remains in the law, appointment of judges and administrators who are supportive of civil rights could give this promise new meaning.

Meanwhile, *Brown*'s vision of integrated education is steadily being dismantled, and *Lau*'s endorsement of language rights is gradually being eroded as the courts question congressional power and curtail private rights to bring suit. At the 50th anniversary of Brown and the 30th anniversary of *Lau*, both were mere shadows of their former selves, and we are reminded that there is no right without a remedy. Perhaps *Brown*'s true legacy remains one of a struggle for equal educational opportunity that can easily be lost if we are not prepared to do battle on several fronts: before the courts, in the hallways of Congress and the offices of administrative agencies, and in the forum of public opinion.

NOTES

[1] A number of different terms are used to refer to students who are not native speakers of English. At the time of the *Lau* decision, the most commonly used term was *limited English proficient*; since that time, *English language learner* and *English learner* have come into common use. Here they are used interchangeably.

[2] Proposition 227 provided for three conditions under which waivers could be obtained: (a) if a student is already fluent in English, (b) if a student is more than 10 years of age, and (c) and if it can be shown that a student has a special need that must be addressed through a different language program. As a result, between 8% and 9% of English learners in California remain in a program that provides instruction at least partially through their primary language.

REFERENCES

Alexander v. Choate, 469 U.S. 287 (1985).

Alexander v. Sandoval, 532 U.S. 275 (2001).

Armor, D. (1996). *Forced justice: School desegregation and the law.* New York: Oxford University Press.

August, D., & Hakuta, K. (1997). *Improving schooling for language minority children.* Washington, DC: National Academy Press.

Baker, K. A., & de Kanter, A. A. (1983). *Bilingual education: A reappraisal of federal policy.* Lexington, MA: Heath.

Bialystok, E. (2001). *Bilingualism in development: Language, literacy, and cognition.* New York: Cambridge University Press.

Bialystok, E., & Hakuta, K. (1994). *In other words: The science and psychology of second-language acquisition.* New York: Basic Books.

Brown v. Board of Education, 347 U.S. 483 (1954).

California Teachers Association v. State Board of Education, 271 F.3d 1141 (9th Cir., 2001).

Coleman, J., Campbell, E., Hobson, C., McPartland, J., Mood, A., Weinfield, F., & York, R. (1966). *Equality of educational opportunity.* Washington, DC: U.S. Government Printing Office.

Crawford, J. (1992). *Language loyalties: A sourcebook on the official English controversy.* Chicago: University of Chicago Press.

Crawford, J. (1998). Language politics in the USA: The paradox of bilingual education. *Social Justice, 25*(3). Retrieved April 22, 2005, from http://ourworld.compuserve.com/homepages/JWCRAWFORD/paradox.htm

Crawford, J. (2004a). *Educating English learners: Language diversity in the classroom.* (5th ed.). Los Angeles: Bilingual Educational Services.

Crawford, J. (2004b). *"No Child Left Behind": Misguided approach to school accountability for English language learners. Retrieved* January 5, 2005, from http://www.ctredpol.org/pubs/Forum

Danoff, M. N., Coles, G. J., McLaughlin, D. H., & Reynolds, D. J. (1978). *Evaluation of the impact of ESEA Title VII Spanish/English bilingual education program* (Vol. 3). Palo Alto, CA: American Institutes for Research.

Development Associates. (2003) *Descriptive study of LEP students and LEP students with disabilities.* Washington, DC: Author.

Eaton, S. (1996). Slipping toward segregation: Local control and eroding desegregation in Montgomery County. In G. Orfield (Ed.), *Dismantling desegregation: The quiet reversal of Brown v Board of Education* (pp. 207–240). New York: New Press.

Gándara, P. (2000). In the aftermath of the storm: English learners in the post-227 era. *Bilingual Research Journal, 24,* 1–13.

Genesee, F., & Gándara, P. (1999). Bilingual education programs: A cross-national perspective. *Journal of Social Issues, 55,* 665–685.

GI Forum v. Texas Education Agency, 87 F. Supp. 2d 667 (W.D. Tex., 2000).

González, G. (1999). Segregation and the education of Mexican children, 1900–1940. In J. Moreno (Ed.), *The elusive quest for equality.* Cambridge, MA: Harvard University.

Greene, J. (1998). *A meta-analysis of the Rossell and Baker review of bilingual education research.* Retrieved December 13, 2004, from http://brj.asu,edu/archives/23v21/articles/art.hmtl

Guardians Association v. Civil Service Commission, 463 U.S. 582 (1983).

Hakuta, K. (1986). *Mirror of language: The debate on bilingualism.* New York: Basic Books.

Keyes v. Denver School District No. 1, 413 U.S. 189 (1973).

Kindler, A. L. (2002). *Survey of the states' limited English proficient students and available educational programs and services: 2000–2001 summary report.* Washington, DC: National Clearinghouse for English Language Acquisition and Language Instruction Educational Programs.

Krashen, S. (1996). *Under attack: The case against bilingual education.* Culver City, CA: Language Education Associates.

Kunen, J. (1996, April 29). The end of integration. *Time,* pp. 39–45.Lau v. Nichols, 414 U.S. 563 (1974).

Mahard, R., & Crain, R. (1983). Research on minority achievement in desegregated schools. In C. Rossell & W. Hawley (Eds.), *The consequences of school desegregation* (pp. 103–125). Philadelphia: Temple University Press.

Méndez et al v. Westminster School District of Orange County et al., 64 F. Supp. 544 (S.D. Calif., 1946).

Milliken v. Bradley, 94 S. Court 3112, 3134–3141 (1974).

Morantz, A. (1996). Desegregation at risk: Threat and reaffirmation in Charlotte. In G. Orfield (Ed.), *Dismantling desegregation: The quiet reversal of Brown v Board of Education* (pp. 179–206). New York: New Press.

National Research Council. (1998). *Preventing reading difficulties in young children.* Washington, DC: National Academy Press.

Orfield, G. (1996). Plessy parallels, back to traditional assumptions. In G. Orfield (Ed.), *Dismantling desegregation: The quiet reversal of Brown v. Board of Education* (pp. 1–52). New York: New Press.

Orfield, G., & Lee, C. M. (2004). *Brown at fifty.* Cambridge, MA: Civil Rights Project, Harvard University.

Ruiz, R. (1984). Orientations in language planning. *Journal of the National Association of Bilingual Education, 2,* 15–34.

Saracho, O. N., & Spodek, B. (2004). Historical perspectives in language policy and literacy reform. In O. N. Saracho & B. Spodek (Eds.), *Contemporary perspectives on language policy and literacy instruction in early childhood education.* Greenwich, CT: Information Age.

Schlesinger, A. (1991, July 8). The cult of ethnicity: Good and bad. *Time,* p. 20.

Slavin, R., & Cheung, A. (2003). *Effective reading programs for English language learners: A best-evidence synthesis.* Baltimore: CRESPAR/Johns Hopkins University.

Steinberg, J. (2000). Increase in test scores counters dire forecasts for bilingual ban. *New York Times.* Retrieved December 15, 2004, from http://www.ourworld.compuserve.com/homepages/JWCRAWFORD/NYT18.htm

Swann v. Charlotte-Mecklenburg Board of Education, 402 U.S. 1 (1971).

Unz, R., & Tuchman, G. M. (1997). *English language for children in public schools.* Unpublished document.

Wiese, A.-M., & Garcia, E. E. (2001). The Bilingual Education Act: Language minority students and US federal educational policy. *International Journal of Bilingual Education and Bilingualism, 4,* 229–248.

Willig, A. (1985). A meta-analysis of selected studies on the effectiveness of bilingual education. *Review of Educational Research, 55,* 269–317.

Chapter 3

How Society Failed School Desegregation Policy: Looking Past the Schools to Understand Them

AMY STUART WELLS
Teachers College, Columbia University

JENNIFER JELLISON HOLME
University of California, Los Angeles

ANITA TIJERINA REVILLA
University of Nevada at Las Vegas

AWO KORANTEMAA ATANDA
Mathematica Policy Research, Inc.

In America we have deemed desegregation too difficult a social process to be dealt with by realtors, bankers, clergymen, and community leaders. We have assigned the task to the children. (Mack, 1968, p. 459)

It is a noteworthy coincidence that the year of publication of this volume, 2005, sits chronologically between the 50th anniversary of *Brown v. Board of Education* in 2004 and the 40th anniversary of *Equality of Educational Opportunity* (also known as the "Coleman report") in 2006. This juxtaposition is symbolic given that, while both the Supreme Court ruling and the congressionally mandated Coleman study ultimately supported school desegregation policies, they differed relatively dramatically in terms of *why*, and these distinctions related to different views of the role of schools in society. It is fitting, then, that this chapter, which argues that we cannot understand the success or failure of school desegregation until we consider the complex relationship between desegregated public schools and the larger society, is wedged between these two important anniversaries.

The strongly worded *Brown* ruling discussed at length the importance of public education in preparing students for their adult lives as workers and citizens. For instance, Chief Justice Warren wrote: "Today, education is perhaps the most important function of state and local governments. Compulsory school attendance laws and the great expenditures for education both demonstrate our recognition of the importance of education in our democratic society" (p. 7).[1]

In contrast, the Coleman report muted the *Brown* decision's interpretation of public education as a paramount institution and argued instead that the variation in school curriculum and facilities and, to a lesser extent, teacher quality accounted for relatively little difference in student achievement, especially among students of color. According to the report, "Attributes of other students account for far more variation in the achievement of minority-group children than do any attributes of school facilities and slightly more than do attributes of staff" (Coleman et al., 1966, p. 322).

Thus, the implication of the Coleman report was that school desegregation policies would help raise the achievement of students of low socioeconomic status (SES) because they would attend school with high-SES students. And while news coverage of the report's central findings varied greatly, the *New York Times* reported that "differences in schools had very little effect on the achievement scores of children with a strong educational background in the home" (cited in Grant, 1973, p. 30). The message was that family background was more important than schools.

Over time, the Coleman report came to be seen as evidence that schools do not matter—at least not as much as people had believed—and that family background, especially parents' education and income, mattered much more (Grant, 1973). Thus, while both the *Brown* decision and the Coleman report advocated for school desegregation, one did so by pointing out how important schools are to students' life chances and the other did so by pointing out the importance of outside-of-school forces, especially family background.[2]

We begin by highlighting this distinction between these two landmark documents because we believe it reflects the ongoing ambivalence in the United States over how much responsibility we can and should place on our public schools to solve problems that the schools themselves did not create, even when the schools have done their share to perpetuate such problems. In many ways, the 12 years between the *Brown* decision and the Coleman report marked one of the first swings of an ongoing political pendulum vacillating between an argument that schools can solve most inequality in our society and an argument that schools do not make much of a difference at all in overcoming inequality in the lives of children. In the years since the Coleman report, we have seen the pendulum swing far back toward the position that schools alone can solve the problems of poor children because, with the right incentives or sanctions, educators can close the achievement gap between privileged and disadvantaged students.

In the first section of this chapter, we trace the history of this pendulum swing from Coleman to the current federal law, No Child Left Behind—from an argument that schools matter very little to a focus on schools as the sole solution to social problems—and consider various political trends that have propelled it, including racial politics and the backlash against school desegregation. We also consider the role of social science research in our collective understanding of what schools can and cannot accomplish and ask why more researchers have not examined schools within their contexts.

In the second section, we consider how and why so little of the post-Coleman research on school desegregation offered a more balanced understanding of the role of schools in society, given what these studies were revealing about the difficulty schools faced in overcoming racial inequality and, at the same time, the relative success of desegregation policies in comparison with other school reform models. We argue that, for the most part, research on school desegregation inadvertently contributed to the swinging pendulum by focusing solely on what schools accomplished or failed to accomplish on their own, despite the challenges they faced in the context of a racially segregated and unequal society. And yet, ironically, nowhere should the relationship between schools and society be more apparent than in communities struggling to implement a policy such as school desegregation that so rubs against the societal norm of racial separation.

In the third section of this chapter, we discuss our own 5-year historical study of six high schools that were desegregated in the 1970s and their now-adult graduates from the class of 1980 to provide a new framework for understanding the intertwined relationship between schools and the larger society. Through this study, we note the many ways in which the local community context of these schools and the broader social context at that time affected educators' and policymakers' efforts to implement school desegregation policies. For instance, we found that the schools and communities we studied often reproduced racial inequality by maintaining the White privilege of the larger society within the context of desegregated schools. Yet, at the same time, these schools provided venues where students and educators crossed the color line in ways they had never done before and many have not done since (Wells, Revilla, Holme, & Atanda, 2004). For the most part, the students of color who attended these schools thought they received a better education than they would have in more racially segregated schools, but they also recalled facing the same kind of discrimination inside these schools that they experienced in the larger society (see Revilla, Wells, & Holme, 2005).

Such research helps to explain the space between the pendulum swings, that is, the places where we can see the impact of schools on their students *and* the impact of society on schools. It allows us to consider a more fluid and iterative relationship between schools and their social context—a relationship in which schools both perpetuate and occasionally circumvent broader inequalities. Through such understandings, we can see schools as places where social reproduction occurs but also where human agency matters and makes a difference in students' lives.

In many ways, this wider-angle lens enabled us to understand that school desegregation policy was not a simple failure, as it has so often been portrayed (Armor, 1995). Rather, we learned that in many ways our society failed school desegregation policy by providing a context that worked against its goals at every turn. We hope our findings will cause policymakers to reconsider the extreme arguments representing the two sides of the pendulum: that schools alone can solve our societal problems and that schools do not matter much at all.

Thus, we use our own work as an example of what happens when researchers examine schools within their social and political contexts and thus explore the complex relationship between schools and the larger society—a relationship that both complicates equity-minded policies such as school desegregation and makes these policies all the more important. In the end, we argue that such studies can best shed light on the many ways in which schools matter and, at the same time, the many ways in which schools' efforts to make changes are compromised by larger social forces.

Finally, we make a case for more educational research that looks carefully at the relationship between schools and society, not just families, as Coleman and others have focused on, but the local and global contexts of schools and families. While we recognize the important role that families play in preparing their children for school and in supporting their education, we think it is naive to talk about families as if they were making child-rearing decisions in a vacuum protected from powerful social forces such as racism, poverty, and a highly competitive form of capitalism. Thus, we argue, there are too few empirical attempts to place educators, students, and parents into a broader social and political context to understand how their local communities and the larger society constrain or enable educational policies and the effects that schools have on children. Throughout this chapter, we discuss some of the methodological reasons for this empirical neglect of context and conclude with suggestions that might help researchers design studies that can answer broader questions.

The point of this chapter, then, is to encourage researchers to consider and conceptualize a more complex and iterative relationship between schools and society. We think that the vacillation between political arguments that place far too much burden on the schools to solve huge societal problems and arguments that "schools don't matter at all"—that only families do—is extremely problematic. Both arguments ultimately erode public support for public education, either because of frustration that schools are not doing enough or because of a lack of belief that they can do anything.

WHEN SCHOOLS MATTER TOO MUCH OR TOO LITTLE: THE SWINGING PENDULUM OF PUBLIC DISCOURSE

In the decade following the Coleman report, despite many protests from educators, the pendulum remained on the "schools don't matter" side of the spectrum. This was due in part to other social scientists, most notably Daniel Patrick Moynihan and Christopher Jencks, who put forth somewhat similar arguments in their writing and public engagement.

For instance, in 1972 Jencks and colleagues published *Inequality*, a book arguing that the most effective way to create greater equality in our society was not through educational reform but through more equal distribution of income. This study, with its focus on structural inequality and social reproduction, discounted the impact of several factors, including family background, cognitive ability, *and* schooling, on adults' economic equality and thus differed somewhat from the Coleman report, which had emphasized family background as it relates to educational outcomes.

As a result, the Jencks et al. (1972) argument was broader than the Coleman report's because it focused on inequality in terms of the income of adults rather than the test scores of students. The authors claimed that while equalizing school resources and opportunities might be an important moral and political goal, the long-term impact on overall equality would be negligible. The headline of a front-page story in the *New*

York Times read "Harvard Study Disputes Impact of Schooling on Future Income" (Tanner, 1972). *Inequality* fueled the "schools don't matter" argument even as its more radical implications regarding income inequality and how to lessen it were ignored.

Meanwhile, Daniel Patrick Moynihan, who served as counselor to President Richard M. Nixon before becoming a senator, strongly supported the findings of the Coleman report, especially its conclusion regarding the importance of the family. According to Grant (1973), Moynihan was interested in the Coleman report because the findings were in sync with his own earlier report on the decline of the Black family. Moynihan's report, however, had been controversial, and he was criticized for what was seen as a negative portrayal of Black families and culture (Grant, 1973).

Thus, Moynihan welcomed the Coleman study because it also spoke to the importance of families, and he worked at getting more attention for the report. Grant (1973) argued that Moynihan "had more to do with the way the Report was received, analyzed and subsequently made an instrument of policy than any social scientist other than James Coleman himself" (p. 32).

Before joining the Nixon administration, Moynihan was part of a team of professors and graduate students at Harvard who reanalyzed the Coleman data and came up with the same findings. Their results were published in a book—*On Equality of Educational Opportunity*—that helped to place the findings of the Coleman report into the public domain (Mosteller & Moynihan, 1972). As Nixon's counselor in the early 1970s, Moynihan brought Coleman's message to federal policymakers (Grant, 1973; Moynihan, 1991). Nixon tried to use the report to justify major cuts to the Department of Health, Education, and Welfare budget and his unwillingness to enforce school desegregation. While he did not succeed in making these cuts in the short run, such arguments gained much attention (Grant, 1973).

Moynihan, Jencks, and Coleman all tried to articulate the educational policy implications of their research. And while they did not always embrace the same goals or agree on the contributions of various factors to inequality, often their messages were interpreted in their simplest forms to mean that schools did not matter, and thus spending more money on public education was fruitless.

Thus, at its best, the Coleman report was seen as a rationale for school desegregation and compensatory education for poor students to help schools do what families were not doing (Moynihan, 1991). At its worst, this research, coupled with the writings of Jencks et al. (1972) and Moynihan (1991), became a rationale for not equalizing highly disparate expenditures across schools and districts, no doubt contributing to the separate and unequal educational system we have today.

Researchers, Educators, and Advocates Respond to Coleman: The Effective Schools Movement

The first attempt to swing the pendulum back in the direction of "schools matter" started with a group of researchers and educators who, in the late 1960s and 1970s, set out to disprove Coleman's conclusions (Bickel, 1983). Ronald Edmonds, an educator and advocate for disadvantaged students, was influenced by the research of James Comer, George Weber, Wilbur Brookover, and Lawrence Lezotte, who were studying the education and development of poor children. In particular, Edmonds drew on Weber's early 1970s research on successful urban schools serving poor students to develop a set of correlates of what came to be called "effective schools": schools that made a difference in the lives of students from poor families (Becker, 1992).

The five correlates—strong administrative leadership; a climate of high expectations; a quiet, orderly atmosphere; an emphasis on basic skills; and educators' awareness of pupil progress through frequent testing—provided the foundation for what would soon become the very popular and widespread "effective schools movement" (Becker, 1992). By the mid-1980s, most states and many school districts across the country were implementing certain aspects of the effective schools reform model.

Most observers of the rise of the effective schools movement credit its success to a deep sense of frustration among educators and advocates that the "schools don't matter" argument was at best exaggerated and at worst disingenuous. Bickel (1983) referred to the origin of this movement as both an effort to dispel the Coleman report and a strong desire among educators across the country "to hear a more hopeful message about the ability of schools to educate children" (p. 3).

Indeed, Edmonds himself provided a very powerful critique of the argument that schools do not matter. In 1979, he wrote that the belief that large differences in students' school performance can be attributed to their social class and family background was popular because of the "many social scientists and opinion makers" who continued to espouse it. This belief, he wrote, "has the effect of absolving educators of their professional responsibility to be instructionally effective" (cited in Becker, 1992, p. 6).

More specifically, the effective schools movement started out as an African American movement and was partially an outgrowth of anger and frustration with the racial inequalities in the educational system and the "White liberal" reliance on school desegregation policies to solve this inequality. Meanwhile, massive White flight from urban school districts sent a clear message to Blacks that racial integration was not a feasible means of bringing about much-needed change in urban schools.

The National Council on Educating Black Children was founded in 1986 to promote the effective schools philosophy. The council's leaders argued that African Americans needed to take the education of their children into their own hands. According to Arnold Cooper (1995), one of the leaders of the council, "The African-American community must ultimately rely upon itself to reinforce a substantive and relevant education for its children."

Yet, the tenets of the effective schools movement, which squarely place the responsibility for educating disadvantaged children back on the schools, resonated with a much larger constituency beyond the African American community. Throughout the 1980s and 1990s, the effective schools movement continued to influence educators and policymakers around the country. For instance, in 1988, Congress passed the Hawkins-Stafford School Improvement Act, which permits school districts to use Chapter 1 (now called Title 1) money for effective schools programs (Bradley, 1989). This act marked the first time effective schools principles were included in a federal law (Snider, 1989).

By 1989, a U.S. General Accounting Office survey estimated that 58% of the nation's school districts had implemented or were planning to implement programs based on "effective schools" research; this was up from only 17% of all school districts in 1984–1985. According to Snider (1989), these findings offered the first official confirmation of the rapid spread of the effective schools movement. According to Richardson (1995), "In sheer numbers, the effective-schools model appears to be one of the most successful efforts at scaling up—spreading a reform idea or practice beyond a few schools."

Thus, what had started out as a grassroots movement within the African American community had, by the 1990s, become far more "mainstream." And in the process of scaling up the effective schools movement, researchers and advocates added new correlates to the original five (Taylor & Bullard, 1995). Helping to fuel the movement's popularity was a growing body of research literature on classroom- and school-level variables that influence student achievement. In a review of the effective schools research, Rowan, Bossert, and Dwyer (1983) argued that this literature went beyond estimating the overall effects of schools on student achievement and instead attempted to identify more specific factors that have an impact. This specificity, Rowan et al. (1983) noted, is what distinguished the effective schools literature from previous studies on school effects, which they said "focused on gross measures of school facilities, funding, and staffing that are far removed from important teaching and learning processes" (p. 27).

Similarly, Wenglinsky (2002), in a more recent review of literature on whether schools matter, noted a methodological distinction between the large-scale quantitative Coleman-era studies, which tended to show few if any school effects, and the qualitative effective schools studies, which emphasized just how much schools do matter:

Quantitative research on whether schools matter has generally supported the notion that the problems of U.S. education lie outside of the schools. . . . A possible reason for the lack of large school effects in quantitative research is the failure of such research to capitalize on an insight from qualitative research: the central importance of the classroom practices of teachers. (p. 2)

Indeed, it is no coincidence that the effective schools movement took off around the time qualitative researchers began to pay close attention to student-teacher interactions and the effects of classroom dynamics, especially teacher expectations, on student achievement, motivation, and self-esteem. Authors such as Brophy and Good (1974) and Rist (1970) published groundbreaking work on teachers and students in their everyday activities and demonstrated the powerful effects of schools on children. Brophy and Good (1974) noted that researchers should focus on actual teachers as they interact with their own students in the context of their classrooms. Then and only then, many qualitative researchers would argue, do we really gain an awareness of school effects or effective schools (see Mehan, 1992).

According to Rowan et al. (1983), the large-scale quantitative research on so-called "gross measures" was not very successful in identifying specific features of school organizations that influence student achievement. They argued that the effective schools research, in contrast, has focused on features of school organization and culture that are "both intuitively sensible and manipulable" (p. 27).

Still, Rowan et al. (1983), like Purkey and Smith (1983), argued that overall qualitative studies of the effective schools movement left a great deal to be desired, especially in terms of generalizability of findings from one school to another. For instance, in their extensive review of effective schools research, Purkey and Smith (1983) noted that these studies generally examined "good" schools or classrooms and their characteristics or compared the characteristics of "high-scoring" and "low-scoring" schools. Purkey and Smith (1983) argued that it is unlikely that adoption of the characteristics suggested in the literature would work in all schools. Furthermore, they noted that these characteristics "may not work as expected in many schools and may in fact be counterproductive in some schools" (p. 440).

Of course, the effective schools movement also had other detractors, including scholars who critiqued the movement for ignoring the social and political context of schools (see Hallinger & Murphy, 1986; Lawrence, 1986). By the 1980s, however, in the midst of the Reagan administration and deep into the political backlash against civil rights policies and the welfare state (see Edsall, 1991), it was clear that examining the social and political context of schools was not on the policy agenda

In fact, as time went on, many of the tenets of the effective schools movement were absorbed into the so-called "excellence" movement that has fueled recent waves of educational reform, most notably the standards and accountability measures that characterize the current era in education (see Taylor & Bullard, 1995). As Richardson (1995) noted, "The emphasis on believing that all children can learn, the central tenet that undergirds effective schools, has become the rallying cry for the current push to raise education standards."

While the leaders of the effective schools movement were justified in their frustration with African American student achievement levels in public schools in the 1970s, it is more than a little ironic that a school reform movement that was originally intended to alleviate the inequality remaining after *Brown* was eventually used by White policymakers to justify the maintenance of a separate and unequal educational system—albeit with high standards for all.

Political Backlash Against the "Schools Don't Matter" Argument

It is difficult to say how strongly or directly the effective schools movement influenced the broader standards and accountability movement that would begin to dominate the educational policy agenda by the late 1980s. Yet, philosophically the central themes of the effective schools movement supported a reform agenda that would place a large part of the burden of solving inequality on the public schools. As stated by Lezotte, one of the founders and advocates of the effective schools movement, in a way it "contributed to the call for standards because we were always asking people where they want to go" (cited in Richardson, 1995).

This connection between the effective schools movement and a standards movement that would call upon schools to solve inequality almost single-handedly began in the early 1980s. According to Cuban (1993), the widely read and politically powerful 1983 report issued by the Reagan administration, *A Nation at Risk*, borrowed the central beliefs of the effective schools movement and gave the movement a political platform. "Effective-schools principles became a national agenda: All children can learn; schools must have high academic standards; for a school to achieve its goals, texts, tests, and the curriculum must be tightly coupled; and, finally, test scores will prove to a skeptical public that schools are accountable."

Thus, by the early 1980s, the pendulum had swung all the way back to emphasizing the crucial role of schools in society. Cuban (1993) noted the irony that, within two decades, "policymaker 'wisdom' on schooling had flip-flopped from schools not making much difference to the local school being the single most important instrument in securing equity and excellence for all children."

Yet, by the 1980s, the message from Washington, D.C., to the schools was highly critical, as *A Nation at Risk* and other reports stressed both the importance of education and the failure of the nation's schools in preparing students for a globally competitive workforce (Cross, 2004). As part of a larger political backlash against many public policies of the 1960s and 1970s such as school desegregation, *A Nation at Risk* set a tone of impatience and intolerance toward public schools while simultaneously placing the burden of solving most of society's problems back on them. For instance, one of the report's most oft-quoted phrases is that "the educational foundations of our society are presently being eroded by a rising tide of mediocrity that threatens our very future as a nation and a people" (National Commission on Excellence in Education, 1983, p. 1).

This rhetoric and the educational "excellence" policy agenda that evolved from it set a tone of public educational failure and the need for higher standards, more requirements, and more sanctions for schools and students. In fact, the central theme dominating educational policy debates for almost 25 years has been that public schools are seen as critical to the future of the nation but woefully inadequate in their capacity to meet the demands of this burden. Most notably, Reagan's second education secretary, the bombastic William J. Bennett, used his position as a bully pulpit to draw attention to what he saw as multiple problems with the public schools (Cross, 2004).

Thus, while the once-grassroots effective schools movement and the then-emerging Reagan administration agenda on education and excellence shared some philosophical roots—namely, they both sought to address a perceived lack of responsibility on the part of schools and educators for student failure—there were several inconsistencies as well. For instance, Boyd (1987) noted that the Reagan administration's strategy for school reform exhibited several weaknesses:

> The national-commission reports suggest that we can change schools by external mandates, that we can, in effect, "legislate learning" by heaping new requirements and accountability demands on schools. But this approach neglects the internal workings of schools and what we have learned from the "effective schools" movement. Instead, it focuses on such matters as course and certification requirements, the length of the school day and year, and supervision of instruction. (p. 3)

Furthermore, as the effective schools movement seemed to fade from the public spotlight in the late 1990s, the so-called excellence movement, which subsequently became the standards and accountability movement, took off and became codified in several pieces of federal legislation beginning with the Goals 2000: Educate America Act of 1994 (Riley, 1995; Schwartz & Robinson, 2000). This landmark legislation provided funding for states to establish standards and tests to measure student progress, creating the apparatus for a more punitive policy of accountability to be put in place.

Such a policy was passed in 2002 when President George W. Bush's educational reform agenda was embraced by Congress and became the No Child Left Behind Act. The cornerstone of this massive legislation is more testing for students and a strict accountability system of sanctions associated with schools' failure to make progress in meeting student outcomes. Furthermore, test score data are broken down by student subgroups defined according to race/ethnicity, poverty, gender, disability, and limited English proficiency. This provision, in theory, will help schools and the government ensure that no children are being left behind (Cross, 2004).

But it has become clear since the outset that the rhetoric of No Child Left Behind has not matched the reality. For instance, some observers have been quick to point out that the sanctions and punishments associated with schools failing to achieve "adequate yearly progress" are laid down upon a highly unequal educational system in which some students—particularly those in high-poverty schools—have access to far fewer resources and opportunities (Darling-Hammond, 2004; Sizer, 2004). To make matters worse, the law has been underfunded since the year it was passed, meaning that such inequalities in the educational system are not being offset by federal funding targeted toward poor students (Robelen, 2004; Sanger, 2003).

Still, in recent years, journalists and policymakers have often argued that the best way to achieve "equity" is not through redistributive policies such as school desegregation but, rather, through policies that hold separate and unequal schools equally accountable for student outcomes. Accordingly, President Bush claimed that his new policy would attack "the soft bigotry of low expectations" ("Bush Warns Against," 1999)—a phrase that connotes the central beliefs of the effective schools movement. But the No Child Left Behind policy itself, grounded in a belief that schools alone can overcome virtually all of the inequality in society, has done little to offset this unevenness in the system (Karp, 2004). The burden was once again laid firmly on the schools' doorstep.

Note the following excerpt from a 2004 U.S. Department of Education newsletter:

"Raise the bar!" "Close the gap!" These enthusiastic exclamations may sound like new-age workout instructions, but to teachers in the era of *No Child Left Behind*, they are familiar educational objectives. And they are achievable, thanks to over a decade of research that has delivered promising school improvement models. (Office of Innovation and Improvement, 2004, p. 1)

Indeed, the larger context of schools—poverty, inequality, and segregation—has been completely missing from recent debates about educational policy (Karp, 2004). For instance, some of the most prominent news coverage of the *Brown* 50th anniversary in spring 2004 focused on how school accountability systems or court cases providing poor schools with "adequate" funding had replaced desegregation as the promise of greater educational equity. Articles in publications such as the *New York Times* (Winter, 2004) and *U.S. News & World Report* (J. E. Barnes, Bentrup, Ekman, & Brady, 2004) ignored, for the most part, the inequalities in the educational system that would not be corrected by providing some poor districts with more "adequate" funding while maintaining a high degree of racial and socioeconomic segregation. While more funding for poor school districts serving poor students of color is worth fighting for, there is no reason to believe that, if all else remains the same—especially the high concentrations of rich and poor students in different rich and poor communities and schools—it will create equal educational opportunities (Orfield & Lee, 2005).

In essence, it appeared as though the *Brown* anniversary commentators were settling for *Plessy v. Ferguson*'s promise of "separate but equal" despite the lack of evidence that such a condition can exist in the field of education. And while the "separate" dimension is not sanctioned by law, it is wholeheartedly supported through many public policies and private practices in a manner that creates outcomes similar to de jure segregation (Drier, Mollenkopf, & Swanstrom, 2004; Massey & Denton, 1993).

But it also seems that as long as accountability systems are in place and there is at least a perception that equality of outcomes is being enforced—even when outcomes remain extremely unequal in a way that reflects so much of the disparity in our society—policymakers and pundits feel they have done justice to the goals of "equity" and "excellence" (see Robelen, 2002, 2004). In fact, many argue that they can achieve more equality than school desegregation policy did by focusing on excellence instead of equity. According to the authors of the *U.S. News & World Report* special issue on the *Brown* anniversary, it was surprising in 2004 that Chief Justice Earl Warren's opinion in *Brown* made little reference to student achievement. Rather, it focused on the psychological damage of segregation and asserted that as long as education is separate, true equality of opportunity cannot exist.

But now, as the racially charged fights over desegregation recede into the past, a new national debate over how to close the minority achievement gap has emerged. Not only is integration hard to achieve, but it is no longer universally assumed to be the key to excellence. If anything, the argument had been reversed:

To have any hope of luring whites into majority-black schools, educators must first raise academic achievement in those classrooms. The 2001 No Child Left Behind Act is the most prominent example of this intellectual shift. The law does not concern itself with how integrated a school is. It simply demands achievement from every student, in every school. (p. 66)

Meanwhile, as policymakers and their proposals maintain some now-far-removed philosophical connection to the effective schools movement in terms of the emphasis placed on the role of schools in serving all students, the so-called "excellence" reform agenda that began in the 1980s and continues today as the standards and accountability agenda does not continue the effective schools focus on within-school relationships and dynamics. Instead, the current agenda appears to use blunt policy tools—new standards, tests, and sanctions—to try to achieve higher student outcomes. In addition, the current educational policy agenda calls for greater privatization, marketization, and competition among schools, another tactic that appears to only exacerbate inequalities across schools (see Wells & Holme, in press).

In this way, the decontextualized coverage of the *Brown* anniversary worked well to absolve White Americans of responsibility for the perpetual segregation and inequality in our society and to lay the blame and burden back on the public schools. These arguments implied that all that was needed to close the achievement gap between White and Asian affluent students and poor Black and Brown students was more standardized testing and punitive measures for schools that do not raise scores (J. E. Barnes, 2004). This is an example of both a misguided and an exaggerated understanding of the role of schools in society: of schools as the single institution that can equalize so many inequalities—those that most adults turn their backs on every day.

The Role of Educational Research in Debates About Schools and Society

As policymakers have been busy creating a more complex and punitive accountability system that mostly ignores the larger context of education, educational researchers have been, for the most part, also ignoring the larger context of schools and thus not challenging the popular paradigm that schools alone (or almost alone) matter. Thus, we must lay some of the blame for this all-or-nothing thinking regarding the role of schools in the laps of educational researchers and ask why so few studies have even attempted to examine schools and student learning in a way that sheds light on the relationship between schools and the larger society.

For instance, we ought to consider why so little research and writing in education have made the connection between low-income students' achievement and the living conditions of these students and their families in our postindustrial society. Furthermore, very little research in education assesses how racism and racial inequality in society as a whole affect the policies we try to implement in schools. And why have educational researchers failed to examine the effects of growing income inequalities coupled with ongoing racial segregation on public education in this country? Why do we not focus on the fluid boundaries between schools and society and at least occasionally ask whether society has failed the schools?

As Riehl (2001) noted in her review of interpretive qualitative studies in the sociology of education, apart from a few neo-Marxism and historical-comparative analyses of education within larger systems, U.S. mainstream sociologists of education have not linked studies of schooling to broader social, political, and economic issues. She wrote: "Not only are the core processes of schooling not subjected to rigorous conceptual and theoretical development, but they are not connected to social theories of a wider scope" (p. 127).

Thus, studies exploring the relationship between schools and society remain the exception, even among sociologists of education, many of whom were studying desegregation in the 1970s and early 1980s. And if most sociologists fail to examine schools within that larger social context, what hope do we have that other researchers in the field of education will do so? Thus, it is far more likely that even those researchers who do fieldwork and collect data inside of schools will not also collect data at the district or community level. At the same time, we know it is rare for researchers who examine the political or social context of schools to set foot inside the schools themselves and think about such connections. As Wells, Hirshberg, Lipton, and Oakes (1995) found in their review of research, "Despite the obvious link between district politics and change within schools, most researchers who study the politics of education at the local level tended to stay outside of schools" (p. 20).

Some of the more notable exceptions to the decontextualized norm in educational research would include Willis's *Learning to Labor* (1977) and MacLeod's *Ain't No Making It* (1995), because they took readers both inside and outside of schools to explain why working-class and low-income boys become disillusioned with the achievement ideology put forth by educators and the larger society. These two somewhat parallel studies—one from the United Kingdom (Willis) and the other from the United States (MacLeod)—explained the larger social and political context associated with young boys and how it shapes their interpretations of school and academic success and their creation of an oppositional identity against the achievement ideology. These studies explain why poor or working-class boys often feel shut out of the so-called meritocratic system of education and mobility and why they resist rather than embrace this system.

For instance, in his insightful ethnography of working-class English boys, Willis (1977) showed us empirically and theoretically how the choices these students make about their schooling and their lives are inextricably tied to their understanding of where they and their families fit into the larger capitalist society and the opportunities available to them as a result. In connecting the lives of these boys inside and outside of schools, Willis (1977) helped his readers understand that students' choices are limited but that, even within these limits, they will exercise the human agency that allows them to participate and to some small degree mold their own social reproduction. Willis (1977) argued that "we need to see what the *symbolic* power of structural determination is within the mediating realm of the human and cultural" (p. 171).

In other words, Willis's contribution to the literature is not simply to help us understand the complex lives and decisions of working-class boys but to help us understand that schools are but one institution that helps these boys make sense of who they are and where they are going. Both Willis and MacLeod helped us appreciate that while schools do matter to these students—in part because they espouse an achievement ideology that these boys penetrate and critique while legitimizing their school failure—clearly their larger social context matters a great deal as well, especially in how they make sense of schools and schoolwork. While neither of these books was written to be part of the "school effects" literature, they both have a great deal to say about the role of schools in the lives of working-class boys and in industrial societies at the end of the 20th century.

Other exceptions to the regularly decontextualized descriptions and analyses of schools and education include the works of well-known author Jonathan Kozol (1991, 1994), who, in a more journalistic way, has shown his readers the extremely problematic link between context and classroom for students situated in the poorest communities and schools. In *Savage Inequalities*, Kozol (1991) took his readers to six disparate cities to examine not only school budgets, sciences labs, and libraries but also the broader social, political, and economic context of poor children and their schools. In this way, Kozol (1991) avoided simply blaming school personnel in these communities for the educational failure of their students (although he did not apologize for educators who were taking advantage of a dismal situation), and he asked difficult questions about how, in a society as affluent as ours, these urban communities and public schools came to be as separate and unequal as they were from wealthy neighborhoods and school districts across the tracks, across the river, or up high on the bluff.

The end result was that Kozol (1991) drew his audience into the world of these schools and their fragile students in a way that helped to provide an understanding of school "failure" as far more complex than unmotivated teachers. For instance, in his chapter on New York City and a school in the Bronx, he first discussed the inequality between the city schools and those of the surrounding suburbs and the inequality *within* the city school system, between the more and less affluent neighborhoods. After setting this scene, Kozol (1991) took us to Public School 261:

In order to find Public School 261 in District 10, a visitor is told to look for a mortician's office. The funeral home, which faces Jerome Avenue in the North Bronx, is easy to identify by its green awning. The school is next door, in a former roller-skating rink. No sign identified the building as a school. A metal awning frame without an awning supports a flagpole, but there is no flag. (p. 85)

The many problematic realities within this unmarked public school—including class sizes of 37, an almost bookless library, and a lack of windows and fresh air—are not less egregious because of the larger context Kozol (1991) provided his readers, but they are seen as more complex than simple laziness or neglect on the part of educators. In fact, Kozol's (1991) powerful argument was that the learning conditions experienced by all of the children described in his book represented a form of societal neglect that can be solved only at a societal level; laws such as No Child Left Behind cannot alone address the issues he presented. Yet, why do so few educational researchers consider this larger context of schools?

In the 1990s, Jeannie Oakes and the first author of this chapter conducted a study of racially mixed schools implementing forms of "detracking." Interviews with parents, school board members, and community advocates showed that much of the struggle over creating more diverse classrooms within schools reflected the larger context of privilege and inequality in the surrounding communities. Thus, parents' and often educators' understandings of which students deserved more challenging curricula and greater opportunities within these schools were strongly related to who had economic and political clout in the district and the school community.

Several publications resulting from that study, including Oakes, Wells, and Associates (1996); Wells et al. (1995); and Wells and Serna (1996), demonstrated the powerful role that context played in local communities' efforts to "detrack" racially diverse schools. These publications made it clear that local political resistance to detracking reform had a major impact on the progress (or lack thereof) of reform-minded educators.

Similarly, Lipman's (1998) book on two racially diverse middle schools in a southern school district that was implementing a "restructuring" reform demonstrates how teachers' practices within schools were embedded in a context of racial and social class struggle and conflict within the local community. In this case study of the district and town context and the two schools nested within, Lipman (1998) wrote: "In Riverton, parents, community members, and teachers viewed restructuring through the long lens of historical struggles over race and class and the dynamics of reform were played out within present-day relations of power and privilege" (p. 4).

In the same vein, Brantlinger's (2003) book on social class and school advantage included extensive interviews with parents, local school officials, and educators in an effort to portray the political power more affluent families have in a small community and how they are able to influence education policy and practice in a manner that advantages their own children. Yet, such empirical work examining these dynamics and how they shape the experiences of students within schools is hard to find (see Riehl, 2001; Wells et al., 1995).

In fact, much of the work that critiques the broader social and racial stratification in our society and discusses the impact of this inequality on public schools is theoretical and conceptual, not empirical. While such work is helpful for scholars who are trying to make sense of our postindustrial society and the ways in which class and race privilege are manifest symbolically, it does not provide insight into how and why educators and school officials are so strongly influenced by this privilege and how such privilege shapes—in both subtle and not so subtle ways—the opportunities available to different students.

Examining each of these empirical contributions to the literature, it appears as though the more labor-intensive qualitative research—namely, case studies and ethnographies—is best able to examine schools and students within their broader context. Yet, historical research can also be more conducive to examining schools in a contextual manner, as we can see from Walker's (2002) extensive review of research on segregated African American schools from 1935 to 1969. The point of this literature review was to challenge popular assumptions about Black schools as universally inferior owing to their lack of resources and lack of parity with White schools.

Yet, Walker's (2002) point was that when we look more closely at these schools via historical research including extensive interviews with former educators, students, and other members of the Black communities that surrounded these segregated schools, we learn something else. We learn of the seamless connections between these schools and the African American communities that supported and sustained them in spite of a larger political and social context of racism, racial violence, and severe oppression. This multilayered story of African American schools and their communities in the middle of the 20th century—before the *Brown* decision was enforced in any meaningful way—demonstrates the many attributes of these schools despite their lack of resources. Walker (2002), in this and other writings, enabled readers to understand how schools are molded by that context and the extent to which African Americans—in the schools and surrounding communities—struggled to make the best of a very bad situation, namely the racist Jim Crow system.

And because this limited literature exists, we know that it is possible for educational researchers to examine schools within their contexts, even if it is not the norm. Yet, we are beginning to see some evidence that, increasingly, more researchers appreciate the need for studies designed to help us better understand the role of schools in society and thus move beyond the simplistic debate over whether or not schools matter.

For instance, one area of educational research in which we now see researchers trying to make these crucial connections is policy research on standards-based reform and accountability. Whether it is school-based researchers who are paying far more attention to the federal, state, and local policy context of the educators and students they study, or whether it is researchers who begin by examining the policy context of schools and then look at the schools themselves, there are greater connections being made (see C. Barnes, 2002; Burch, 2002; Carnoy, Elmore, & Siskin, 2003; Little & McLaughlin, 1993).

Furthermore, despite the political trend of the past 25 years to place a large amount of responsibility on the schools, there is mounting evidence and analysis suggesting the pendulum needs to shift back toward the middle of the schools do not matter/schools are all that matter spectrum. Such research—some of which has been well publicized—reminds us of how student outcomes are influenced by forces external to schools, especially parents and families, but also the social conditions in which these families exist.

Several recently published books, including those of Abigail and Stephan Thernstrom (2003) and Richard Rothstein (2004), point to the importance of family background and child-rearing practices in discussions about achievement gaps across racial and socioeconomic lines. These two publications, which have received a fair amount of attention, summarize other research on the achievement gap between Black and White students. And while there are important distinctions between them, both of these books have broadened the debate from simply an argument that schools alone are responsible for closing large gaps that often begin well before kindergarten.

The Thernstroms well-publicized book, *No Excuses* (2003), offered a somewhat odd mix of arguments on these issues. For instance, one section of the book praised a handful of educators and schools helping low-income students of color achieve, implying that they are the exception and not the rule in the field of education. Then, after critiquing most educators, the authors blamed African American parents for not fostering home environments that help their children succeed in school. They presented statistics, for example, on the number of hours that Black versus White and Asian students spend watching television. They were also highly critical of many Black parents' child-rearing techniques. In the end, the Thernstroms (2003) blamed not only Black parents but also the public schools and policies that support them for the Black-White (and Black-Asian) achievement gap. Yet, what is missing from the Thernstroms' book, as well as the popular press coverage of school desegregation and educational inequality more generally, is a thoughtful critique of the ways in which *larger* social forces—forces larger than the family unit—affect policies designed to provide poor students and students of color equal educational opportunities.

Rothstein (2004), in contrast, argued that social-class differences deeply affect students' educational outcomes. Yet, his argument went well beyond class-related distinctions in child-rearing practices to talk about inequality writ large in our society and its impact on schools and children. For instance, he documented evidence that the lack of health and dental care, substandard housing, and poor nutrition characteristic of low-income students' lives all have profound influences on these students' learning in schools—so much influence that school reform alone cannot close the gap: "As is argued in this book, the influence of social class characteristics is probably so powerful that schools cannot overcome it, no matter how well trained are their teachers and no matter how well designed are their instructional programs and climates" (p. 5).

Although Rothstein (2004) praised educators who work hard to help disadvantaged students succeed and was quick to point out that improving education is an important goal, he was clearly trying to move the debate beyond the ideology that schools can "do it alone." At the same time, he cautioned that his argument should not be interpreted to mean that "schools don't matter."

What is so refreshing about Rothstein's (2004) argument is that he clearly implicated institutions other than public schools and Black parents in explaining the inequality of student outcomes. His policy recommendations included universal health and dental care for children, more stable housing for the working poor, and more equal distribution of income. These are not the typical set of educational policy recommendations, but Rothstein (2004) presented evidence that improving poor students' lives in these ways could increase their achievement. In fact, he wrote: "If the nation can't close the gaps in income, health, and housing, there is little prospect of equalizing achievement" (p. 131).

A handful of other recent publications have put forth similar arguments. For instance, Levin and Belfield (2002) argued that while the educational achievement of students is dependent on both family and school, it is much more dependent on the former than the latter. While these authors focused mainly on the role of families and the home-school relationship, they pointed out that "more than 90 percent of a child's waking hours from birth to the age of eighteen are spent outside of school in an environment that is heavily conditioned, both directly and indirectly, by families" (p. 2).

The demand for a broader focus on what is failing and why in terms of the academic achievement of low-income students and students of color is also heard in Noguera's (2003) *City Schools and the American Dream:*

Educational problems in poor inner-city neighborhoods cannot be addressed without also responding to the social and economic conditions in the communities where schools are located. It is unfair and unrealistic to expect schools to raise test scores and focus narrowly on the task of educating children when a broad array of unmet nonacademic needs (e.g. food, housing, and health care) invariably affect their ability to learn. (p. xiii)

Another recently published book, *Supplementary Education,* edited by Gordon, Bridglall, and Meroe (2004), stated quite boldly that schools alone cannot close the achievement gap between White and Asian students, on the one hand, and African American and Latino students, on the other. This book called for far more political support for supplemental programs such as after-school care and youth development programs.

Similarly, in *Unequal Childhoods* (2003), Lareau looked carefully at children's lives outside of schools in an effort to explain differences in child-rearing practices across social classes and how the highly scheduled lives of middle- and upper-middle class children advantage them in school and in their adult lives. While this book primarily focused on parenting and the role of the family vis-à-vis the school, it also discussed the institutional arrangements and the class structure and privilege that allow some children to have so many more after- and outside-of-school learning opportunities.

And finally, in her 2005 book *Radical Possibilities,* Jean Anyon was not shy about the need for policymakers to address poverty and all of its related variables—jobs, wages, housing, and so forth—before we can hope for more equal educational outcomes. This book, although not an empirical study of the policy context as it relates to the daily experiences of students and educators in poor schools (Anyon's, 1997, earlier writing did do this), provides ample evidence that the current conditions of poor schools and families cannot be transformed by educational policies alone.

Despite the compelling arguments put forth by these authors, their perspective is swimming against a tide that says schools should solve most of the problems in society, and if they fail to do so, it must be because schools are bad and educators are poorly trained, lazy, or uncaring. It is as if once policymakers argue that schools matter, then somehow the prevailing wisdom is that they are *all* that matters—or at least the only thing that matters that can be fixed by public policy. Thus, major cuts in welfare and Medicaid, coupled with policymakers' unwillingness to ensure that all children have access to preschool, an "adequate" K–12 public education, health care, or livable housing, occur alongside punitive educational policies that demand schools close the gap between poor and nonpoor students in terms of achievement (see Brown, 2003; Halpren, 1995; Noguera, 2003; Rothstein, 2004).

Clearly, what we need is additional research and writing on the iterative relationship between a society that neglects many of its poor children of color and the schools that are left to solve the problems of those children. If there had not been such a dearth of research exploring these issues over the past 25 years, perhaps our public policies would be different today. In particular, if more of the school desegregation literature had considered the challenges schools faced in trying to institute an ostensibly antiracist policy in the midst of widespread racism, we may well have learned a different set of lessons from the integration efforts that were the legacy of *Brown*. Perhaps the discussions around the 50th anniversary would have been different—more focused on how to tackle racial inequality and the ongoing racism that drives today's rampant de facto segregation. In the following section, we review a large portion of the research literature on school desegregation to try to understand why this work—which in many ways began with the Coleman report—rarely placed desegregated schools or students into a larger context.

LOOKING FOR CONTEXT IN THE SCHOOL DESEGREGATION LITERATURE: SO LITTLE, SO LATE

In theory, the body of research on school desegregation, perhaps more than most areas of educational research, should provide a great deal of insight into the role of schools within society and not simply focus on educational outcomes in a decontextualized way. We say this for two reasons. First, much of this work was conducted by sociologists of education, whose focus we would expect to be broader owing to the nature of their discipline. Second, given the racial tension and political resistance to school desegregation symbolized in the angry, mob-like actions of Whites in places such as Little Rock, Arkansas (see Beals, 1994), researchers studying this policy should have been attuned to the significant contextual issues surrounding its implementation.

Prior to launching our 5-year study of the relationship between the social and political context of districts and schools involved in school desegregation and the long-term lessons learned by students who attended these schools in the late 1970s, we combed the desegregation literature to see who, if anyone, had done something similar. We were not trying to answer simple questions about whether or not school desegregation "worked." Rather, we wanted to understand how the specific contexts of these schools and the details of the policies that made them racially diverse shaped the experiences of their students.

We learned through our literature review that most of the earlier school desegregation research either had ignored context completely and focused only on student outcomes or had talked about the politics of desegregation in one district or across the country without connecting that political context to the lives of students and educators in the schools. A smaller subset of the literature included studies examining just one school more in depth and sometimes relating schools' stories to their local political context. But for the most part, these in-depth qualitative studies focused on what was happening *inside* the schools as students and educators grappled—or failed to grapple—with important issues of race.

While much of this prior research has helped to answer some very important questions about school desegregation policy, as we describe subsequently, there was a gaping hole in the literature; namely, far too few desegregation studies have examined how an educational policy that goes against the grain of a racially segregated and unequal society is affected by that context. To explain the gaps in the large body of school desegregation literature, we have organized our review into three categories that emphasize important differences in the scope of this research. Thus, beyond the basic quantitative demographic studies of school-level racial makeup and students' exposure across racial groups (see, for instance, Frankenberg, Lee, & Orfield, 2003; Orfield & Lee, 2005), we see three major categories of school desegregation research: (a) student outcomes, (b) within-school relations and experiences, and (c) political context/public opinion.

These three categories can help us understand that most studies have focused on one important part of the overall school desegregation experience. The problem is that very few studies have transcended these categories and looked, for instance, at how the political context of school desegregation may influence students' experiences within schools. As Braddock (2004) has noted, social science research on school desegregation has rarely been embedded in rich theories of social mobility, community power, or discrimination.

Because we use narrow theoretical perspectives to generate research on school desegregation effects, social researchers have failed to direct the policy debates on this issue toward a renewed public interest in the contemporary meaning of American ideals such as opportunity, social justice and individual rights. (p. 5)

Student Achievement and Outcomes Without the Context

While many researchers have measured interracial contact in desegregated schools, the bulk of school desegregation research has examined the academic achievement of students in racially mixed schools (see Clotfelter, 2004; Crain & Mahard, 1978; Levin, 1975; Wells, 2001). According to Crain and Mahard (1978), in an extensive review of the literature:

The effect of desegregation on the performance of black and white students on achievement tests has received an undeserved emphasis in the desegregation literature. There are over a hundred studies of achievement test performances following desegregation. When this is contrasted with the number of studies on other aspects of desegregation, the emphasis is embarrassing. (p. 17)

In terms of methodology, the Coleman report profoundly shaped the subsequent research on school desegregation. For instance, much of the early research on school desegregation that followed the Coleman report in the late 1960s and 1970s was similar in design and thus examined student outcome data using quantitative analyses in which the racial makeup of schools was the dependent variable.

Thus, most of these student achievement studies were "input-output" studies that examined the relationship between the racial composition of a school (the input) and student achievement as measured by test scores (the output) (Crain & Mahard, 1978; see also Crain & Mahard, 1983). Such studies tell us very little about what was happening inside of schools—in the so-called "black box"—let alone anything about the local context of these schools and how issues of race and class affect the social and political dynamics of their communities.

In fact, this student achievement research generally included no consideration of the conditions of desegregation: whether protests or school boycotts occurred, whether students were in fear of their safety, or how desegregation shaped and was shaped by the actions and attitudes of educators in desegregated schools. The degree to which White teachers in racially mixed schools welcomed African American students or believed that they were as smart as White students was not discussed in these studies, although such factors may well have affected student test scores (Crain & Mahard, 1978; Orfield, 1975; Schofield, 1989 ; St. John, 1975). As Crain and Mahard (1978) argued:

If desegregation occurs under certain conditions, the short-run effects will not be positive. Student performance can be affected by community conflict, by school desegregation that is not reinforced by neighborhood integration, and by the racial attitudes of black and white students and staff. (p. 22)

Furthermore, these studies were not able to consider the many different types of desegregation plans. Thus, there was no information about whether the students were reassigned by their districts under a mandatory desegregation plan or whether they volunteered to be transferred to a more desegregated school. Nor was there recognition of the age at which students were desegregated or how long they had been in desegregated schools (Crain & Mahard, 1978). In addition, this early literature was not able to calculate the prevalence of *within*-school segregation via tracking or the extent to which Black and White students were exposed to the same curriculum (St. John, 1975).

The lack of information on these very important contextual elements significantly lessens the implications of these input-output studies, which for the most part were inconclusive. Clearly, other research suggests that these contextual variables matter a great deal and that caring educators who believe in African American and Latino students' ability and help to build their confidence make a huge difference in how these students thrive or fail in desegregated settings (see Delpit, 1995; Foster, 1997).

Indeed, in their review of desegregation research that focused on academic achievement, Crain and Mahard (1978) found that the very small number of studies that did include data on what was going on in the community and the schools were the most helpful and gave the test-score data more meaning. For instance, they reported that one or more of the following variables could influence student performance: type and scope of the plans, community reaction, staff preparation for desegregation, grade levels at which students were desegregated, and the curricula provided in the schools. Crain and Mahard (1978) concluded that several favorable conditions must exist before desegregation has beneficial achievement effects on African Americans students. (They also noted that none of the research revealed that desegregation had a negative effect on White students.)

For instance, they found that if Black students transferred into schools with better facilities, better teachers, high expectations for all students, a flurry of in-service programs for teachers, new curricula, and so forth, they were more likely to experience major achievement gains. Thus, Crain and Mahard (1978) argued that large numbers of academics have been fascinated by what they considered to be the most intellectually interesting question: "All else being equal, will the mixing of races alone result in higher black achievement? That question cannot be answered because in the real world, desegregation is never an 'all else being equal' situation" (p. 49).

Given that most of the school desegregation research on student achievement outcomes did not factor in these contextual variables of desegregation across different states, towns, or schools, it is not at all surprising that the results of these studies were inconclusive (Crain & Mahard, 1978; Schofield, 1989; St. John, 1975). While the majority of these studies showed that African American students' achievement—as measured by test scores—improved with school desegregation and that White students' achievement levels rarely if ever declined in racially diverse schools, this literature left us with very little understanding of *how* or *why* these results occurred or *where* and *when* achievement was greater (see Crain, 1976).

Basically, this early post-Coleman school desegregation research was trying to answer whether schools and thus school desegregation mattered, with a focus solely on students' test scores—often after only limited exposure to desegregated schools. This focus grew out of the belief that the goal of desegregation was mainly to raise Black students' test scores. While raising the achievement levels of students whose families had faced discrimination for centuries is definitely a worthwhile goal, this focus tended to downplay the fact that school desegregation is a legal remedy for the racial discrimination that Whites had instituted and supported for so long (see Wells, 2001; Wells & Crain, 1997).

Thus, what appeared to be a limited impact of school desegregation on student outcomes may have been more of an indictment of White educators', policymakers', and parents' failure to embrace school desegregation policy as a remedy designed to challenge their racial privilege. In other words, a more contextualized study of student outcomes in this early era of school desegregation research may have yielded critical insights into how this racial privilege was simply reproduced within desegregated schools, albeit in a kinder and gentler form.

The Long-Term Effects Research: Positive Findings but Little "How" or "Why"

A second body of work focusing on the so-called long-term effects of school desegregation on students' life chances, mobility rates, and adult accomplishments also comprised mostly input-output studies. This work, while very helpful to us in framing our study, was mostly quantitative research examining the experiences of African Americans and the effects of their school experiences on their adult lives. Conducted mainly in the 1970s and 1980s, this work explored the ways in which the racial balance of a graduate's school (the input) correlated with various postsecondary variables such as college attendance and career and housing choices (the outputs).

Thus, these studies share many of the strengths and shortcomings of the research described earlier on student achievement within desegregated schools. In other words, the long-term effects research for the most part did not provide information on the conditions of school desegregation that African American students experienced. Yet, at the same time many of the "outputs" measured by these studies were quite impressive.

For instance, in a review of 21 studies on the long-term effects of school desegregation, Wells and Crain (1994) found that Black graduates of racially integrated schools were more likely to have higher occupational aspirations and expectations and to be aware of the steps they needed to take to obtain their goals. This finding suggests that professional information flows through institutions and social networks, which are often racially segregated (see DuBois, 1935; Granovetter, 1973).

The long-term effects literature also showed that African American graduates of desegregated high schools were more likely to attend predominantly White universities and more likely to work in integrated environments (see Braddock, Crain, McPartland, & Dawkins, 1986). Also, with one exception, this research revealed that these graduates end up completing more years of education, earning higher degrees, and majoring in more "nontraditional" occupations than graduates of all-Black schools (Braddock & McPartland, 1987; Wells & Crain, 1994).

The final set of findings from the long-term effects literature demonstrates that Black graduates of desegregated schools are more likely to work in white-collar and professional jobs in integrated corporations and institutions (see Wells & Crain, 1994). While the findings just described are quite encouraging in terms of the impact of desegregation on African Americans' life chances, this quantitative, survey-based research tells us very little about *how* or *why* these outcomes occurred among graduates of desegregated schools. Thus, in considering the perennial question regarding the pendulum swing discussed earlier, this research cannot tell us whether these findings reflect the effect of the desegregated schools per se (e.g., their resources, curricula, and teachers) on African American students, whether they reflect the peer influences that Coleman described, or, quite possibly, both.

In other words, if we are to analyze the findings from this research and suggest, as we did earlier (see also Wells & Crain, 1994), that the social networks formed in desegregated schools are likely to assist African Americans in leading more educated, lucrative, and integrated adult lives, then we would have to assume that peer effects are a critical part of their school experience. Still, we would not want to rule out the impact of other within-school factors, including the racial attitudes of educators, the school's academic press, and the school's reputation in the community and with higher education institutions.

Yet, this quantitative long-term effects literature does not allow us to draw conclusions about school effects because it does not include the needed information about the daily experiences of these adults when they were in school, local political reactions to school desegregation, or educators' efforts (or lack thereof) to make schools more equal or fair along racial lines. A more recent book by Eaton (2001) fits into the category of the long-term effects of school desegregation literature, but it was a qualitative study that entailed in-depth interviews with 65 African American graduates of an urban-suburban voluntary transfer program in Boston known as METCO. These adult graduates of the METCO program had, as children of color growing up in Boston, been assigned to predominantly White and mostly affluent suburban schools. What this study lacked in breadth it made up for by helping us understand, through the eyes of the adults who lived through it, *how* and *why* this educational journey from Boston to the suburbs was meaningful.

Interestingly enough, Eaton's (2001) findings echoed and extended some of the powerful themes of the quantitative long-term effects literature just described. For instance, she found that METCO graduates felt far more comfortable in racially diverse and predominantly White settings than their friends and family members who lacked such desegregated experiences. She also found that the METCO graduates tapped into powerful social networks in their suburban schools and that information about postsecondary school experiences, including the college application process and job opportunities, flowed through these networks.

The African American graduates in Eaton's study (2001) also talked about the downsides of participating in METCO, including the racial discrimination they faced in the suburban schools, the assumptions many White students and educators made about their families and backgrounds, and a sense of disconnection from their own communities. Still, overall, nearly all of the adults interviewed said that they would repeat their METCO experiences again if they had the chance. Such decisions, Eaton (2001) wrote, were "influenced . . . by their discoveries that the exposure they had in suburbia comprised fair approximations and decent preparation for life as blacks in white-dominated America" (p. 21).

Eaton's (2001) book gives us an in-depth look at how and why urban-suburban school desegregation in the Boston metropolitan area changed the lives of graduates of desegregated schools. Still, because Eaton (2001) interviewed METCO graduates who attended different suburban schools in different districts during different years, this study did not provide any analysis of the suburban schools or their local communities. Thus, the only understanding of the "context" of the schools and how the METCO program was accepted or rejected comes from the interviews with the METCO graduates from these different schools and eras. As a result, this book does not provide a clear sense of how the experiences of students in desegregated schools related to the social and political context of those schools. While we certainly learn that school desegregation matters from this long-term effects literature, it is still not clear exactly why.

The Intergroup Relations Research:
Getting Along One Desegregated School at a Time

Another body of school desegregation literature—often called the intergroup relations literature—was, in the late 1960s and early 1970s, also composed primarily of quantitative input-output studies that attempted to assess "the effect" of school desegregation on indicators of relations between Blacks and Whites "such as racial attitudes or the formation of close friendships" (Schofield, 1991, p. 381). In many ways, this research was grounded in the belief that "schools matter" not simply because they teach children to read and do math—the value added measured on standardized tests—but also because they develop children socially and emotionally. Thus, these researchers examined the social skills and relationships students develop in desegregated schools, which are important while the students are in school as well as after they graduate and enter the adult world.

In fact, Schofield (1989) noted that while student achievement data are critical, schools do more than teach academic subject matter: They have a profound potential for shaping individuals and their social networks. Schofield (1989) cited the Jencks et al. book, *Inequality* (1972), which "demonstrated that academic achievement does not have the kind of overwhelming impact on later occupational successes that might justify making it the exclusive focus of most research on the outcomes of desegregated schooling" (p. x).

In her extensive review of this intergroup relations literature, Schofield (1991) discussed different historical periods of school desegregation and the type of intergroup relations research that was conducted in each, noting that up until the late 1960s there was relatively little school desegregation and thus little evidence of its social consequences. Between 1968 and 1975, the research on intergroup relations in desegregated schools grew rapidly, but most of it involved cross-sectional portraits focusing on students' racial attitudes at one moment in time (Schofield, 1991). Nor was there much discussion of the context of these students and their schools or the ways in which schools were working against larger forces of racism in society. Thus, like the research on student achievement and desegregation mentioned earlier, the focus of the intergroup relations research up until the mid-1970s was "clearly . . . on outcomes rather than on the processes that might account for these outcomes" (Schofield, 1991, p. 344).

For instance, Schofield (1991) noted that many of these earlier researchers did not indicate whether the schools studied were desegregated via mandatory, voluntary, or residential "neighborhood" desegregation. Nor did they indicate whether the classrooms within desegregated schools were resegregated, with mostly White students in the higher-level classes and most of the African American or Latino students in the lower-level classes. Such resegregation within racially diverse schools is common and has multiple implications for so-called "intergroup" relations (Oakes, 1985). But if researchers examine intergroup relations only as an outcome variable and do not pay attention to within-school resegregation, they may be far too quick to conclude that "desegregation"—as a poorly defined "input" variable—has a negative effect on intergroup relations when it may actually be the resegregation of students within nominally desegregated buildings that hampers such relations.

As a result of these shortcomings, reviews of this earlier research failed to draw any hard and fast conclusions about the effects of desegregation on students' racial attitudes and their relations across racial lines. Schofield (1991) noted that this inconclusiveness was due in large part to researchers' unwillingness to frame their work theoretically in a way that would help readers better understand the role played by desegregated schools in shaping how students interact along racial lines:

Typically, researchers study a particular example of desegregation and look for changes in students' attitudes or behaviors that can be attributed to their desegregated experiences. Because they bring no theoretical framework that would suggest what characteristics of the desegregated setting might relate to those changes, most researchers have paid little attention to what the desegregated setting was actually like. (p. 359)

At the end of her extensive review of this intergroup relations research, Schofield (1991) argued that those who study these delicate issues in desegregated schools should ask "What is going on here?" and pay more attention to the social processes that lead to the various "outcomes." Examples of studies that have provided such insights include those that have examined one or two desegregated schools in depth, paying far more attention to what is going on within these schools.

In fact, Schofield was one of a small group of researchers who, in the late 1970s, took their work inside schools to study desegregation up close and in depth in a small number of cases. These later studies gave readers a more holistic view of what was going on within schools and how intergroup relations shaped and were shaped by different learning environments, student success, and the self-esteem of students, particularly students of color. While more limited in scope, this literature focused on the structures and cultures of desegregated schools and how they influence relationships between students and educators and between different groups of students. These mostly qualitative studies, including the work of Grant (1988), Metz (1978, 2003), Oakes et al. (1996), Patchen (1982), Rist (1970), Schofield (1989), and Wells and Crain (1997), raise important issues about which types of school desegregation policies and practices are most effective in creating successful schools.

In particular, these qualitative studies help to illustrate the problems related to within-school segregation or the process of placing African American students in lower-level classes resegregated from their White peers. Some of this work highlights complex issues related to teachers' attitudes and beliefs about the ability of Black students to succeed as well as their willingness to talk about race (in particular, see Metz, 1978, 2003; Oakes et al., 1996; Rist, 1970; Schofield, 1989).

Furthermore, many of these qualitative, intergroup relations studies provide important information about the local context of desegregated schools and thus about how these schools shaped and were shaped by that context. Some of the studies included interviews with local officials responsible for implementing school desegregation. Others provided at least basic demographic or historical data on the surrounding communities and school districts. For instance, in Metz's revised edition of *Different by Design* (2003), she wrote that the book's story of three urban magnet schools in the early 1980s remains timely because she examined these schools' internal "processes and realities" while looking,

as little research until very recently has done, at the interplay of school-level organizational processes and the policies and specific decisions at the district level. *[The book] explores processes in the conduct of school district decision making that balance district-level needs and district political processes against the educational welfare of students in individual schools.* . . . While current pressures on districts are quite different, the links and disjunctions between districts and schools that the book explores still reveal much about the fundamental character of, and processes in, the relationship between districts and schools. (pp. viii–ix, italics added)

Similarly, in Grant's (1988) study of one racially diverse and demographically unstable school that he called Hamilton High, he provided much of the historical background and contextual information needed to help readers understand how things got to be the way they are in this school and its local community. Furthermore, Grant (1988) made the much-needed connections between the tensions and changes taking place within this increasingly diverse public high school and the many layers of policies and political pressures that have shaped the school's demographics and culture.

As helpful as this intergroup relations research is, for the most part, researchers either employed quantitative data that provided little insight into the local context of schools or engaged in in-depth qualitative studies of individual schools that offered a detailed portrait of what it was like to be a student or educator in these schools but little insight into the role of the broader context in shaping those experiences (Schofield, 1991). While most of these qualitative studies provided helpful in-depth examinations of one school, it was clear to us that what was missing from the literature was a systematic study of many schools across different district and community contexts.

Political Context Studies and Opinion Polls: Looking at Context but Not the Schools

In addition to the desegregation research mentioned earlier, there have been a few notable studies of the politics of school desegregation and several opinion polls throughout the years that have included questions about desegregation and racially diverse schools. This research tells us a great deal about the political contexts of desegregation but usually does not connect these broader contexts to the experiences of students and educators or how politics have compromised the goals of desegregation at the school and classroom levels. Thus, these studies only partially shape our understanding of how and why schools matter.

Politics of Desegregation Research: The Context Without the Schools

While the work of Coleman, Jencks, and Moynihan was receiving a great deal of attention, other studies that offered different and more complex perspectives were overlooked in the policy debates. One of the best examples of this was a study of nine local communities struggling with the issue of school desegregation. This set of qualitative case studies was published in a 1968 book, *Our Children's Burden*, edited by Raymond W. Mack. This research, like the Coleman report it was intended to supplement, had been commissioned by Congress in Section 402 of the Civil Rights Act of 1964. In fact, Mack wrote that he worked with James Coleman and his coauthor Earnest Campbell to design this study of nine communities in a way that might "put flesh on the bones of the survey data by learning something from observation and unscheduled interview about definitions of situations and the interactional contexts of the data sought by survey methods" (1968, p. xi).

These case studies offer often riveting portraits of the struggles and tensions within the nine communities undergoing school desegregation. The authors of these chapters provided important historical and demographic information on these towns and districts to help readers better understand the political barriers to meaningful desegregation. For instance, in his chapter on Riverside, California, Duster (1968), a sociologist, wrote about Whites' resistance to desegregation. He quoted a White woman who stood up at a public hearing on desegregation to say "We have the right to discriminate. We've earned it. This is American, not Red country, where the state tells you what to do and think" (p. 35). She received applause from many people in the audience.

These contextual data are critical to our understanding of the political opposition to school desegregation, and thus they help explain the extent of the "burden" we placed on children and educators when we asked schools to do what no other institution in society—with the exception of the military—was willing to do. Hence, the title of the book and the central finding highlighted in the introduction—"Americans are asking their children to bear the brunt of the difficult social process of desegregation" (Mack, 1968, p. xiii)—speak to this important theme. Still, the scope of the Mack (1968) study did not allow inclusion of data collection within the schools themselves, the places where the students and teachers bore that burden. It was a study of the local politics surrounding school desegregation.

Similarly, Crain's (1969) landmark study, *The Politics of School Desegregation,* examined the role of school boards in the school desegregation process in 15 cities. The main finding was that the most important factor determining the behavior of the school boards in these cities was the influence of the local civic elite: the businessmen and other nongovernmental local leaders who participated in city decision making (p. 3).

Crain's collection of political case studies, like those in the Mack (1968) book, provided valuable insights into the local political contexts of desegregated public schools. Still, this study, similar to Mack's book, did not examine what was actually happening within the schools—or even within the school districts, for the most part. In fact, Wells and Crain (1997) wrote in their book analyzing the St. Louis desegregation plan almost 30 years later that the city of St. Louis had, when Crain (1969) wrote his book, looked politically progressive as local leaders embraced the *Brown* decision and banned de jure segregation, but the reality in the schools and neighborhoods was far more problematic.

For instance, they found that during the period that Crain (1969) was describing, the St. Louis school board was also redrawing neighborhood school boundaries to exclude Black neighborhoods from White schools' attendance boundaries. Meanwhile, the Black schools were severely overcrowded, and at least once, when Black students were reassigned to a White school, they were on their own separate floor of the school, their school day started and ended at different times than for the White students, and there were separate White and Black recesses and lunch times (see Wells & Crain, 1997). Thus, had Crain (1969) tried to connect the talk of the local political elites in St. Louis to a systematic study of what was actually happening within the schools and neighborhoods, he would have offered a far less optimistic view of school desegregation in that city in the 1960s.

Another seminal book on school desegregation that fits the politics of education paradigm is Hochschild's *The New American Dilemma* (1984). In her thoughtful analysis of Whites' resistance to school desegregation policies and the many ways in which racism is symbiotic with the American dream—as opposed to being an anomaly in an otherwise equal society—Hochschild (1984) captured the national political context of desegregation. Her central argument was that incremental approaches to implementing school desegregation will never work in a society in which many Whites have benefited from racial inequality and segregation for so long. This political analysis provides an important framework to help researchers, educators, students, and parents who struggle on a daily basis to make school desegregation work in schools and communities. But Hochschild is a political scientist whose expertise is analyzing opinion poll data and other primary sources and drawing new insights from them. She did not explore the multiple ways in which this political context affects schools and local communities or how the struggles at those sites might shape the experiences of educators and students.

The Hochschild (1984) book was similar in this way to a spate of books published in the period leading up to the 50th anniversary of the *Brown* decision. Most of these books were political, legal, or historical analyses of *Brown* and its legal legacy and significance (see, for example, Bell, 2004; Cashin, 2004; Klarman, 2004; Ogletree, 2004). These books, like Hochschild's (1984), help readers place the *Brown* decision and subsequent efforts to desegregate schools into a larger perspective that speaks to the past and present direction of this country in terms of racial equality and public policy.

Empirical evidence drawn from local desegregated school sites would help in making such macro-micro connections between the politics of the local context and the schools. Case studies of school desegregation in particular towns or school districts stand the best chance of doing this. And yet, for the most part such in-depth case studies do not do this. Rather, they tend to focus on the local political context or on legal battles or court orders related to the district they are studying.

For example, Gaillard's (1988) *The Dream Long Deferred,* focusing on the Charlotte school desegregation case, provides a rich and detailed description of the struggle in that city to come up with a politically and logistically viable student assignment plan after many false starts. But Gaillard (1988) did not, for whatever reason, explore what was happening inside the schools so profoundly affected by this plan. In any event, Gaillard's (1988) focus on the court case and the political fallout from that case is not unusual in terms of how most case studies of single towns or districts are conducted. For instance, in another, even more detailed study of the Charlotte case, Douglas (1995) provided a powerful analysis of the legal and political developments in the city's two-decade fight to first resist and then implement a school desegregation plan.

Many of the local case studies of school desegregation across different contexts are similarly focused on the local political and often legal battles over desegregation. They often provide invaluable data on student demographics and other quantitative data on resources, enrollment, and so forth, but they do not offer an analysis of what is happening inside the schools affected by these legal battles and demographic shifts (see, for instance, Orfield et al., 1996).

Of course, there is also a body of research examining White flight from desegregating school districts that is based mostly on demographic data. Much of this work has been conducted by expert witnesses for legal teams trying to limit or dismantle school desegregation plans across the country. This research attempts to prove the strong and causal relationship between school desegregation and White flight (see Armor, 1995, for a review). On the opposing side of the debate, other researchers have made the claim that the relationship between White flight and school desegregation is overblown and that a great deal of White flight occurs in cities with neighborhood school assignments (see Orfield & Monfort, 1988; Orfield et al., 1996). While this research is very important in terms of the demographic shifts taking place within and around school desegregation policies, it does not help us understand what White flight looks like at the school or community level or how people make sense of their school choices as they relate to race.

Some of the case studies of individual locales provide insight into the experiences of particular people involved in school desegregation. For instance, Lukas's (1985) account of school desegregation in Boston portrayed the court order and its aftermath through the eyes of three families. Similarly, a more recent case study of desegregation in Austin, Texas, focused on the 18 teachers who were the first to be reassigned to historically segregated schools at the outset of desegregation (Wilson & Segall, 2001). Walker's (2005) historical work linked the grassroots efforts of African American teachers in Georgia to the larger legal and political struggle for desegregation and equal educational opportunities for Black students.

Meanwhile, the Wells and Crain (1997) study of the urban-suburban school desegregation plan in metropolitan St. Louis explored the experiences of different African American students from the city: those who remained in city schools, those who transferred to suburban schools, and those who transferred to the suburbs and then returned to city schools. This book, therefore, provided the legal history and local political context of this unique school desegregation plan as well as insight into the impact of the plan on individual students and the schools they attended. As a result, the book offered some insight into the relationship between the broader context and the schools, educators, and students whose daily lives were affected by desegregation.

The problem with these case studies is that even when they do go more in depth to look at the impact of desegregation on students' or educators' lives, they tend to focus on only one city or district or one school desegregation plan, often leaving the reader wondering whether the phenomena they describe are anomalies or themes and issues that emerge across different sites. The next section provides data on the political context writ large as measured via public opinion polls.

Public Opinion Polls: Research Focusing on What People Say but Not What They Do

Beyond the literature on the effects of school desegregation on the achievement and opportunities of African American students or on local politics, there is a body of literature on attitudes toward racially mixed schools. This literature provides insights into broader public perceptions of school desegregation and thus helps to explain what happens in local contexts and in schools themselves; however, this research does not, in itself, make connections to these experiences. In other words, it tells us what people *say* and not what they actually *do.*

For instance, Orfield's (1995) review of literature on public opinion and school desegregation showed that recorded attitudes had changed relatively dramatically in the 40 years since the *Brown* decision. In fact, the percentage of Americans of all races who believed that the Supreme Court was right in its *Brown* decision increased from 63% in the early 1960s to 87% in the mid-1990s. And in the South, where only 19% of people agreed with the landmark ruling in 1954, only 15% in the 1990s said that they did *not* agree with the ruling. This marks a dramatic shift in attitudes in the region of the country that has experienced the most school desegregation.

Furthermore, there is a great deal of evidence from the past 20 years that the majority of Americans say they see some value in having their children attend racially diverse public schools. For instance, a 1994 Gallup poll revealed that the percentage of Americans who believed that "more should be done to integrate schools" had risen rapidly in a short time span, from 37% in 1988 to 56% in 1994. Among African Americans, 84% supported efforts to achieve integrated schools (Orfield, 1995).

And then there is the Public Agenda (1998) report *Time to Move On,* which included polling data and argued that today most parents put academic achievement ahead of racial integration as the priority for their children—as if integration and achievement were mutually exclusive. Yet, despite the authors' simple conclusion in this report, closer examination of their data reveals a picture that is far more complex. For instance, toward the end of the report, the polling data show that 80% of Black parents and 66% of White parents surveyed said that it was either "very important" or "somewhat important" that their child's school be racially integrated. In fact, only 10% of Black parents and 16% of White parents said that it was "not important at all" for their children to attend racially diverse schools. Echoing these national findings in a city that has seen much racial strife in the past several years, a poll conducted in the greater Cincinnati area showed that 80% of Whites and 90% of Blacks believe children develop better when they attend schools with children of another race (see Pilsher, 2001).

Among people who have had first-hand experience with desegregation, the findings are positive. A 1978 survey of graduates of desegregated schools showed that 63% of Blacks and 56% of Whites believed their school desegregation experience had been "very satisfactory." Only 8% of Blacks and 16% of Whites said the experience was "unsatisfactory" (Orfield, 1995, p. 663).

These polling data suggest that public opinion toward racially mixed schools has become more favorable—at least in the abstract—at the same time judges and policymakers have led the way toward dismantling school desegregation policies. Thus, we need to better understand how these stated opinions interact with the lived experiences of students, educators, and parents in desegregated schools. Somewhere between what people say in opinion polls and the choices they make and support in their daily lives is the underlying story of school desegregation in the United States.

Clearly, while the body of research literature on school desegregation is quite expansive, what has been missing is a study of how school desegregation policy was shaped and compromised by its social and political context and how these influences in turn shaped the personal experiences of students and educators in desegregated schools. In fact, our study, discussed subsequently, is the first to look carefully across different communities at the relationship between the social and political contexts of different racially diverse schools, including their desegregation policies and the experiences of students and educators.

Using this broader framework in a study of six racially diverse schools during the late 1970s and the lives of their graduates today, we questioned the value of placing all of the burden of equalizing society on public schools or on Black parents. To paraphrase the Honorable Judge Robert L. Carter, who was one of the lead NAACP attorneys on the *Brown* case, segregated public schools are but a symptom of a larger disease: the disease of racism in our society.

THE UNDERSTANDING RACE AND EDUCATION STUDY: QUESTIONS AND METHODS FOR LOOKING AT DESEGREGATED SCHOOLS WITHIN THEIR CONTEXT

In 1999, we set out to conduct in-depth case studies of six high schools within districts that had undergone some form of desegregation by the late 1970s. We planned to examine these schools in light of political and historical trends and to conduct lengthy interviews with at least 40 class of 1980 graduates from each site.

Our study was designed to answer qualitative research questions about how the broader policy contexts of these schools shaped their students' experiences and understandings. Furthermore, we wanted to know how the 1980 graduates of these schools understood their school experience and its effect on their lives—their racial attitudes, educational and professional opportunities, personal relationships, and social networks. We set out to learn how and why these desegregated schools mattered in the lives of their students and how school effects were mediated by larger social forces. Qualitative historical case studies of these schools and their graduates within local political contexts were the mechanisms we chose to answer these interpretive questions.

Data Collection

We designed a three-tiered data collection strategy: Tier 1 consisted of the historical case studies of the six high schools; Tier 2 entailed interviews with graduates of the class of 1980 from each high school; and Tier 3 involved in-depth "portraits" of at least four of the graduates interviewed during Tier 2 from each high school.

Tier 1: Historical Case Studies

The first tier of our data collection involved historical case studies of the high schools and their social and political contexts in the late 1970s and early 1980s. These historical case studies were based, in part, on interviews with community members, lawyers, elected officials, and educators who were involved in the six schools during that time. In addition, we collected an array of historical documents, such as school board minutes, newspaper articles, yearbooks, and legal documents, to help piece together the stories of what was happening in these six schools during the study period.

Our goal in choosing the six communities in which we would conduct the historical case studies was to find school districts across the country that varied in terms of their size and region, the racial/ethnic make up of their general population and public school students, the social class of their residents, and the ways in which their schools became desegregated. We wanted districts with significant school desegregation plans, but, to better understand the role that context plays in this process, we wanted their contexts to be different. We came up with an initial list of about 20 potential districts by asking school desegregation experts from different regions of the country for suggestions.

We chose the following six communities to study: Austin, Texas; Charlotte, North Carolina; Englewood, New Jersey; Pasadena, California; Shaker Heights, Ohio; and Topeka, Kansas. These cities vary not only in terms of their geographic locations but also in terms of how and why their public schools became racially diverse. In some, there was court-ordered mandatory student reassignment. In others, the high school(s) became desegregated via efforts to create racially diverse residential areas.

Thus, each of these six school districts had at least one high school that was racially mixed[3] during the late 1970s and early 1980s. In the four districts with more than one high school, we ended up choosing among these schools on the basis of the racial and social-class composition of their enrollments and the role they played in desegregation programs within each district. We wanted the high schools across the six sites to be diverse in terms of these criteria. The six schools selected were as follows.

- *Austin High School, Austin, Texas (Austin Independent School District):* This school was desegregated via majority-to-minority transfers from several attendance areas. Its racial makeup during the 1970s was 15% African American, 19% Hispanic, and 66% White.
- *Dwight Morrow High School, Englewood, New Jersey (Englewood Public Schools):* Dwight Morrow was desegregated by receiving White students from Englewood Cliffs High School via a sending-receiving plan. It was already somewhat integrated as the only public high school serving the racially diverse town of Englewood. Busing and reassignment began at the elementary level. The school's racial makeup during the 1970s was 57% African American, 7% Hispanic, and 36% White.
- *John Muir High School, Pasadena, California (Pasadena Unified School District):* John Muir was originally desegregated by drawing from several diverse attendance areas; in the 1970s, it was desegregated via mandatory busing. Its racial makeup during the 1970s was 50% African American, 11% Hispanic, 34% White, and 5% Asian/Pacific Islander.
- *Shaker Heights High School, Shaker Heights, Ohio (Shaker Heights City School District):* Shaker Heights was desegregated as the only high school in a district experiencing an influx of African American students from Cleveland. Efforts were made to integrate neighborhoods, and student reassignment began at the elementary level. The school's racial makeup during the 1970s was 39% "minority" (mostly African American) and 61% White.
- *Topeka High School, Topeka, Kansas (501 School District):* This school was desegregated via assigned attendance areas; student reassignment began at the elementary and junior high levels. Its racial makeup during the 1970s was 20% African American, 8% Hispanic, 69% White, 1.4% American Indian, and 1.4% Asian.
- *West Charlotte High School, Charlotte, North Carolina (Charlotte-Mecklenburg Schools):* This historically black school was desegregated via a court order reassigning students from White high schools. Its racial makeup during the 1970s was 50% African American and 50% White.

Interestingly enough, both John Muir High School and Dwight Morrow High School had enrollments that were less than 50% White by the late 1970s. Both of these schools, along with West Charlotte High School, have experienced massive White flight since the class of 1980 graduated and are now predominantly African American and Latino. Meanwhile, Austin High School, Shaker Heights High School, and Topeka High School have managed to remain relatively more stable, with a shrinking but still significant White population. Yet, as we note later, both Austin and Shaker Heights are quite possibly on the verge of losing the majority of their White students. This leaves Topeka High School as the only one of the six that promises to maintain some White-Black-Latino diversity for the next several years.

Tier 2: Interviews With Graduates

The second tier of data collection consisted of semistructured, in-depth, and open-ended interviews with a sample of 40 to 50 students who graduated in 1980 from each of the six high schools. We chose to study the class of 1980 because these students entered kindergarten in the fall of 1967, when Lyndon B. Johnson occupied the White House and Martin Luther King Jr. was still alive. Thus, these students entered public schools across the country full of hope and promise regarding civil rights, and they traveled through the educational system at a time of tremendous change. On their first day of school, the federal government was poised to finally force hundreds of school districts to implement the *Brown v. Board of Education decision*. Thirteen years later, they would graduate from public schools that were, on average, far more desegregated than those they had entered.

Thus, we chose this class because its members experienced many of the peak years in American school desegregation. By 1988, efforts by the Reagan and Bush administrations to dismantle school desegregation policies had begun to pay off, and resegregation was on the rise. National data show that members of the class of 1980 were therefore more likely, on average, to have classmates of other races than were students in any class before them or in classes of the past 15 years.

Our research suggests that the late 1970s was a particularly pivotal moment in the history of school desegregation policy across the country. By this time in many towns, the initial protests and racial conflict that occurred when students were first reassigned to desegregated schools in the early 1970s had subsided to some degree. According to many people we interviewed, the late-1970s era was a relatively sedate time when strong and vocal opposition to desegregation had died down. The promise of a new, more racially integrated society was still alive, at least in school districts that had not already lost most of their White students.[4]

At the same time, this was a transitional period, following Watergate and the Vietnam War. A conservative political movement would soon change the policy agenda in education and other public policy arenas. By the time the class of 1980 graduated from high school, in the midst of the Iranian hostage crisis, a major recession, and a severe oil shortage, Ronald Reagan's presidential campaign was already fueling a powerful backlash against the Great Society policies of the 1960s and 1970s (Edsall, 1991).

Thus, the class of 1980 was born at the tail end of the baby boom and during the civil rights movement but came of age during the Reagan years. Over the nearly 25 years following their high school graduation, many in this cohort sought jobs and a college education, married, bought homes, had children, met new friends, and joined new organizations. Meanwhile, the public schools gradually became more racially segregated, and little progress was made in reducing the level of segregation in other realms of society.

Given their historical context, we thought that the members of the class of 1980 had an important story to tell. We sampled the graduates from each school purposively to reflect the range of diversity of the students in their class, particularly in terms of race, ethnicity, social class, residential neighborhood, academic success, and level of school involvement. We also made a concerted effort to interview graduates who had moved away from their hometowns, either by phone or by traveling to nearby towns. In addition, we interviewed small numbers of nongraduates—those who had either dropped out or transferred out of the schools before graduating. Numbers of graduate interviews conducted, by race, were as follows: White, 136; African American, 79; Latino, 21; Asian, 2; and mixed race, 4. In addition, 26 "portrait interviews were conducted.

Our interviews with the graduates elicited, as only qualitative research can, their understandings of how their lives were affected by their experiences in racially diverse high schools. In particular, we asked the graduates about their educational opportunities, friendships, and networks while attending their racially diverse high schools.

Tier 3: Portraits of Graduates

The third and final tier of data collection for this study involved a much more detailed and in-depth examination of the lives of 4 to 6 graduates from each site. Once we had learned about the history and politics of the context of the high school and interviewed a broad range of students from the class of 1980, we selected between 4 and 6 of these graduates who embodied the major themes emerging from each site. They also reflected the racial diversity of the class of 1980 at their particular school. Each of the 26 graduates we interviewed a second time provided us with ample information to construct a "portrait" of their experiences at their high schools (see Lawrence-Lightfoot & Davis, 1997).

Overview of Data

A total of 540 interviews were conducted, among them 268 interviews of graduates (242 initial interviews and 26 portrait interviews). Our open-ended interviews with policymakers, activists, school officials, lawyers, educators, and graduates focused, for the most part, on the effects of school desegregation on their communities, schools, and lives. We also collected yearbooks, newspaper clips, district documents, and historical documents in libraries and schools from each of the sites.

Data Analysis

As we conducted interviews with approximately 80 people at each site (for a total of 540 interviews) and collected file cabinets full of historical documents, we began data analysis through analytical memos and many pages of field notes. We also wrote case reports about each site for our advisory board meetings. Each interview was fully transcribed and coded according to both within- and cross-case themes that emerged over the course of the study. These themes and subthemes were challenged, merged, and rewritten throughout the course of our data coding process. Our ongoing analysis of these coded data, along with our review of historical documents, portrait transcripts, and field notes, allowed us to develop outlines and a framework for our main findings. The quotations presented here were taken from the corresponding sections of the coded data documents. Thus, each theme or subtheme represented a large body of data, primarily concurring or dissenting quotations derived from hundreds of interviews. The quotations presented, therefore, portray a sentiment or understanding far greater than each utterance.

The findings described here were drawn from our larger analysis, which included five major themes. The two themes discussed subsequently speak most directly to the relationship between schools and their contexts and thus allow us to contemplate the ways in which schools do and do not matter.

FINDINGS FROM A STUDY OF SCHOOLS WITHIN THEIR CONTEXT: WHY SCHOOLS COULD NOT, ON THEIR OWN, FULFILL THE PROMISE OF *BROWN*

Hochschild and Scovronick (2003) argued that school desegregation was, in many ways, a successful public policy as measured by various outcomes, including African American achievement and cross-racial relations, but that politically it was a failure. Whites never strongly supported public policies that took away their freedom to choose where and with whom their children attended school. Meanwhile, many African Americans and Latinos have grown weary of the various ways in which White resistance to desegregation manifests itself inside desegregated schools and districts, often making the goal of equal educational opportunity an elusive one.

Key findings from our study help explain how the context influenced the school community. The stories of the schools we studied and their graduates exemplify the challenges public schools faced as educators tried to facilitate racial integration amid a highly segregated and unequal society. Indeed, our argument, based on these hundreds of interviews and extensive document collection, is that while the racially mixed public schools of the late 1970s were doing more than other institutions in our society to bring people of different racial/ethnic backgrounds together and foster equal opportunity, they did not come close to fulfilling the promise of *Brown v. Board of Education*. Rather, our in-depth study shows that these schools and the districts in which they were located reflected the racial inequality of their local communities and the larger society even as some educators struggled to alter that inequality through equity-minded policies.

Important answers to the *why* questions that emanate from this central argument are grounded in the local contexts of these six high schools. Clearly, we have learned—as no other study on school desegregation has shown in a systematic manner—that the specific context and demographics mattered in the daily experiences of educators and students in racially diverse schools.

Thus, the high schools located in more politically liberal communities and those with larger Black populations were more likely to offer a small number of courses in African American history or Swahili than other high schools. Also, we found more cross-racial friendships in high schools with larger middle-class Black student populations and more interracial dating in the three schools located in more socially liberal communities. Context and demographics also influenced the schools' reputations, the degree of White flight and racial tension, and the commitment of educators.

Yet, while these local distinctions are important, the fact that there are differences across these contexts makes the common, cross-site themes even more powerful because, at each of the sites, policymakers and educators did as little as was legally possible to upset the status quo. This resistance to change was manifest in similar practices across the six districts: forcing Black students to bear most of the burden of desegregating, providing significant incentives to Whites who agreed to participate, and segregating students within racially mixed schools through tracking practices and unequal information and access regarding the most challenging classes.

Through the experiences of educators and students in racially diverse schools in the 1970s, we can help readers understand the many ways in which the promise of *Brown* remained unfulfilled as White privilege was upheld—sometimes in a very de facto manner—within the context of these schools and communities. Such an analysis creates a context for the experiences of the graduates; this is why desegregation had a profound impact on the students and educators, but also why the society as a whole limited the impact that desegregation could have on the students.

Our study, because it looked at several schools within their particular contexts, illustrates how difficult it was for the people in these schools to live up to the goals of school desegregation given the larger societal forces, including housing segregation, economic inequality, and racial politics, working against them. In this way, we can better understand the political failure of school desegregation policy—a policy that accomplished enough to earn the animosity of most White Americans and, as a result, faced too much resistance and White flight for African Americans and Latinos to continue to fight for it.

At the same time, in other publications from this study, we have documented how deeply committed some of these actors—both educators and students—were to trying to bring about change. We captured their memories of many "integrated moments" (connections and experiences) in which they crossed the color line, moments that would not have occurred if not for school desegregation. Furthermore, we learned that despite the social forces working against school desegregation, virtually all of the graduates we interviewed said that desegregation was "worth it" and that they would do it again if they had the chance. And yet, their current lives are far more segregated than their high schools were (see Holme, Wells, & Revilla, 2004; Wells, Holme, Revilla, & Atanda, 2004a, 2004b, in press).

Thus, we argue that the school desegregation policies and efforts that existed in these schools were better than nothing but simply not enough to change the larger society single-handedly. In this way, our study speaks to larger lessons about the role of schools in society and the futile but worthwhile efforts of lawyers and judges to use schools as a tool for social change. The social and economic inequalities across color lines that had accumulated in the United States by the late 1970s—inequalities that are still severe today—reproduced themselves within these racially diverse schools, leaving some students with far fewer opportunities. The boundaries between the schools and their social and political context proved to be as porous as the will to change society through the schools.

Efforts to dismiss school desegregation as a "failed policy"—or, worse yet, a "failed social experiment"—are highly misleading. Indeed, in many contexts, even getting Black, White, and Latino students and educators into the same building was a major feat. And the fact that most of these students said, more than 20 years later, that they valued the experience and would do it again speaks to the importance of the struggle in which these schools were engaged. Indeed, despite the degree of resegregation that occurred, many African American and Latino students said that their schools did matter in their lives—that they benefited from their association with more prestigious and well-resourced schools. Far from being a failure, therefore, school desegregation was never fully implemented, and thus racial integration was never achieved. Thus, our study advances an important point made by John Hope Franklin: "The real tragedy of contemporary race relations . . . is not that integration failed but that it was barely tried" (cited in Applebome, 1995, p. 34).

In the following two sections of this chapter, we highlight two of the most powerful themes (and several subthemes) to emerge from our data that illustrate the powerful connections between these schools and their local communities—and society in general. More detailed discussions of these themes, as well as additional themes, can be found in Wells et al. (in press).

The Power of White Privilege in Racially Mixed Schools and Districts: The Broader Social Context of Desegregation

The theme of the power of White privilege and how it undermined school desegregation policies and practices in these six communities illustrates the distance between the intent behind school desegregation policies—to vindicate 14th Amendment rights of African Americans and Latinos—and the actual results these policies achieved. In all of the six school districts we studied, powerful Whites were able to maintain their privileged status even in the context of an equity-minded reform movement such as school desegregation.

In each of these communities and schools, policymakers and educators tried to make desegregation as palatable as possible for middle-class White parents and students. On a political level, this made perfect sense. The idea was to stave off White and middle-class flight, which would leave the public schools politically and economically vulnerable. However, in concentrating on appeasing White parents, school districts often disregarded the needs of both students of color and poor students (see Wells et al., 2004).

Across the school districts studied, therefore, we saw the disillusionment of African American and Latino advocates, educators, parents, and students as they began to give up on a "remedy" they once thought would solve many educational problems for students of color. While they acknowledged many gains that resulted from efforts to desegregate public schools and create more diversity within these educational institutions, they voiced clear disappointment about how little progress had been made overall and the price that communities of color had to pay to accommodate the demands and threats of Whites. In the end, in each of these communities, the tide of racial inequality and segregation was more powerful than the efforts to reverse it.

We broke down this broad theme of White power and privilege into two subthemes that help illustrate the larger point: (a) White resistance and threat of flight led to Black school closings and the burden of busing being placed on Blacks and (b) "green"—meaning resources and opportunities—follows "white." In the following, we describe each of these subthemes briefly (for more detail, see Wells et al., 2004).

White Resistance and Threat of Flight

Other writings on school desegregation have demonstrated that African American—and, to a lesser extent, Latino—students have almost always borne most of the burden of busing when students are reassigned to achieve racial balance (Adair, 1984; Bell, 1987, 2004; Shujaa, 1996). We also know that far more Black schools were closed down and Black teachers were fired, all in the name of school desegregation that would take place almost exclusively on "White turf." What we learned from our qualitative study is more of the story of *how* this happens: how Whites resisted desegregation plans that looked any different, plans that would have equalized school closings or student travel across racial lines.

There are many quotations in our data on White resistance to school desegregation and how politically effective that resistance was. For instance, a former school board member in Austin, Texas, noted, when asked about the perspective of White parents on the school desegregation process:

Look, we weren't here when the Civil War was fought, we had nothing to do with that. This is 1970, and we're 35 years old and have a child 10 years old or 5 years old going to school, and that's all we want, is our kid to go to school, and we didn't fight the war between the states and we had nothing to do with discrimination against anybody. We just live in a particular neighborhood. A school is right down the road. We want to go to that school right down the road.

Thus, one of the ways in which White privilege manifested itself in these local contexts was through a sense of entitlement about neighborhood schools and a denial that anything was wrong with the highly segregated system in which students attended schools "right down the road." Of course, there was no simultaneous effort, except in Shaker Heights, to address the extreme housing segregation and inequality that left most of the neighborhood schools single-race schools.

In some of the settings we studied, there was almost a sense of self-righteousness in the way Whites made sense of their opposition to desegregation—that they did not deserve to be treated in this way and that it was their obligation to fight integration. For instance, in Pasadena, desegregation sparked a conservative backlash on the part of many Whites in the district, who in turn elected a radically conservative school board. What is notable about these board candidates is that they were successful in large part because they blamed desegregation for the more liberal social climate of the late 1960s and early 1970s. They also crusaded against the "looser morals" and liberalization of the curriculum in the schools. By turning their opposition to desegregation into a crusade for values and a moral order, they appealed to many White conservative voters (many of whom did not have children) who voted for these anti-busing candidates. These far-right candidates (some were rumored to be associated with the John Birch Society) promised not only to end desegregation but to restore "discipline" and a fundamental curriculum in the district.

Once elected, these board members not only actively fought the desegregation order, they embarked on a book banning campaign and established several back-to-basics "fundamental" schools of choice in the district. All of this made the possibility of meaningful school desegregation within Muir High School difficult at best. With a school board that was not supportive of integration, racially mixed schools—their educators, parents, and students—were left to sink or swim on their own.

To make matters worse, Pasadena and Englewood experienced dramatic White flight from the public schools during the era we studied. In Pasadena in particular, new private schools cropped up and White enrollment in the district—especially at Muir High School—plummeted. As a Muir math teacher who had been there for many years explained, "Pasadena is a mecca for private schools. I don't know whether you know that or not. They're all over the place and . . . White flight. That's what it was called, White flight. It was just . . . yeah, there you go. That's what happened. . . . I mean, that was in the newspaper every other day, White flight."

This resistance to school desegregation—whether it was school board elections or White flight or protesting—gave White parents and community members greater leverage in terms of what school desegregation would look like and who would bear the burden of the disruption that would come with it. According to one of the lawyers for the Black plaintiffs in the Charlotte school desegregation case:

> The big problem I had with all of them was that we kept compromising and placing a greater burden on Black parents than we did on others . . . the court purposely decided to take away Grades 1, 2, 3, or K through 3 from the inner city and put them all out in the suburbs, so that White kids wouldn't have to go to school in the inner city and that supposedly made it easier for White parents to send their kids to school.

In Pasadena, the burden of desegregation was placed largely on young Black children. The plan paired Black and White elementary schools in different parts of town, and children would be slated to attend Grades K–3 in one part of town and then Grades 4–6 in the other; the idea was that students would be able to attend their neighborhood school for half of their elementary career. Not coincidentally, the K–3 centers were always in the White areas, so not only did the youngest kids of color have to travel farthest in the early years, by 4th grade many White parents had pulled their kids out of school before they could go to schools located in the minority areas of town.

In Austin, where several different school desegregation plans were drawn up before one was adopted, White students simply did not show up when they were reassigned to a historically Black high school. As a former Austin school board member explained, "We tried in Austin, as a result of the court extending the order, to say that all the kids had to get on the bus, not just the minority kids—all the kids get on the bus. Well, of course as soon as the buses started running the other way, the big push was to dismantle the program of desegregation."

When busing White students to the Black and Latino side of town did not work, the district tried using voluntary measures to desegregate the schools—more specifically "majority to minority" transfer plans. But once again, the movement of students was unidirectional, as another former Austin school board member noted: "The majority to minority transfer rule did not meet the test of integration, because all the burden for moving was on the minorities. No White guy would say 'I want to go into a minority school.'"

Of course, these practices had major implications for what happened once students got to their desegregated schools—who was on whose turf and which parents were already connected and in control—in ways that affected the students' daily experiences and the African American and Latino communities' perception of the benefit of the plan (see Wells et al., in press). If we had simply studied these six high schools without a better sense of their contexts and the political struggles swirling around them, we might have come to different conclusions about what was happening inside them and why.

"Green" Follows "White"

The political leverage and clout that White parents brought to the table in school district struggles over how to desegregate schools carried over once students were reassigned to racially diverse schools and decisions were made about how resources and opportunities were to be distributed across and within schools. For instance, at West Charlotte High School, the only high school in Charlotte that had been a Black school before desegregation and was not shut down when the buses rolled, things changed when the White students arrived. Several teachers and administrators we interviewed attested to the new equipment and renovations suddenly bestowed upon the school once White students—notably, affluent White students—were assigned there. But the changes within West Charlotte High School went beyond bricks and mortar. As one Black graduate noted:

By the time that I got there and then we started going to school with the White kids, it [West Charlotte] changed. It became a place where everybody wanted to be. They started upgrading it and things like that and to me I felt like they catered more to the White kids and parents. . . . Maybe it was in an effort to make them a part of everything. It just seemed like they were just taking over everything. They were the head of the student council and all of that kind of stuff.

Such evidence that "green follows white" was positive for African American students, who suddenly had greater access to resources by virtue of being in schools with

White students, but it was also a reminder that the political system was driven by White privilege and the demands more powerful families made on the system.

Yet, even more problematic were instances in which there were huge *within-*school inequalities in desegregated schools as students of different racial backgrounds had unequal access to the most challenging curricula. In fact, we learned that one of the most common practices in desegregated schools was the creation of high-track or gifted classes. These tracks were promoted simply as the classes in which the most advanced students could be challenged academically. But the racial overtones and implications cannot be ignored, as in school after school these top-level classes were almost entirely White.[5]

We recognize that many factors affected the resegregation of students within desegregated schools, such as the unequal schooling that Black and Latino students had received prior to desegregation and the higher poverty rates of their families. But our data also suggest that White students were given more information about and easier access to honors, advanced placement, and other advanced classes.

Some practices labeled students as "gifted" as early as kindergarten and then channeled them through the grade levels in the "appropriate" classes. More subtle forms of sorting students entailed teacher recommendations and support to get into the best classes. Whatever the method, all six of the schools and districts managed to create incredible and consistent levels of within-school segregation.

A White 1980 graduate of Shaker Heights High School who was in all high-level classes said that "this [advanced placement] thing . . . was actually also like a school within a school." This graduate noted that, while it was not always exactly the same 20 students in every class, "it would be very unusual to see somebody, like a new face, in one class that you didn't see in any other class" (cited in Wells et al., 2004).

At Dwight Morrow High School, which was only 36% White by the time the class of 1980 arrived, the more "academically stringent" the class, the lower the number of Black students enrolled, according to a White graduate who had been in all high-level classes. He noted that in his advanced placement biology class there were one or two Black students, and in calculus there was only one—in a school that was almost 60% Black. He recalled that there were "two societies going on at the academic level."

At Dwight Morrow, even when African Americans did well in regular-level classes, teachers and counselors were sometimes reluctant to promote them to the high-track classes. According to one such African American graduate, "Dwight Morrow, in terms of academics, it was integrated, but it was segregated. And what happened was, once you got labeled that was pretty much it."

An African American parent and teacher at Dwight Morrow High School noted that back in the 1970s, Black parents had to "fight real hard" to get their children into the National Honor Society, even when Black students had higher grades than White students. She recalled one Black mother in particular who had a high-achieving daughter:

Even though she knew that her child had the highest grade level . . . they didn't accept her child. And she went all the way to the state, and she had threatened that if she had to go to the federal government about it, she would because she thought it was unfair.

In Pasadena at Muir High School, the tracking system resegregated the school's class-rooms. According to graduates and educators, classes at Muir were very divided along the lines of race—advanced placement or honors classes were mostly White and higher income (with a few Asian students), while the regular track was racially mixed. Graduates noted that tracking seemed even more severe in the math department: While the English classes had a few students of color, the upper-track math classes were almost all White, with a few Asian students. As reported by one teacher, this tracking started early on in the district. In elementary and especially middle schools, students were tested into a "gifted and talented program" (or the MGM program—"mentally gifted minors") that was predominantly White, and by high school students of color were so far behind that they were locked out of the upper-track classes. According to this teacher:

Because segregation existed in the middle school, the students of color had not had an opportunity before that court order to participate at the middle school in honors programs in large numbers. So it followed that they would not be in the high school program for 5 years because you have to bring them up, you know, through the rest of the levels of honors, so they're prepared to do honors.

Possibly the most revealing memory of tracking and race came from a former English teacher at West Charlotte High School. This now-retired instructor told us about her first year at West Charlotte, when it was still an all-Black school. She recalled that the students in the all-Black honors classes were some of the brightest students she had ever taught. She did not think at the time the school desegregated that the Black students who came in and quickly filled most of the seats in those classes. She said that today she often wonders "What did happen to [those high-achieving Black students] when the school became integrated and the high-level classes [became] predominantly White?" (Wells, Holme, Revilla, & Atanda, 2004a). Interestingly enough, a reform movement to "detrack" schools and create more access to high-level curricula came along in the 1990s, well after the class of 1980 had graduated and after the schools in this country were already becoming more racially segregated (see Oakes et al., 1996).

Effects of Segregation in the Larger Society on Meaningful Integration Within Schools

The second major theme from our findings that speaks to the powerful relationship between schools and their context is one that explains how the racial segregation and inequality in the local communities perpetuated segregation friendships and social networks within the schools. Thus, we argue that there are several ways to interpret lunchroom segregation within desegregated schools (see Tatum, 1998), and one is to consider who students see and interact with outside of school. In the case of students who live in very segregated neighborhoods and lack access to much mass transportation—circumstances that describe the lives of most teenagers in the United States—it is easier to understand why close friendships within racially diverse schools are more often than not same-race friendships.

For the most part, the graduates of the six schools we studied talked about having friends or acquaintances of other races, but their very best friends—those they spent the most time with outside of school—were primarily of the same race. As one Shaker Heights graduate noted, "Even though it was an integrated area, I noticed that most of the Whites hung with the Whites and most of the Blacks hung with the Blacks. But we still had friends within them and you would still talk and be nice to people."

Furthermore, in the predominantly White schools in which Black or Latino students were being bused "in" from elsewhere, the popular White students—usually the more affluent White students—"ruled" the school social realm. As one affluent White graduate of Austin High told us: "We ruled the school. We were *the* group. We were it. We just were all very involved in school. We all loved going to school, it was a great place to be, that's why." In describing her clique of girlfriends from the affluent west side of town, this same graduate noted: "What did we call ourselves? I know some schools, they call them the 'socios,' but we weren't 'socios.' I don't remember what we called ourselves—'West Austin rich bitches,' that's what some people called us."

Thus, not only did the social stratification from the community and larger context filter into the schools—as it does in single-race schools as well—but the racial dimension and the segregated neighborhoods added another layer of complexity. According to an African American graduate of Topeka High School who was popular and was a star athlete at the school, the White and Black students stuck to themselves outside of school:

You know, pretty much during that time period, you know, that's probably . . . you didn't really go over to the White kids' house. I mean, it wouldn't have been a problem I don't think, but you know, just transportation-wise and just being able to get there sometimes and you know, just all the things that maybe go with being a mom or a dad and trying to learn those people's families, or not knowing those families you usually didn't go over there really.

The vast majority of graduates we interviewed hung out with other students from their neighborhoods outside of school. As an African American graduate of West Charlotte High school noted:

I just felt more . . . comfortable being with my own . . . I should say [pause] I can get comfortable around anyone basically. I know after school there were two guys that I saw because we were all in the same neighborhood. I didn't drive over to the east side of town to hang out. I hung out with the people in my neighborhood.

Particularly among the White graduates, there was often a "fear" of the unknown Black neighborhoods. A White West Charlotte graduate recalled that, outside of school, it was not racially mixed. When asked why, she said that her parents probably would not have allowed her to go to a party in a Black neighborhood. "You know, they just would have said, 'No, you can't come.' And I think, you know, parties at that time pretty much spread by word of mouth and . . . I don't remember . . . seeing Black friends from school at parties that were in this neighborhood."

Thus, for the most part, the students in these desegregated schools stepped over color lines only when they were inside the schools, if they did it there; outside of school, these color lines continued to divide them. They often found that their interracial friendships in school went only "so far"—in many instances, they did not feel welcome or comfortable in the homes of students of different racial or ethnic backgrounds. One White Austin High graduate recalled the first time she invited a Latina friend home with her after school:

I can remember bringing her to my house and asking her to stand outside for just a few minutes, and I went in and called my mother and asked if I could have a friend come in. . . . She said yes, and I said, "Well, she's Mexican. Would that still be okay?" My mother said, "Rita only." I mean . . . it wasn't an open door policy.

Furthermore, this translated into a post–high school life of increased racial segregation. When asked why he was not in contact with any of his Black friends from high school, a White alumnus of Dwight Morrow said, "I think I went off with my White world, and . . . people live lives for the most part along color [lines]." Sitting on his back porch in a mostly White upper-middle-class suburb, he grew more frustrated as he compared his current life to the days when he was close to many of his Black classmates:

We went to school with each other . . . we got along nice, we all threw our hats up together, and then we don't talk [to] or see each other anymore, so I think we failed. . . . We didn't make the world an integrated place, it's just not. They forced people to go to school together, but they don't force you to live together, so other than that—the races, where do they commingle? Tell me.

Such testimonies lead us to wonder how much blame we can place on the public schools for "failing" in regard to school desegregation when, indeed, they were often one of the only institutions—or *the* only institution—in their communities struggling with these deep-seated issues and inequalities. This larger context of the struggle to desegregate schools and students was best captured by a study that examined racially mixed schools within their local context and thus documented the porous boundaries between schools and society.

CONCLUSION: WHERE DO WE GO FROM HERE?

The central point of this literature review and the excerpts from our findings regarding desegregated schools is to help fellow educational researchers reconsider how to frame their research in a way that does justice to the impact of the local context on within-school practices. Similarly, we call on those who study local policy and political contexts to connect to the lived experiences of educators and students within schools. And we call on those who study schools and their "outputs," cultures, or relations to question how their findings are shaped by the larger context of schools in the 21st century.

Only by looking at educational policy and practice from both sides of the looking glass will we see clearly how profoundly schools *matter*—and that how they matter most is through their struggles against and their reinforcement of inequality in the larger society. Yet, this kind of research requires us to rethink our methodology, to consider moving beyond the quantitative-qualitative dichotomy and conducting more mixed-method research that would speak to school "outcomes" as well as the broader contexts of schools (see Chatterji, 2004).

Such studies could be designed as historical or sociological case studies of particular places at a particular time. But multiple sources of data—demographics and other statistics, test scores, surveys, in-depth interviews, observations, documents, and so forth—would provide a more holistic picture of what is taking place within schools and why. This comprehensive research is expensive and labor intensive but extremely valuable. It has the potential to answer important questions about how much educational policy and practice can accomplish, especially when policies or practices go against the grain of U.S. society—when, for instance, they challenge long-held assumptions about race, class, or student ability or present a cooperative as opposed to a competitive paradigm. When educational policies and practices do not have the intended effects we had hoped for, we must ask how these policies stand vis-à-vis other social forces and consider the tide they are swimming against before weighing their success or failure.

More specifically, at this half-century mark since the *Brown* ruling, we must once again consider the extent to which the public schools failed to successfully desegregate versus the extent to which our society failed to support desegregation in these schools. At the same time, we must celebrate the successes along the way: the improved achievement of African Americans during the peak years of integration and the more positive racial attitudes of graduates of racially diverse schools and the country as a whole. Also, we must celebrate the accomplishments of individual educators and students within a context that pushed against the success of their lived experiences and constantly tried to dismantle what they had done.

This never-ending struggle against larger social forces that work against school desegregation and racial equality and integration more broadly must be acknowledged as an important act of human agency amid imposing social structures of inequality and oppression. In reality, White and Black students were never supposed to sit next to each other in schools or learn from each other. The history of our country has and continues to work against such experiences, and yet there are spaces where this occurs and where meaningful experiences transform people's lives. But the struggle is never over, and these experiences *and* their larger contexts are what educational researchers must capture.

We close with a quotation from an administrator in Charlotte who served as the principal of West Charlotte High School in the late 1970s, when it was racially balanced—about 50% African American and 50% White. Today, West Charlotte High School is less than 5% White. According to this administrator:

I think the biggest lesson that I learned from it was that it was never over, that there was never a point when we achieved it [integration]. . . . And it is never truly achieved; it is something you have to constantly work at, because there are so many outside influences and so many background influences that put us back to where we were.

NOTES

[1] While both the *Brown* decision and the Coleman report discounted the effect of "tangible factors," including school buildings and resources, on the educational opportunities of children and justified school desegregation as a solution to broader social ills, their conclusions were grounded in distinct arguments about the impact of schools—versus other social forces—on the lives of children.

[2] The *Brown* ruling also addressed the social psychological effect of segregation on "hearts and minds" and the importance of an African American student's ability "to study, to engage in discussions and exchange views with other students." This freedom to associate with other students seemed to matter to the Warren court, however, because it takes place within an institution so critical to children's life chances.

[3] By "racially mixed," we mean between 40% and 75% of any one race and no more than 25% off the racial balance of the city or town for any one race.

[4] We realize that after 1974, when the U.S. Supreme Court ruled in *Milliken v. Bradley* that court-ordered urban-suburban school desegregation was possible only when plaintiffs could prove that suburban districts helped to create racial segregation in cities, the possible impact of school desegregation on poor urban school districts was highly limited. But for the students who were "living" school desegregation during this later era at the end of the 1970s, things were better, more hopeful, and certainly calmer in their communities than they had been before.

[5] For prior research on the role of tracking in racially mixed schools, see Oakes et al. (1996).

REFERENCES

Adair, A. V. (1984). *Desegregation: The illusion of Black progress.* Lanham, MD: University Press of America.

American Association of School Administrators. (1992). *An effective schools primer.* Arlington, VA: Author.

Anyon, J. (1997). *Ghetto schooling: A political economy of urban educational reform.* New York: Teachers College Press.

Anyon, J. (2005). *Radical possibilities: Public policy, urban education, and a new social movement.* New York: Routledge.

Applebome, P. (1995, September 26). Opponents' moves refueling debate on school busing. *New York Times,* pp. A1, A12.

Armor, D. J. (1995). *Forced justice: School desegregation and the law.* New York: Oxford University Press.

Barnes, C. (2002). *Standards reform in high poverty schools: Managing conflict and building capacity.* New York: Teachers College Press.

Barnes, J. E. (2004, March 22). Now the focus shifts from integration to achievement for all. *U.S. News & World Report,* pp. 67–75.

Barnes, J. E., Bentrup, N., Ekman, M., & Brady, M. (2004, March 22). Unequal education. *U.S. News & World Report,* p. 66.

Beals, M. P. (1994). *Warriors don't cry.* New York: Pocket Books.

Bell, D. (1987). *And we are not saved: The elusive quest for racial justice.* New York: Basic Books.

Bell, D. (2004). *Silent covenants: Brown v. Board of Education and the unfulfilled hopes for racial reform.* New York: Oxford University Press.

Bickel, W. E. (1983). Effective schools: Knowledge, dissemination, inquiry. *Educational Researcher, 12*(4), 3–5.

Bossert, S. T. (1988). School effects. In N. J. Boyan (Ed.), *Handbook of research on educational administration* (pp. 341–352). New York: Longman.

Boyd, W. (1987). President Reagan's school-reform agenda. *Education Week.* Retrieved June 14, 2005, from http://www.edweek.org/ew/articles/1987/03/18/2525boyd.h06.html? querystring=Boyd

Braddock, J. (2004, August). *Sociologists and the fight against racial segregation.* Paper presented at the annual meeting of the American Sociology Association, San Francisco.

Braddock, J. H., Crain, R. L., McPartland, J. M., & Dawkins, R. L. (1986). Applicant race and job placement decisions: A national survey experiment. *International Journal of Sociology and Social Policy, 6,* 3–24.

Braddock, J. H., & McPartland, J. M. (1987). How minorities continue to be excluded from equal employment opportunities: Research on labor market and institutional barriers. *Journal of Social Issues, 43,* 5–39.

Bradley, A. (1989, June 21). Black educators hail rapid progress of their 'effective schools' blueprint. *Education Week,* p. 7.

Brantlinger, E. (2003). *Dividing classes: How the middle class negotiates and rationalizes school advantage.* New York: Routledge/Falmer.

Brophy, J., & Good, T. (1974). *Teacher-student relationships: Causes and consequences.* New York: Holt, Rinehart & Winston.

Brown, M. K. (2003). Ghettos, fiscal federalism, and welfare reform. In S. F. Schram, J. Soss, & R. C. Fording (Eds.), *Race and the politics of welfare reform* (pp. 47–71). Ann Arbor: University of Michigan Press.

Brown v. Board of Education, 347 U.S. 483 (1954).

Burch, P. (2002). Constraints and opportunities in changing policy environments. In A. M. Hightower, M. S. Knapp, J. A. Marsh, & M. W. McLaughlin (Eds.), *School districts and instructional renewal.* New York: Teachers College Press.

Bush warns against the "soft bigotry of low expectations." (1999). *Education Week.* Retrieved June 14, 2005, from http://www.edweek.org/ew/articles/1999/09/22/03bushs1.h19.html? querystring=soft%20bigotry

Carnoy, M., Elmore, R., & Siskin, L. (2003). *The new accountability: High schools and high-stakes testing.* New York: Falmer Press.

Cashin, S. (2004). *The failures of integration: How race and class are undermining the American dream.* New York: Public Affairs.

Chatterji, M. (2004). Evidence on "what works": An argument for extended-term mixed-method (ETMM) evaluation designs. *Educational Researcher, 33*(9), 3–13.

Clotfelter, C. T. (2004). *After Brown: The rise and retreat of school desegregation.* Princeton, NJ: Princeton University Press.

Coleman, J. S., Campbell, E. Q., Hobson, C. J., McPartland, J., Mood, A. M., Weinfeld, F. D., & York, R. L. (1966). *Equality of educational opportunity.* Washington, DC: U.S. Government Printing Office.

Cooper, A. (1995). Educating African-American children: Higher than hope. *Education Week.* Retrieved November 30, 2004, from http://www.edweek.org/ew/articles/1995/11/01/ 09cooper.h15.html?querystring=Cooper

Crain, R. L. (1969). *The politics of school desegregation.* Garden City, NY: Anchor Books.

Crain, R. L. (1976). Why academic research fails to be useful. *School Review, 84,* 337–351.

Crain, R. L., & Mahard, R. E. (1978). Desegregation and Black achievement: A review of the research. *Law and Contemporary Problems, 42*(3), 17–55.

Crain, R. L., & Mahard, R. E. (1983). The effect of research methodology on desegregation-student achievement: A meta-analysis. *American Journal of Sociology, 88,* 839–854.

Cross, C. T. (2004). *Political education: National policy comes of age.* New York: Teachers College Press.

Cuban, L. (1993). A national curriculum and tests: Charting the consequences. *Education Week.* Retrieved September 27, 2004, from http://www.edweek.org/ew/articles/ 1993/07/14/41cuban.h12.html?querystring=Cuban,%20Larry

Darling-Hammond, L. (2004). From "separate but equal" to "No Child Left Behind": The collision of new standards and old inequalities. In D. Meier & G. Wood (Eds.), *Many children left behind* (pp. 3–32). Boston: Beacon Press.

Delpit, L. (1995). *Other people's children: Cultural conflict in the classroom.* New York: New Press.

Douglas, D. M. (1995). *Reading, writing and race: The desegregation of the Charlotte schools.* Chapel Hill: University of North Carolina Press.

Drier, P., Mollenkopf, J., & Swanstrom, T. (2004). *Place matters: Metropolitics for the twenty-first century.* Lawrence: University Press of Kansas.

DuBois, W. E. B. (1935). Does the Negro need separate schools? *Journal of Negro Education, 4,* 328–335.

Duster, T. (1968). Violence and civic responsibility: Combinations of "fear" and "right." In R. W. Mack (Ed.), *Our children's burden* (pp. 1–41). New York: Vintage Books.

Eaton, S. F. (2001). *The other Boston busing story.* New Haven, CT: Yale University Press.

Edsall, T. B., with Edsall, M. D. (1991). *Chain reaction: The impact of race, rights, and taxes on American politics.* New York: Norton.

Foster, M. (1997). *Black teachers on teaching.* New York: New Press.

Frankenberg, E., Lee, C., & Orfield, G. (2003). *A multiracial society with segregated schools: Are we losing the dream?* Retrieved September 27, 2004, from http://www.civilrightsproject.harvard.edu/research/reseg03/reseg03_full.php

Gaillard, F. (1988). *The dream long deferred.* Chapel Hill: University of North Carolina Press.

Gordon, E. W., Bridglall, B. L., & Meroe, A. S. (Eds.). (2004). *Supplementary education: The hidden curriculum of high academic achievement.* Lanham, MD: Rowman & Littlefield.

Granovetter, M. S. (1973). The strength of weak ties. *American Journal of Sociology, 78,* 1360–1380.

Grant, G. (1973). Shaping social policy: The politics of the Coleman report. *Teachers College Record, 75,* 17–54.

Grant, G. (1988). *The world we created at Hamilton High.* Cambridge, MA: Harvard University Press.

Hallinger, P., & Murphy, J. F. (1986). The social context of effective schools. *American Journal of Education, 94,* 328–355.

Halpren, R. (1995). *Rebuilding the inner city: A history of neighborhood initiatives to address poverty in the United States.* New York: Columbia University Press.

Hochschild, J. (1984). *The new American dilemma: Liberal democracy and school desegregation.* New Haven, CT: Yale University Press.

Hochschild, J., & Scovronick, N. (2003). *The American dream and the public schools.* New York: Oxford University Press.

Holme, J. J., Wells, A. S., & Revilla, A. T. (2004). Learning through experience: What graduates gained by attending desegregated high schools. *Equity and Excellence in Education, 38,* 14–24.

Jencks, C., Smith, M., Acland, H., Jo Bane, M., Cohen, D., Gintis, H., Heynes, B., & Michelson, S. (1972). *Inequality.* New York: Basic Books.

Karp, S. (2004). NCLB's selective vision of equality: Some gaps count more than others." In D. Meier & G. Wood (Eds.), *Many children left behind* (pp. 53–65). Boston: Beacon Press.

Klarman, M. (2004). *From Jim Crow to civil rights: The Supreme Court and the struggle for equality.* New York: Oxford University Press.

Kozol, J. (1991). *Savage inequalities: Children in America's schools.* New York: Crown.

Kozol, J. (1994). *Amazing grace: The lives of children and the conscience of a nation.* New York: HarperPerennial.

Lareau, A. (2003). *Unequal childhoods: Class, race and family life.* Berkeley: University of California Press.

Lawrence, A. (1986). *Schooling, the school effectiveness movement, and educational reform.* Melbourne, Victoria, Australia: Deakin University Press.

Lawrence-Lightfoot, S., & Davis, J. H. (1997). *The art and science of portraiture.* San Francisco: Jossey-Bass.

Levin, H. M. (1975). Education, life chances, and the courts: The role of social science evidence. *Law and Contemporary Problems, 39,* 217–240.

Levin, H. M., & Belfield, C. R. (2002). Families as contractual partners in education. *UCLA Law Review, 49,* 1–27.

Lipman, P. (1998). *Race, class, and power in school restructuring.* Albany: State University of New York Press.

Little, J. W., & McLaughlin, M. W. (1993). *Teachers' work: Individuals, colleagues, and contexts.* New York: Teachers College Press.

Lukas, J. A. (1985). *Common ground: A turbulent decade in the lives of three American families.* New York: Alfred A. Knopf.

Mack, R. W. (Ed.). (1968). *Our children's burden.* New York: Vintage Books.

MacLeod, J. (1995). *Ain't no making it* (2nd ed.). Boulder, CO: Westview Press.

Massey, D., & Denton, N. (1993). *American apartheid: Segregation and the making of the underclass.* Cambridge, MA: Harvard University Press.

Mehan, H. (1992). Understanding inequality in schools: The contribution of interpretive studies. *Sociology of Education, 65,* 1–20.

Metz, M. H. (1978). *Classrooms and corridors: The crisis of authority in desegregated secondary schools.* Berkeley: University of California Press.

Metz, M. H. (2003). *Different by design: The context and character of three magnet schools* (2nd ed.). New York: Teachers College Press.

Milliken v. Bradley, 418 U.S. 717 (1974).

Mosteller, F., & Moynihan, D. P. (Eds.). (1972). *On equality of educational opportunity.* New York: Random House.

Moynihan, D. P. (1991). Educational goals and political plans. *Public Interest, 102,* 32–84.

National Commission on Excellence in Education. (1983). *A nation at risk.* Washington, DC: U.S. Department of Education.

Noguera, P. (2003). *City schools and the American dream: Reclaiming the promise of public education.* New York: Teachers College Press.

Oakes, J. (1985). *Keeping track: How schools structure inequality.* New Haven, CT: Yale University Press.

Oakes, J., & Wells, A. S., & Associates. (1996). *Beyond the technicalities of school reform: Policy lessons from detracking schools.* Los Angeles: Graduate School of Education and Information Studies, University of California, Los Angeles.

Office of Innovation and Improvement. (2004). *Americans' choice lifts students to reach the achievement bar.* Washington, DC: U.S. Department of Education.

Ogletree, C. J. (2004). *All deliberate speed: Reflections on the first half-century of Brown v. Board of Education.* New York: Norton.

Orfield, G. (1975). How to make desegregation work: The adaptation of schools to their newly-integrated student bodies. *Law and Contemporary Problems, 39,* 314–340.

Orfield, G. (1995). Public opinion and school desegregation. *Teachers College Record, 96,* 654–670.

Orfield, G., Eaton, S., & Harvard Project on School Desegregation. (1996). *Dismantling desegregation.* New York: New Press.

Orfield, G., & Lee, C. (2005). *Why segregation matters: Poverty and educational inequality.* Cambridge, MA: Civil Rights Project, Harvard University.

Orfield, G., & Monfort, F. (1988). *Racial change and desegregation in large school districts.* Washington, DC: National School Boards Association.

Patchen, M. (1982). *Black-White Contact in Schools: Its Social and Academic Effects.* West Lafayette, IN: Purdue University Press.

Pilsher, J. (2001). Schools: It's the color of money. *Cincinnati Enquirer.* Retrieved June 13, 2005, from http://enquirer.com/editions/2001/09/05/loc_schools_its_color_of.html

Plessy v. Ferguson, 163 U.S. 537 (1896).

Public Agenda. (1998). *Time to move on: African-American and White parents set an agenda for public school.* New York: Author.

Purkey, S. C., & Smith, M. S. (1983). Effective schools: A review. *Elementary School Journal, 83,* 426–452.

Revilla, A. T., Wells, A. S., & Holme, J. J. (2005). "We didn't see color . . .": The salience of colorblindness in desegregated schools. In M. Fine, L. Weis, L. P. Pruitt, & A. Burns (Eds.), *Off white* (pp. 284–301). New York: Routledge.

Richardson, J. (1995). Next generation of effective schools looks to districts. *Education Week.* Retrieved September 6, 2004, from http://www.edweek.org/ew/articles/1995/04/12/29effect.h14.html?querystring=Richardson

Riehl, C. (2001). Bridges to the future: The contributions of qualitative research to the sociology of education. *Sociology of Education, 74*(Suppl.), 115–134.

Riley, R. W. (1995). Reflections on Goals 2000. *Teachers College Record, 96,* 380–388.

Rist, R. (1970). Student social class and teacher expectations: The self-fulfilling prophecy in ghetto education. *Harvard Educational Review, 40,* 70–110.

Rist, R. C. (1979). *Desegregated schools: Appraisals of an American experiment.* New York: Academic Press.

Robelen, E. (2002, January 9). ESEA to boost federal role in education. *Education Week,* pp. 1, 28–29, 31.

Robelen, E. (2004, September 29). "No Child" remains at top of Bush record. *Education Week,* pp. 1, 23–24.

Rothstein, R. (2004). *Class and schools: Using social, economic, and educational reform to close the Black-White achievement gap.* Washington, DC: Economical Policy Institute.

Rowan, B., Bossert, S. T., & Dwyer, D. C. (1983). Research on effective schools: A cautionary note. *Educational Researcher, 12*(4), 24–31.

Sanger, D. E. (2003). Bush defends financing for schools. *New York Times.* Retrieved September 6, 2004, from http://www.nytimes.com/2003/09/09/politics/09BUSH.html?ex=1064133497&ei=1&en=40edb153596f5cda

Schofield, J. (1989). *Black and White in school.* New York: Teachers College Press.

Schofield, J. (1991). School desegregation and intergroup relations: A review of the literature. In G. Grant (Ed.), *Review of research in education* (Vol. 17, pp. 335–409). Washington, DC: American Educational Research Association.

Schwartz, R. B., & Robinson, M. A. (2000). Goals 2000 and the standards movement. In D. Ravitch (Ed.), *Brookings papers on education policy 2000* (pp. 173–214). Washington, DC: Brookings Institution Press.

Shujaa, M. J. (1996). *Beyond desegregation: The politics of quality in African American schooling.* Thousand Oaks, CA: Corwin Press.

Sizer, T. R. (2004). Preamble: A reminder for Americans. In D. Meier & G. Wood (Eds.), *Many children left behind* (pp. xvii–xxii). Boston: Beacon Press.

Snider, D. (1989). Survey confirms the rapid spread of "effective schools." *Education Week.* Retrieved September 6, 2004, from http://www.edweek.org/ew/articles/1989/09/27/09070022.h09.html?querystring=Hawkins%20Snider

St. John, N. (1975). *School desegregation: Outcomes for children.* New York: Wiley.

Tanner, D. (1972, September 8). Harvard study disputes impact of schooling on future income. *New York Times,* p. A1.

Tatum, B. D. (1998). *Why are all the Black kids sitting together in the cafeteria?* New York: Basic Books.

Taylor, B., & Bullard, P. (1995). *The revolution revisited: Effective schools and systemic reform.* Bloomington, IN: Phi Delta Kappa Educational Foundation.

Thernstrom, A., & Thernstrom, S. (2003). *No excuses: Closing the racial gap in learning.* New York: Simon & Schuster.

Walker, V. S. (2002). Valued segregated school for African American children in the South, 1935–1969: A review of common themes and characteristics. *Review of Educational Research, 70,* 253–285.

Walker, V. S. (2005). Organized resistance and Black educators' quest for school equality. *Teachers College Record, 107,* 355–388.

Wells, A. S. (2001). The "consequences" of school desegregation: The mismatch between the research and the rationale. *Hastings Constitutional Law Quarterly, 28,* 771–797.

Wells, A. S., & Crain, R. L. (1994). Perpetuation theory and the long-term effects of school desegregation. *Review of Educational Research, 64,* 531–555.

Wells, A. S., & Crain, R. L. (1997). *Stepping over the color line: African American students in White suburban schools.* New Haven, CT: Yale University Press.

Wells, A. S., Hirshberg, D., Lipton, M., & Oakes, J. (1995). Bounding the case within its context: A constructivist approach to studying detracking reform. *Educational Researcher, 24*(5), 18–24.

Wells, A. S., & Holme, J. J. (in press). Marketization in education: Looking back to move forward with a stronger critique. In N. Bascia, A. Cumming, A. Datnow, K. Leithwood, & D. Livingston (Eds.), *International handbook of educational policy.* New York: Springer.

Wells, A. S., Holme, J. J., Revilla, A. T., & Atanda, A. K. (2004a). *How desegregation changed us: The effects of racially mixed schools on students and society.* New York: Teachers College, Columbia University.

Wells, A. S., Holme, J. J., Revilla, A. T., & Atanda, A. K. (2004b). Against the tide: Desegregated high schools and their 1980 graduates. *Phi Delta Kappan, 85,* 670–679.

Wells, A. S., Holme, J. J., Revilla, A. J., & Atanda, A. K. (in press). Tackling racial segregation one policy at a time: Why school desegregation only went so far. *Teachers College Record.*

Wells, A. S., Revilla, A. T., Holme, J. J., & Atanda, A. K. (2004). The space between school desegregation court orders and outcomes: The struggle to challenge White privilege. *Virginia Law Review, 90,* 1721–1748.

Wells, A. S., & Serna, I. (1996). The politics of culture: Understanding local political resistance to detracking in racially mixed schools. *Harvard Educational Review, 62,* 93–118.

Wenglinsky, H. (2002). How schools matter: The link between teacher classroom practices and student academic performance. *Educational Policy Analysis Archives, 10*(12), 1–31.

Willis, P. (1977). *Learning to labor: How working class kids get working class jobs.* New York: Columbia University Press.

Wilson, A. V., & Segall, W. E. (2001). *Oh, do I remember!: Experiences of teachers during the desegregation of Austin's schools, 1964–1971.* Albany: State University of New York Press.

Winter, G. (2004, May 17). 50 years after *Brown,* the issue is often money. *New York Times,* pp. A1, A19.

Chapter 4

African American Principals and the Legacy of *Brown*

Linda C. Tillman

University of North Carolina at Chapel Hill

The year 2004 was filled with celebrations and commemorations of the 50th anniversary of the *Brown v. Board of Education* decision. There were a significant number of conferences that featured experts from education, law, sociology, and civil rights organizations who spoke of promises fulfilled and unfulfilled 50 years after the historic decision. This volume contributes to the American Educational Research Association's recognition of the *Brown* decision, which also included the Brown Lecture in Educational Research (Gordon, 2004) and the DeWitt Wallace Reader's Digest Distinguished Lecture (Ladson-Billings, 2004). Much of what was written, presented, and discussed during the jubilee year focused on historical accounts of events leading up to *Brown*, court-ordered desegregation efforts, the displacement of Black educators after the *Brown* decision, and the current state of African American education 50 years after this landmark case.[1] Indeed, our thinking has been stimulated regarding the impact of the *Brown* decision on education today, particularly for African Americans.[2]

One aspect of the *Brown* legacy that is underdeveloped in the literature is the significance of the leadership of African American principals in pre-K–12 education both before and after *Brown*. Pre-*Brown* African American principals were committed to the education of Black children, worked with other Black leaders to establish schools for these children, and worked in all-Black schools, usually in substandard conditions. Post-*Brown* African American principals helped to implement desegregation and educate African American children in the face of resistance. Today these men and women are primarily employed in large, urban school districts and continue to work for the social, emotional, and academic achievement of African American students. Yet, many of the historical and contemporary contributions of African Americans have not been documented in the traditional literature on educational leadership and administration.[3]

Our knowledge of the contributions of African American school leaders has been enhanced by the work of scholars such as Anderson (1988), Franklin (1984, 1990), Savage (2001), Siddle Walker (1993a, 1993b, 1996, 2003), and Ward Randolph (1997). However, research by and about African Americans in school leadership positions has not become a dominant strand in the scholarship on educational leadership, leaving gaps in terms of an African American perspective (Banks, 1995; Bloom & Erlandson, 2003; Coursen, Mazzarella, Jeffress, & Hadderman, 1989; Dillard, 1995; Tillman, in press-a). It is worth noting that, during the commemoration of the 50th anniversary of *Brown,* no special issues were published in the four major educational administration journals identified by Leithwood and Duke (1999)— *Educational Administration Quarterly, Journal of School Leadership, Journal of Educational Administration,* and *Educational Management and Administration*[4]—that focused on the importance of the *Brown* decision to school leadership.

A forthcoming special issue of *Educational Administration Quarterly,* "Pushing Back Resistance: African American Discourses on School Leadership" (Tillman, in press-b), will include perspectives on *Brown* and its significance to educational leadership. In addition, race and culture as factors in school leadership, topics that have not been extensively discussed in the educational leadership literature, will be consistent themes in this special issue. The issues of race and culture in educational leadership are particularly relevant given the increasing number of African American principals and students in pre-K–12 education and the need to investigate issues that may be specific to African Americans in school leadership positions, including same-race and cultural affiliation; leadership styles; recruitment, hiring, and retention of African American leaders; instructional supervision; leadership in urban schools[5]; and the relationship between African American school leadership and African American student success. This special issue will be the first full issue in the *Educational Administration Quarterly* to focus specifically on African Americans in school leadership, and it represents an attempt to broaden the discussions on school leadership generally, and to establish a body of work on African Americans in school leadership specifically, in the mainstream school administration literature.[6]

The 1954 *Brown v. Board of Education* decision is significant with respect to African Americans in the principalship for several reasons. First, teachers, principals, and parents were the most important influences in the education of Black children in the pre-*Brown* era of schooling. Thus, discussions about the *Brown* decision and the education of Blacks cannot be held absent discussions about the roles played by the central figure in the school: the Black principal. As the research reviewed here will reveal, it was the Black principal who led the closed system of segregated schooling for Blacks, primarily in the South. The Black principal represented the Black community; was regarded as the authority on educational, social, and economic issues; and was responsible for establishing the all-Black school as the cultural symbol of the Black community. Second, the work of Black principals in the post-*Brown* era has contributed to the theory and practice of educational leadership. As this review will also reveal, the leadership of post-*Brown* African American principals is similar to that of their pre-*Brown* predecessors. Finally, the *Brown* decision is significant with respect to Black principals because one of the goals of the decision was to remedy educational inequities and thus allow Black principals to continue their work under improved social and educational conditions. It is ironic that the *Brown* decision resulted in the firing and demotion of thousands of Black principals, mostly in the southern and border states. As a result, Black principals were often denied the opportunity and authority to act on behalf of Black children in the implementation of desegregation.

Culture appeared to strongly influence the leadership of pre- as well as post-*Brown* African American principals. Tillman (2002) defined *culture* as "a group's individual and collective ways of thinking, believing, and knowing, which includes their shared experiences, consciousness, skills, values, forms of expression, social institutions and behaviors" (p. 4). The research reviewed here reveals that in the closed system of segregated schooling, as well as in post-*Brown* resegregated schools (Orfield & Lee, 2004), Black principals considered the cultural norms of the Black community in their leadership practices. The work of scholars such as Lomotey (1989a, 1993), Dillard (1995), Siddle Walker (1993a, 1996), and Bloom and Erlandson (2003) points to the importance of culture in the leadership of African American principals. For example, Dillard wrote that principals have three cultural management roles: interpreting, representing, and authenticating school culture and relationships. Dillard, citing the conclusions of Mitchell, Ortiz, and Mitchell (1987) in their work on the notion of cultural management, noted that "particularly helpful were their conclusions that background, culture, religion, gender and other identities serve to develop particularized experiential views of schooling and leadership for the school principal" (p. 545). Finally, Dillard noted that "both nurturing and protecting African American children has historically included authoritative and direct ways of interacting, guided specifically by explicit, ethical, social, and *cultural rules and expectations*" (p. 551, italics added). While the importance of culture, particularly with respect to racial and ethnic group membership, is not fully developed in the traditional educational leadership literature, this review will show that an emphasis on culture as a factor in the leadership of Black principals dates back to the pre-*Brown* era of schooling.

OUTLINE OF THE PRESENT DISCUSSION

The specific focus of this chapter is African American principals in pre-K–12 education in the pre- and post-*Brown* eras. It is not my intent to present a comprehensive review of the broad range of topics in the field of educational leadership. Rather, I reviewed published research on Blacks in the principalship and identified major themes in the literature. The research is interdisciplinary, including work from the fields of history, sociology, education, and, more specifically, educational leadership/administration. While a great deal of the empirical work on Blacks in educational leadership/administration can be found in unpublished dissertations (see, for example, Hobson-Horton, 2000; Loder, 2002; Shotwell, 1999; Wells, 1991; White, 1995), this review is based on published research and does not include dissertation research on Blacks in the principalship.

The chapter is organized into three sections. In the first section, I discuss historical research on Blacks in the principalship in the pre-*Brown* era and the impact of

Brown on the displacement of Black principals. In the subsequent section, I discuss research on Blacks in the principalship in the post-*Brown* era. This work includes case studies, ethnographic research, and an emerging body of research on African American female principals. I conclude the review by summarizing major themes across the studies, discussing the impact of the absence of race in educational leadership, and recommending directions for future research.

The presentation and analysis of the research in this review may be considered "different" from what is traditionally offered in "standard" literature reviews in educational research. However, this difference is consistent with the methodological approaches used by the researchers discussed. Several of the authors discussed in this review note that their findings offer a counternarrative to what is written in traditional educational research (Bloom & Erlandson, 2003; Dillard, 1995, Lomotey, 1989a, 1993; Siddle Walker, 1993a, 1996). These authors rely heavily on the narrative approach and recount participants' stories—stories that, as the authors point out, may not be valued outside of these specific racial and cultural experiences. They are stories of vision, hope, persistence, pride, opportunity, disappointment, racism, sexism, segregation, desegregation, resegregation, and survival. The approaches taken by the researchers are intended to place the experiences of African American principals at the center of the inquiry rather than at the margins (Tillman, 2002).

Collectively, the research in this review yielded four consistent themes: (a) resistance to ideologies and individuals opposed to the education of Black students, (b) the academic and social development of Black students as a priority, (c) the importance of the cultural perspectives of the Black principal, and (d) leadership based on interpersonal caring. These themes are not linear. Rather, they overlap, and several themes may be found in each study. In addition, the themes cut across the pre- and post-*Brown* eras. There may be tensions in some of the themes; that is, they are not without contradictions and at times may appear to be in conflict within and across the research. A possible limitation of this review is that much of the research focuses on the positive aspects of Blacks in the principalship and "good schools." However, as did Sowell (1976) and Siddle Walker (2003), I chose to highlight scholarship on Black principals in the pre- and post-*Brown* eras that will "expand the narrow lens through which Black leadership has historically been viewed" (Siddle Walker, 2003, p. 59).

HISTORICAL PERSPECTIVES OF THE BLACK PRINCIPALSHIP

The work of Black educators is historically and culturally significant. A tradition of excellence in Black school leadership and an agenda for the education of Blacks date back to the 1860s (Anderson, 1988; M. Foster, 1997; Franklin, 1990; Pollard, 1997; Savage, 2001; Siddle Walker, 2000, 2001; Watkins, 2001). Black educators helped to build and operate public and private schools, secured funding and other needed resources, worked with the Black community, and served dual but complementary roles as educators and activists for the education of Black children. From a cultural standpoint, the educational philosophies of Black principals generally reflected the collective ethos of Black communities that believed education was the key to enhancing the life chances of their children. Particularly in many small southern towns, the all-Black school was the institution that reinforced community values and served as the community's ultimate cultural symbol (Dempsey & Noblit, 1996).

Thus, even while schools were segregated, they were "valued" by the Black community (Siddle Walker, 2000). Indeed, while separate school systems were the order of the day in the pre-*Brown* era, Black educators taught and nurtured an important segment of the Black community: its children. Henig, Hula, Orr, and Pedescleaux (1999) noted that "by the second half of the twentieth century, black teachers and principals were important role models and respected leaders in their communities. They also comprised a significant proportion of the African-American community's middle-class" (p. 44). Education was one of the few vocations open to middle-class Blacks in the pre-*Brown* era (M. Foster, 1997; Orfield, 1969; Pollard, 1997; Siddle Walker, 2000, 2001), and, because of their profession, Black principals served as models of "servant leadership."[7] Black principals demonstrated an ethos of service "which obligated those who acquired literacy to transfer this knowledge to others in the Black community" (Savage, 2001, p.173).

The historical literature on Black principals focuses primarily on two areas: the lives and work of Black principals in the pre-*Brown* era and the employment status of Black principals immediately after the *Brown* decision. The sections to follow discuss research in these two areas.

THE BLACK PRINCIPAL IN THE PRE-*BROWN* ERA

Much of the scholarship on the lives and work of Black principals who led schools just after slavery into the early 1950s has been written by historians and is typically based on archival research and interviews. The majority of this scholarship has focused on the principal's role in the education of Blacks in the South in the pre-*Brown* era. The tasks of building and maintaining schools for Black children were taken on by Blacks who assumed leadership roles and functioned as heads or principals of common schools as well as all-Black institutions such as Hampton and Tuskegee institutes (Anderson, 1988; Butchart, 1988; Franklin, 1990; S. N. Jones, 2003). For example, Zion School, one of the first all-Black schools in the South, was established in December 1865 and operated with an all-Black teaching and administrative staff (Anderson, 1988). Anderson (1988) wrote that Black southerners were freed during the same time that education for Whites "was transformed into a highly formal and critical social institution" (p. 2). Blacks gained access to education under a different set of circumstances than Whites, for whom education was an entitlement. Anderson described systems of public and private education designed and implemented for and by Black southerners between 1860 and 1935. Two types of schools established and maintained by ex-slaves were common schools and Sabbath schools. Sabbath schools, for example, were church sponsored, were open in the evening and on weekends, and provided literacy instruction to ex-slaves. According to Anderson, schooling for Blacks in the South was for the most part effective given the segregated context and hostility toward educated Blacks. Indeed, one of the most prominent themes in the history of Black Americans during this era was their persistent struggle to participate in an educational system that would ensure their continued freedom and grant them entrée into a democratic society. Anderson noted:

> The short range purpose of Black education in the post-slavery era was to provide the masses of ex-slaves with basic literacy skills plus the rudiments of citizenship training for participation in a democratic society. The long-range purpose was the intellectual and moral development of a responsible leadership class that would organize the masses and lead them to freedom and equality. (p. 31)

One of the earliest-known Black principals was Booker T. Washington, who headed Hampton Institute in Virginia and later Tuskegee Institute in Alabama. Students who attended Hampton and Tuskegee were typically older and had been denied the opportunity to participate in structured education in the years immediately after slavery. Washington was principal during a period of history when the education of ex-slaves was primarily controlled by White philanthropists and industrialists who believed that Blacks should be trained (rather than educated) in skills that would benefit the economic development of the South. As principal, Washington established a manual labor program at Hampton Institute in 1879 (Washington, 1901/1993). The program operated at night after students had worked for 10 hours a day, 6 days a week, 11 months a year for 2 years. The Hampton manual labor program was "designed as an ideological force that would provide instruction suitable for adjusting blacks to a subordinate social role in the emergent New South" (Anderson, 1988, p. 36). Basic skills in reading, writing, and computation were discouraged; rather, Black students received instruction in cooking, sewing, and farming and were taught Christian morals. As the principal, Washington was given a great deal of authority to implement his own vision for educating Blacks, a vision that was consistent with the wishes of the White power structure. He often disagreed with Black leaders and Black educators who fought to provide Blacks with the same type of liberal arts and classical education received by Whites. Washington is credited with designing, implementing, and supervising the education of many Blacks, as well as raising money to modernize two schools that would later become premier all-Black institutions. However, his alliances with wealthy and influential Whites and his willingness to compromise the rights and the future of Blacks make him one of the most controversial figures in the struggle for the education of Blacks.

From the 18th century through the 1950s, educated professional elites such as ministers, journalists, and politicians provided leadership in the struggle to educate Blacks (Franklin, 1984, 1990). Throughout the antebellum era, African American minister-educators were particularly instrumental in opening schools in the North and the South. As principals or headmasters, these individuals held a strong belief that while Blacks could be stripped of their money, civil rights, and property, the knowledge they acquired through education could not be taken away. Jeremiah Burke Sanderson served as a principal-teacher in all-Black public schools in Stockton and San Francisco, California, from 1859 through 1874. While studying for the ministry, Sanderson became an outstanding educator and advocate for the schooling of Black children. In 1826, Daniel Payne, an African Methodist Episcopal bishop, started a school in Charleston, South Carolina, for free Black children and adult slaves. The school was closed in 1834 when Whites became fearful that free Blacks might have access to and be influenced by abolitionist literature. The South Carolina legislature passed a law that prohibited free Blacks from having "any school or other place of instruction for teaching any slave or free person of color to read or write" (Franklin, 1990, p. 43). Payne left Charleston and moved north, where he became an influential minister-educator. He later founded Wilberforce College (now Wilberforce University) in Xenia, Ohio, the oldest college affiliated with the African Methodist Episcopal Church.

The agency of African American teachers and principals in Franklin, Tennessee, between 1890 and 1967 was the subject of research conducted by Savage (2001). In this pre- and post-*Brown* account of the education of Blacks, Savage defined *agency* as "self-reliance, proactive actions, and self-determining philosophies that result from a 'centeredness' within one's community" (p. 172). Savage's research documented the work of African American principals at "four continuously operating African American schools located on the same property in Williamson County just 15 miles south of Nashville, Tennessee" (p. 171). Findings indicated that African American principals "did more with less" (p. 171) in regard to providing an education for Black students. That is, even without money or resources, Black principals operated and maintained schools for Black children. Savage noted that Black principals operationalized agency in three ways: (a) developing resources (acquiring money, materials, and other resources to ensure the success of the school), (b) performing extraordinary services (maneuvering district policies, introducing new curricula and activities, and instilling in Black children resiliency, self-reliance, self-respect, and racial pride), and (c) focusing on the school as the center of the community (transforming schools into the cultural symbol of the Black community). Thus, the concept of agency comprised a range of purposeful strategies designed to foster Black self-reliance and empowerment and to resist opposition to the education of Black children.

The eight African American principals included in Savage's study were agents of change who served collectively for more than 80 years. While the leadership styles of the principals were somewhat different, Savage found a common theme in their stories: They worked to provide schooling to African American children in the face of hostile conditions. Their passive and direct resistance to overt hostility included working around discriminatory policies (such as lack of resources and efforts to stop the spread of Black schools) and leading significant curricular change (such as adding academic courses to existing manual labor programs). In addition, they had worked to improve the quality of teachers in all-Black schools by recruiting qualified teachers trained in prestigious Black institutions such as Fisk and Tennessee State universities located in nearby Nashville. Educating Black children was the impetus for their actions, and the notion of "doing more with less" was the core of their agency in preparing students for immediate and future success.

African American women also played exemplary roles in the education of Blacks in the pre-*Brown* era (Alston & Jones, 2002; Franklin, 1990; Hine & Thompson, 1998; S. N. Jones, 2003; Perkins, 1987). Educated African American women opened schools in the North and the South and served dual roles as teachers and principals. Jeanes Supervisors were female principals who served as teachers and principals from 1907 through 1967. They were both teachers and principals, and their duties included introducing new teaching methods and curricula, organizing in-service teacher training workshops, and serving as assistants to county superintendents of schools. Among the most famous African American female principals who worked in the late 19th and early 20th centuries were Sarah Smith, Fannie Jackson Coppin, Anna Julia Cooper, Nannie Helen Burroughs, and Mary MacLeod Bethune. Sarah Smith was named principal of the African School in Brooklyn, New York, in 1863 and was the first African American female principal in the New York public school system. Mary Shadd Cary became a principal in the Washington, D.C., school system in 1869. Fannie Jackson Coppin was principal of Philadelphia's Institute for Colored Youth from 1869 through 1904 and was one of the most influential Black educators of the late 19th century. Under Coppin's leadership, the institute served as the premier example of African American intellectual achievement (Perkins, 1987). The institute was considered one of the best secondary schools in the country, and students were exposed to a curriculum that included the classics. It was also considered a training ground for teachers who would teach in the segregated schools of the South. Coppin's vision for excellence in Black education was evidenced in the educational and professional achievements of the more than 5,000 students with whom she worked during her long tenure at the institute. Her efforts represent one of the earliest examples of the link between African American school leadership and African American student achievement.

Anna Julia Cooper, one of the few Blacks to earn a graduate degree in the 19th century, was recruited to teach at the M Street School in Washington, D.C., the city's only Black high school, and became the principal in 1902 (Cooper, 1892/1988). Cooper's tenure at the M Street School was marked by many accomplishments. When she became principal the school, she was faced with promoting an agenda for Black education that was counter to Booker T. Washington's vocational and industrial program. As noted earlier, Washington's program was viewed by many Whites as the model for educating Blacks, and his philosophy had won the approval of influential Whites who believed in the intellectual inferiority of Blacks. But Cooper fought to build and maintain a curriculum and school culture that prepared students for college and beyond. She defied her White supervisor and prepared M Street students to attend prestigious universities such as Harvard, Brown, Oberlin, and Dartmouth, and under her leadership the school became accredited by Harvard. Her commitment to preparing Black children to attend postsecondary institutions and her refusal to yield to the White power structure and sexist atmosphere in the school and larger community were factors that led to her dismissal as principal. A former student at M Street School noted that Cooper should have expected hostility from males:

You must also remember that as far as the Negro population of Washington was concerned, we were still a small southern community where a woman's place was in the home. The idea of a woman principal of a high school must account in some part for any reaction Dr. Cooper felt against her. (M. H. Washington, 1988, p. xxiii)

According to Franklin (1990), African American female educators participated in similar types of professional and social activities as African American men in the 19th century. However, Cooper's tenure as principal at the M Street School suggests that African American female educators were subjected to various forms of gender discrimination with respect to their supervisory roles. While Cooper was well trained for the principalship, exhibited strong leadership skills, and shared the philosophies of many of her African American male counterparts, the opposition she faced was similar to that experienced by other African American women (e.g., female minister-educators) in the pre-*Brown* era.

The historical literature reveals that African American principals were central figures in segregated schooling and the African American community (Anderson, 1988; Franklin, 1990; Pollard, 1997; Savage, 2001; Siddle Walker, 2000, 2001). They served as connections to and liaisons between the school and the community. As principals, they encouraged parents to donate resources to schools, helped to raise funds for schools, and served as professional role models for teachers and other staff members. For example, Black principals in the pre-*Brown* era modeled professionalism by attending professional conferences and meetings and earning graduate degrees. They also served as instructional leaders and not only provided a vision and direction for the school staff, but also transmitted the goals and ideals of the school to a philanthropic White power structure.

As liaisons to the White community, African American principals often requested funding, resources, and other forms of support for all-Black schools. Black principals enjoyed a significant degree of authority and autonomy that was largely the result of the indifference and neglect of all-White school boards and White superintendents. Whites' lack of interest in the education of Black children (as opposed to training them for manual labor) usually led to the Black principal becoming the ultimate decision maker at the school site. Because segregated schools were primarily closed systems that were important only to Blacks, Black principals could hire and fire teachers, implement programs, and raise money for needed resources. However, these principals had no real power outside the Black community. According to Siddle Walker (2000), they "could consult with the White community, but [they] held little power to make policy decisions" (p. 275). Black principals understood and worked within the existing power dynamics and acted as "middle men."

Understanding the importance of developing an educated Black community, these individuals held themselves accountable for the academic achievement of Black children and adults who attended all-Black public and private schools. Principals in segregated schools "provided counter education to Whites' expectations" (Siddle Walker & Archung, 2003, p. 22) and understood that their own progress was directly linked to the academic, social, economic, and political progress of African Americans as a race.

THE *BROWN* DECISION AND DISPLACEMENT OF BLACK PRINCIPALS

Was the loss of employment for Black principals one of the (un)intended and (un)anticipated consequences (Tillman, 2004a) of desegregation after *Brown*? The *Brown* decision was intended to remedy the inequities of segregated schooling, and, ideally, the decision would provide a more equitable context for Black principals to continue the important work of educating Black children. But the tradition of excellence in African American school leadership was dramatically changed by desegregation, particularly in the South. While some Black principals retained their positions after the historic *Brown v. Board of Education* decision, desegregation had a devastating impact on the closed structure of Black education and thus the professional lives of thousands of Black principals (Ethridge, 1979; Pollard, 1997; Tillman, 2004a, 2004b; Valverde & Brown, 1988; Yeakey, Johnston, & Adkison, 1986).

In his essay "Another Vanishing American: The Black Principal," James (1970) observed that Black principals were "prime victims" of the move from a dual to a unitary system of schooling. Black principals were often the only formally educated Blacks in the community. More important, Black principals had a direct impact on the lives of the students they served; as role models, they provided images that would inspire and motivate Black students. In the post-*Brown* era, displacement of Black principals meant that they were demoted or fired. James noted that, in many instances, Black principals were transferred to central office positions such as coordinators of federal programs or were "given some other title completely foreign to all known educational terminology, a desk, a secretary, no specified responsibilities or authority, and all this with a quiet prayer that [they would] somehow just go away" (p. 20). Because one of the roles of Black principals was to provide a training ground for Black leaders, James lamented that their threatened extinction had dramatic implications for Black leadership in the future. According to James, the loss of Black principals was "catastrophic."

The system of separate, segregated schooling usually favored Black principals (Yeakey et al., 1986). That is, because professional employment opportunities outside of this system were almost nonexistent, the maintenance of a segregated system of schooling ensured Black principals a professional role in the lives of Black children and in the Black community. The dismantling of this system interrupted their favored status. According to Yeakey et al.:

Since racial patterns in most communities, especially those in the South[,] did not countenance blacks supervising whites in any capacity, much less teaching, principals of formerly black schools usually were reassigned as assistants to white principals or as central office supervisors. (1986, p. 122)

The literature on the impact of *Brown* on Black principals is not as prominent as that on Black teachers.[8] Research on the employment status of Black principals is often incorporated into larger studies of Black educators. For example, Ethridge's (1979) study of the employment status of Black educators after the implementation of desegregation focused on teachers, principals, supervisors, and central office personnel. Records on the displacement of Black principals were poorly kept, and Ethridge noted that "the lack of effective data collection throughout the first fourteen years of desegregation will prevent the true impact of the *Brown* decision on Black educators from ever being really known" (p. 222).

Some of the earliest research on the displacement of Black principals was conducted by Hooker (1971), Coffin (1972), Ethridge (1979), Abney (1980), and Valverde and Brown (1988). Hooker's survey of 11 southern states revealed that between 1967 and 1971, the number of Black principals in states such as North Carolina, Virginia, and Arkansas dropped dramatically. For example, the number of Black principals in North Carolina dropped from 620 to 40.

The years 1954 through 1965 were the most devastating for Black principals (Ethridge, 1979). During the period immediately after the *Brown* decision, Whites believed that Black principals had been ineffective in educating Black children. Expert witnesses who testified during a series of postdesegregation legal proceedings called for the dismantling of all-Black schools and replacing Black principals with Whites. For example, Oklahoma, Missouri, Kentucky, West Virginia, Maryland, and Delaware closed the majority of their all-Black schools between 1954 and 1965, and more than 50% of the Black principals in these states were dismissed. More than 6,000 Black principals were needed to reach equity and parity nationally, and Ethridge concluded that "thousands of educational positions which would have gone to Black people in the South under a segregated system have been lost for them since desegregation" (p. 231).

Abney (1980) speculated that the all-White makeup of Florida school boards as well as control by White superintendents in many of the state's districts figured prominently in the demotion and firing of Black principals. He studied the status of Black principals in Florida during the school years 1964–1965 and 1975–1976 and found that, in 1964–1965, Black principals were employed in each of the 67 school districts in Florida. Ten years later, 27 of these districts had no Black principals, even though the Black school-aged population had increased. Florida added 165 public schools in the 1975–1976 school year but fired or demoted 166 Black principals.

School districts in Florida were also grouped according to the percentage of minorities in the state's general population. Thus, in most instances, when the percentage of minorities in the school population was compared with the percentage of Black school principals, the relative number of Black principals was low. This deficiency was "alarming when one considers the fact that 27 of 67 school districts in Florida do not have a single black public school principal, in spite of a significant number of minority group members in the general and pupil populations" (p. 401).[9]

Black principals were being threatened with extinction as a result of desegregation (Fultz, 2004a). Fultz cited a 1971 U.S. Senate Select Committee on Equal Educational Opportunity report revealing that Black principals were being eliminated with "avalanche-like force and tempo" (p. 28). Demotions and firings of Black principals proceeded by four primary means: (a) demoting Black principals to teaching or non-teaching positions, (b) downgrading their schools to lower grade levels, (c) allowing them to retain their title but with no real power, and (d) giving them "paper promotions" to central office positions with no influence. These practices forced Black principals to work almost exclusively in elementary and junior high schools and to work in schools where decision-making authority was allocated to a White assistant. Consequently, Black principals were removed as authority figures at the school-site level. Such practices occurred primarily in southern and rural areas, and Black principals who retained their positions usually worked in urban districts with large populations of Black students.

Patterns of displacement of Black principals also negatively affected the pool of Black teachers who could be mentored for the principalship, effectively eliminating advocates for the recruitment, hiring, and promotion of Black teachers to principal positions (Karpinski, 2004). Demotions and firings of Black principals reflected the deep-seated segregationist ideology of the South, and White southerners with turn-of-the-century attitudes about Black inferiority would not tolerate Black principals supervising students and teachers in integrated schools. In racially charged communities, displacement of Black principals removed them from having any authority over policy-making and instructional leadership and made it difficult for students, parents, and community members to negotiate with the White power structure. The Georgia Teacher and Education Association (1970; cited in Siddle Walker, 2003) referred to the massive displacement of Black principals as "outer-gration." One of the (un)intended consequences of the *Brown* decision was that Black principals were forced out of the profession (Tillman, 2004a), leading to what Cecelski (1994) has called the "decimation" of Black principals. While there have been modest increases in the number of Black principals since the early 1970s, they continue to be underrepresented relative to the number of Black students in the population. In the 1999–2000 school year (the latest year for which data are available), Black principals represented only 9.8% of all principals nationally (National Center for Education Statistics, 2004).

Dempsey and Noblit (1996), in their discussion of school desegregation, noted that "we acted as if we were ignorant of the fact that desegregation was disproportionately burdening . . . African Americans with the bulk of busing, with the closure of African American schools, and with the demotions and firing of African American educators" (p. 115). Yet, history and research illustrate that displacement of Black principals was one of the negative effects of the *Brown* decision. That is, one of the consequences of the desegregation of America's schools was the loss of Black principals, and thus the exclusion of voices and perspectives that were critical to the education of Black children. Not only were positions lost in the numerical sense, but, more important, there was a loss of a tradition of excellence, a loss of Black leadership as a cultural symbol in the Black community, and a loss of the expertise of educators who were committed to the education of Black children.

As the research reviewed in this section indicates, the displacement of Black principals had the immediate effect of disrupting the education of Black children and the stability of the Black community. Desegregation placed Black principals, teachers, students, and parents in an unfamiliar space. The racist context of schooling for Blacks became more obvious and more pronounced. Black principals now had no control over the education of their students and no longer served as the liaison between the Black community and the White power structure. While Black principals typically had had no real voice in policy-making outside of the school itself, the *Brown* decision left them almost completely powerless. Schools were now controlled by Whites, many of whom were resistant to integration. Whites mounted three forms of resistance to integration: (a) States undermined the *Brown* decision by ignoring the mandate and implementing inequitable funding structures; (b) agents of resistance such as White Citizens Councils demonstrated in protest of integration in many southern cities and proposed plans to close all public schools rather than accept integrated schools; and (c) strategies were used to keep Black educators in subordinate positions so that Blacks would have no control or voice in schools (Siddle Walker, 2003).

Several themes are evident in the research on pre-*Brown* principals: the education of Black children as a priority, resistance to ideologies and individuals opposed to the education of Blacks, and the importance of the cultural perspectives of Black principals. Black principals such as Booker T. Washington, Fannie Jackson Coppin, and Daniel Payne were instrumental in establishing schools, garnering resources, and educating Blacks in the period just after slavery. While their individual philosophies may have differed, they shared a collective will to educate Blacks and uplift the race. These Black principals were also agents of change as they fought against theories of inferiority and blatant resistance to the education of Blacks both in their speech and in their actions. In both passive and overt ways, they challenged a White power structure that would deprive Blacks of their right to participate in the free society designed by and for Whites. Racial pride, self-esteem, and self-respect were instilled as a form of passive resistance to theories of inferiority, while the introduction of academic and classical curricula and the recruitment of qualified teachers represented more overt forms of resistance to ideologies and individuals who would keep Blacks in subservient positions.

The cultural perspectives of Black principals were also a consistent theme in the research. Principals were the central figure in the school and the community, and their leadership represented the racial and cultural norms of the Black community and an ethos of service. Their work reflected a cultural heritage of self-determination (Franklin, 1990), a vision for the future of Blacks, and a framework for the work of Black principals who would succeed them. Siddle Walker (2003) emphasized the importance of the cultural perspectives of the Black principal: "The perspective of the Black principal is central to explaining how the segregated Black schools were able to fight the demon of racism by helping Black children believe in what they were capable of achieving" (p. 59).

Tensions exist in the research on pre-*Brown* Black principals. First, while these principals were dedicated to the uplift of the race, they worked in schools that were never adequately funded and lacked essential resources. Consequently, their leadership was, to a great degree, defined by a constant struggle to access buildings, money, and the other resources necessary to produce an educated class of Blacks. Second, pre-*Brown* educators had differing philosophies regarding the most appropriate education, that is, manual training versus an academic education. This was particularly the case in the debates between leaders such as Booker T. Washington and Anna Julia Cooper. In some ways, these ideological struggles resulted in class distinctions among Blacks. Educators such as Fannie Jackson Coppin and Anna Julia Cooper led elite all-Black schools in the North that produced an educated class of Blacks who would go on to become doctors, lawyers, and teachers. Their leadership represents early evidence of the relationship between principal leadership and student achievement. Conversely, Booker T. Washington led schools in the South that largely produced Blacks who were trained in manual labor skills and who would always work in the southern economy. Washington's philosophy that Blacks would receive no training that would place them on equal parity with Whites contributed to tensions among Black educators.

Finally, consistent with the time period, most of the pre-*Brown* principals were men. While the contributions of Black female principals are acknowledged in the research, it was expected that the principal would be male and that he would be accorded recognition and respect based on his gender. These expectations suggest that Black women who aspired to the principalship faced a sexist environment. However, the post-*Brown* period would see a gradual shift in the demographics of the principalship, and more Black women would lead schools (particularly at the elementary level) two decades after the *Brown* decision. Despite these tensions, collectively the research indicates that the leadership of African American principals in the pre-*Brown* period offers a framework for discussing the work of post-*Brown* principals.

BLACK PRINCIPALS IN THE POST-*BROWN* ERA

Black principals in the post-*Brown* era faced different types of challenges than their predecessors. In the desegregated schools of the South and North, the roles of Black principals were more complex. Rodgers (1967), in his study of Black high schools, described African American principals variously as superintendents, supervisors, family counselors, financial advisors, community leaders, employers, and politicians. Scholars conducting research on the education of Blacks in the post-*Brown* era have often focused on the importance of the leadership of Black principals. The research outlined in this section includes ethnographic and case study research on good schools (Lightfoot, 1983; Sowell, 1976), leadership role identity (Lomotey, 1989a, 1993), relationships between segregated schools and the community (Siddle Walker, 1993a, 1996), caring forms of leadership (Lyman, 2000), and African American women in the principalship (Bloom & Erlandson, 2003; Dillard, 1995; Doughty, 1980; Reitzug & Patterson, 1998).[10] As with the themes identified in the literature, these topics overlap. For example, Dillard's research on the leadership of an African American female principal also represents research on a caring leader. The focus of Lightfoot's research is good high schools, but the leadership styles of the principals of these schools are also a consistent theme in her work. Thus, readers will note the overlapping topics in much of the research described in this section.

Sowell (1976) sought to determine the factors that contributed to "black excellence, its sources, and its wider implications for contemporary education and for social policy in general" (p. 7). Sowell studied six all-Black high schools and two all-Black elementary schools. The high schools were selected from Horace Mann's (1970) list of Black high schools with the highest number of alumni with earned doctorates from 1957 through 1962. The two elementary schools in the sample had records of academic achievement.[11] Principals in each of the schools examined were instrumental in students' academic and professional achievement. Two factors were prominent in Sowell's research: a history of educational excellence at each of the schools and strong leaders who were committed to the education of Black children.

Sowell's study is instructive because it offers a historical look at each school: The research not only focused on the prominence of the schools in the pre- and early post-*Brown* periods but also documented their decline after *Brown*. The public schools examined in the study, similar to the cities in which they were located, were victims of the transformation of urban cities. These cities, which once were centers of educational, economic, and social excellence, were now characterized by crime, poverty, and decay. Their public schools, which once boasted high test scores, numerous academic awards, service to the Black community, and the development of Black professionals, were now being defined by low test scores, locations in decaying neighborhoods, lack of parental support, and discipline problems.

One of the schools, Booker T. Washington High School in Atlanta, Georgia, was illustrative of such changes. The principal at the time of the study noted that the neighborhood surrounding the school was no longer a stable middle-class area but was now considered a neighborhood of lower socioeconomic status, and the school was plagued by poor academic performance, with student test scores below the national average and below those of other high schools in Atlanta. The principal believed that the school needed more than money to address these problems. She talked about absence of human resources and, particularly, lack of parental involvement as major problems. Sowell concluded that academic achievement was more than mastery of subject matter; it also included order and respect in the school. More important, the character and ability of the principal were the critical factors in the success of the school and its students.

Sowell's research suggests that the leadership issues facing principals in the pre- and early post-*Brown* periods were similar in some ways and different in others. Leadership in the pre-*Brown* period was defined to a significant degree by de jure segregation, and principals responded primarily to the wishes of the close-knit community of the day. Leadership in the post-*Brown* period evolved amid the changing demographics and dynamics of large urban cities.

Lightfoot (1983) sought to define "good high schools" in case studies of six urban, suburban, and elite schools.[12] Good schools were "described as good by faculty, students, parents, and communities; [they] had distinct reputations as fine institutions with clearly articulated goals and identities" (p. 23). Strong, effective leadership is one of the foundations of the effective schools movement, and the principal, as the instructional leader, sets the tone for the school, decides on instructional strategies, and organizes and distributes school resources (Dantley, 1990; Edmonds, 1979). Lightfoot's view of good high schools included a broader perspective of "effectiveness" than what is described in the effective schools literature. According to Lightfoot, "goodness" (or effectiveness) cannot be measured on the basis of a single indicator of success such as test scores; rather, it includes "people, structures, relationships, ideology, goals, intellectual substance, motivation, and will" (p. 23). A consistent theme in each of the case studies is the significant role of the principal in the culture of a "good" school. Lightfoot argued that the principal holds the ultimate responsibility for creating the vision, mission, goals, and objectives of the good high school. Furthermore, she described the impact of each principal's leadership philosophy and leadership style on the teachers, students, and community.

One of the schools described in Lightfoot's study was George Washington Carver Comprehensive High School in Atlanta. Carver is a public school located in a lower socioeconomic neighborhood, and at the time of Lightfoot's study it had "long been known as a dumping ground for Atlanta schools" (p. 11). However, it had begun to make noticeable progress under the leadership of its new African American principal, Norris Hogans, an energetic, passionate individual who was fighting against the negative history of the school and was determined to build a new image of its students, teachers, parents, and staff. Hogans wanted to "undo old perceptions, reverse entrenched habits, and inculcate new behavioral and attitudinal forms" (p. 15). A former elementary school principal, he was selected to "save Carver from total demise" (p. 31). His passion and commitment were considered catalysts for change in a school where change was badly needed.

Hogan's leadership style was considered to be authoritarian. For example, some teachers and students described Hogans as unwilling to negotiate or share power in decisions that affected the entire school community. Yet, teachers and students agreed that his philosophy and decisions were critical to achieving positive results. Hogans believed that schools were transformational institutions responsible for providing students with discipline and safety—resources that were unavailable to them in their homes and communities—and opportunities for meaningful and productive lives at school and in the larger society. Hogans also believed that schools should demand excellence from students: "I think we don't expect enough from our students. We seem to be content if they score two years below grade level" (p. 35). Hogans's belief that students could be successful both academically and professionally led him to address the issue of student achievement in direct ways. He encouraged teachers to set high standards for student achievement and discipline and preached a philosophy that exposure to professions such as business, industry, medicine, and law could be instrumental in developing the aspirations of African American students. Such purposeful exposure to the world of work would link their aspirations to their achievement in the classroom.

In an effort to achieve these goals, Hogans formed the Explorers Program at Carver High. The program was designed for 10th-grade students and included monthly field trips to major businesses and agencies in the Atlanta area. The purpose of the field trips was to teach students how these businesses operated, orient them to careers offered in such businesses, and provide guidance that would help them make informed career choices. As with the Boy Scout tradition, which served as an example for the program, the Explorers Program stressed honor, honesty, and rigor—characteristics that Hogans promoted as part of the Carver High School image.

Hogans's vision for the school was an ambitious one given the urban school context of his leadership: He wanted students to experience and benefit from a comprehensive education that would provide them with both technical and academic instruction. He believed that students should be exposed to a threefold curriculum (general, vocational, and academic) that would prepare them for positions as laborers as well as positions in professions such as education and medicine. His philosophy was similar to that of Booker T. Washington, one of his heroes. As did Washington, he believed in the value of vocational and technical training for economic stability; however, he did not share Washington's belief that education and employment opportunities for Blacks should be limited to vocational/manual labor fields.

Teachers, students, and parents at Carver were hopeful that Hogans's leadership would be a significant factor in helping students become "industrious, hard-working citizens" (p. 312). Good attendance, a relative lack of discipline problems, a safe and orderly environment, and high employment rates after graduation were viewed as indicators of school success. Under Hogans's leadership, the school had made great strides in each of these areas, and he had led the school through "impressive changes, the progress from terrible to much better" (p. 313). According to Lightfoot, the standards of goodness were being met as a result of Hogans's leadership. While indicators of goodness were evident, Lightfoot also found that there was much more work to be done to achieve other, less measurable standards of goodness such as civility, poise, and ambition, characteristics that students would need in the world outside of school.

Lightfoot noted that "an essential ingredient of good schools is strong, consistent and inspired leadership" (p. 323) and a school culture defined by the vision and purposeful actions of the principal. Hogans was described as a strict authoritarian leader who was both loved and feared by students, teachers, and staff. This description might lead one to assume that Hogans was uncaring and insensitive toward students and the community. However, according to Lightfoot, Hogans was an example of an authoritarian, father figure who, above all, had a strong commitment to the social and academic success of Black children. She noted that he embodied three dominant images associated with the literature on school leadership: Principals are disproportionately male, they are usually former coaches or jocks, and they are father figures. Hogans, a former athlete, was illustrative of the coach and father figure.

The post-*Brown* era brought about an emphasis on effective principal leadership as a catalyst for student achievement (see, for example, Hallinger & Heck, 1996; Murphy, 1988; Witziers, Boskier, & Krüger, 2003). Researchers attempted to define the specific kinds of direct and indirect leadership (Hallinger & Heck, 1996) that established a school culture of success and enhanced student achievement. Some of this research particularly focused on African American students who had lagged behind their White peers since the advent of school reform efforts, including the standardized testing movement (Anderson, 2003).

Lomotey (1989a) conducted research focusing on the significance of African American principals in the educational success of African American students. Lomotey sought to determine the ways in which the leadership styles of African American principals directly influenced the academic achievement of African American students. The study was conducted in "more successful African-American schools": those that "possess the qualities suggested by the research on principal leadership and academic achievement" (p. 6). Three African American elementary school principals who worked in predominantly African American schools were the subjects of the study. The schools were deemed "more successful" than other African American schools because third and sixth graders scored higher in math and reading on the California Assessment Program over a 2-year period. A central question guided the research: "What kind of leadership do African-American principals exhibit in more successful African American elementary schools?" (p. 6). Data were derived from interviews with teachers and principals and from observations of principals in their daily work. In addition, questionnaires were used to investigate teachers' perceptions of how principals implemented four components of principal leadership that were consistent with the school administration literature: (a) developing goals, (b) harnessing the energy of the staff, (c) facilitating communication, and (d) being involved in instructional management.

Principals in Lomotey's study exhibited more than one leadership style. For example, all of the principals placed the education of children as their first priority. However, only two engaged in assertive forms of leadership while establishing a school climate and culture that motivated teachers to focus on the academic achievement of all students. Their leadership styles were consistent with descriptions offered in the educational administration literature. The third principal practiced a more indirect form of leadership and delegated much of the responsibility in each leadership component to support staff. The two principals who engaged in all four components of principal leadership were central figures in the school who performed traditional leadership functions leading to the maintenance of organizational goals. These principals accepted the goals of the organization, facilitated cooperation among staff members, developed and implemented effective communication with their staffs, and actively engaged in curriculum planning, teacher supervision, and student assessment. Lomotey argued that principals who adopt and use all four components of principal leadership help promote the goals of schools: determining how information is disseminated, deciding whose ideas and values are privileged, and controlling the behaviors of others.

The most prominent finding in Lomotey's (1989a) study was that each principal demonstrated a "commitment to the education of African-American children, a compassion for, and understanding of, their students and the communities in which they work, and a confidence in the ability of all African-American children to learn" (p. 131). These principals were committed to the education of African American students and were concerned not only with helping students move successfully from grade to grade but also with enhancing their life chances. They understood that being African American was not enough; they had to exhibit compassion for African American children and their communities. Lomotey posited that because these qualities were shared by each of the principals, this finding

> raises the question of the significance, for African-American principals, of these three characteristics in relation to the four qualities that I sought to explore. It is possible that, given the unique characteristics of these African-American schools (e.g., economic, academic, cultural, and social), these three qualities supersede all others in importance in bringing about success. (p. 131)

Lomotey concluded that principal leadership is critical to the successful schooling of African American students.

In a later study, Lomotey (1993) applied the frameworks from his 1989 study of principals in successful schools to case studies of two African American female elementary principals.[13] Both principals worked in schools that were pilot sites for an African and African American curriculum infusion project. The study focused on the principals' role in facilitating the implementation of the infusion project. In this study, Lomotey referred to the four components of principal leadership as the *bureaucrat/administrator* role identity and the qualities of commitment, confidence, and compassion as the *ethno-humanist* role identity. Specifically, the primary goal of a principal who assumes a bureaucrat/administrator role identity is "schooling": facilitating the movement of students from grade to grade. The primary goal of a principal who assumes an ethno-humanist role identity is "education": meeting a set of cultural goals.

Findings revealed that both principals exhibited the qualities of commitment, compassion, and confidence and were concerned about education issues related to the development of the whole child. As members of the same cultural group, the principals were committed to providing an equitable education to African American children, were confident that these children would excel academically, and showed compassion and understanding for the children and their families. Their goals and actions were purposeful: As leaders, they were committed to ensuring the "perpetuation of African-American culture" (p. 410). For example, both principals were committed to providing African American students with opportunities to learn about African and African American history and culture. More important, the principals were committed to helping students "develop positive self-concepts and generally to feel good about themselves and their people" (p. 410).

Lomotey pointed out that while principals are administrators (i.e., they perform various administrative functions), they are also members of distinctive cultural groups, and principals who believe their cultural affiliation is important to their work will make a distinction between their bureaucrat/administrator and ethno-humanist role identities. Lomotey acknowledged that such a distinction could be viewed as conflicting but noted: "Consequently, but not at all unexpectedly, the personal (ethno-humanist) and professional (bureaucrat/administrator) role identities were often intertwined" (p. 410). The principals in this study merged the two identities in their work and balanced "schooling" and "education" to help African American children achieve academic excellence.

Siddle Walker (1993a, 1993b, 1996, 2003) investigated the relationships between segregated African American schools and their communities in the South. Her ethnographic and case study research examined how communities supported schools, how schools supported their communities, and the implications such relationships might have for contemporary school reform efforts. In her award-winning book, *Their Highest Potential: An African American School Community in the Segregated South* (1996), she documented the pre- and post-*Brown* periods of segregated schooling at Caswell County Training School (CCTS) in rural North Carolina. The school educated children from 1934 to 1969, and a central focus of Siddle Walker's investigation was the work of dedicated educators who believed that their jobs extended from the classrooms into the community. A mutually dependent relationship existed between CCTS and the community. The school held itself accountable to the wishes of the Black community, and community members provided financial and other forms of support for the school. Siddle Walker's work represents a counternarrative to earlier work depicting all-Black schools as deficient (see, for example, H. V. Brown, 1960; Clark, 1963; Kluger, 1977). She noted that while such depictions were not completely inaccurate, they often excluded the perspectives of Black principals and in-depth and thoughtful analyses of how they established and maintained schools for Black children. Furthermore, these depictions overlooked "any suggestion that not all education for African-American children during segregation was inferior" (p. 162).[14]

Similar to the terminology used by Lightfoot (1983), Siddle Walker (1993a) described CCTS as a "good school" on the basis of the school's and the community's belief that it provided a positive social and cultural environment for learning. Siddle Walker acknowledged the inequities as well as the "goodness" of CCTS:

My description of why CCTS was perceived as a good school is not meant to validate the inequities or minimize the discrimination that existed in this and other segregated schools, where parents were overly burdened to create for themselves the educational facilities and opportunities schools boards often denied them (Anderson, 1988; Bullock, 1967). Rather, I offer this case as representative of the many other southern African-American schools whose communities were also pleased with their schools, but whose histories have been lost and whose value is understood now only by former teachers, principals, parents, and students. (p. 162)

Open-ended interviews were conducted with former teachers, students, parents, and administrators, and themes of goodness in the school-community relationship were explored. In the segregated South, the Black school principal was a key figure in establishing and maintaining standards of goodness. Black principals were committed to the social and academic achievement of students and developed relationships with parents, the broader Black community, and the White establishment to achieve their goals. The segregated school environment often served as a second home for Black students; it was an environment where they were taught, nurtured, supported, and corrected. As the central figure in the school, the African American principal provided vision, leadership, and guidance to students, teachers, and other staff members.

The principal of CCTS was Nicholas Longworth Dillard, highly regarded by the community as well as Black and White educational leaders. As an African American principal in a segregated school environment, Dillard worked to ensure that the school kept its commitment to educating African American children by providing support and encouragement and insisting on high academic standards. Dillard prided himself on being very knowledgeable about educational issues and sought to expose students to a well-educated teaching staff. By 1954, the majority of the teachers at CCTS had earned postgraduate certification. Dillard served as principal of CCTS from 1933 to 1969, and during his tenure he instituted more than 53 "extracurricular clubs and activities to enhance student leadership and development" (p. 162).

As the principal, Dillard played a critical role in developing the instructional and physical aspects of the school. By 1938, the student population of CCTS had grown to more than 600, and the school was moved to a 10-room building. Later, Dillard would be instrumental in planning, designing, and supervising the construction of a modern 27-room school that opened in 1951. Parents and the community supported the construction of the school by donating almost $8,000 in equipment. This monetary support was evidence of Dillard's positive relationships with parents and the community.

Dillard promoted student achievement primarily in indirect ways. For example, he established an environment that was conducive to student achievement. One strategy for promoting student achievement was to promote parental involvement. Dillard regularly communicated with parents and used activities such as Parent-Teacher Association (PTA) meetings to report to them about the education their children were receiving at CCTS and ways they could help their children. He reinforced the school's expectations for the students and encouraged parents to attend school-related events. In interviews, parents recalled that the success of every student was Dillard's first priority. He conveyed this message to teachers and required them to attend professional development meetings and conferences. Teachers were also required to attend PTA meetings, which provided parents with the opportunity to establish positive relationships with teachers. Similar to other accounts of Black principals in segregated schools, Dillard rarely appeared before the White board of education. He was aware that, as an employee, his sphere of authority was primarily confined to the school site. Thus, he prepared parents to make requests for the school before the school board, supporting them in their roles as advocates for Black children. Such actions, while illustrative of indirect forms of principal leadership, were consistent with a time period not yet dominated by an emphasis on school reform.

As the "principal leader of a Black high school" (Siddle Walker, 2003, p. 62), Dillard helped to develop a positive relationship with the Black community, and his leadership style is illustrative of the ethic of care in educational leadership (Starratt, 1991), where his goals and actions showed in concrete ways that he cared for every student and was committed to their success. Dillard's goals and actions were also consistent with "interpersonal caring" in regard to the successful schooling of African American students (Siddle Walker, 1993b). This interpersonal caring included providing students with psychological, sociological, and academic support.

Students were transferred to integrated schools when court-ordered desegregation closed CCTS in 1969. A parent who attended PTA meetings after desegregation lamented that, in the new school, teachers rarely were present at these meetings, and the meetings were more focused on problems in the school than on the needs of students and what could be done to address them. She noted:

> You just didn't see any teachers hardly. What few teachers came said, "you don't just walk up to teachers and ask how your child is doing; you have a conference." They said we were not supposed to ask about any [concerns] about our children [in the presence of] of anyone else. We were used to when we were there at the PTA meeting, we could just talk. (p. 178)

The racial and cultural mismatch between the Black parents and students and the White principal and majority White teaching staff led to barriers between the school and the community. As noted by Lomotey (1987, 1989a, 1993), same-race affiliation and membership in a distinct cultural group (e.g., African American) are significant factors affecting how principals interact with parents and students. In addition, Lomotey concluded that it is often the case that individuals with similar values, beliefs, and cultural norms (such as teachers, principals, parents, and students) communicate more effectively.

In *How Do They Know You Care? The Principal's Challenge,* Lyman (2000) presented a case study of Kenneth Hinton, the principal of an early childhood education center located in a low-income, racially and ethnically diverse city in the

Midwest. Lyman conducted an in-depth qualitative investigation of this caring leader and analyzed his contributions to the school environment. Hinton was chosen for the study because he was well respected and epitomized a caring attitude toward students, teachers, parents, and the community. The study framework was based on four perspectives of caring: (a) Caring both gives purpose and is purpose (Mayeroff, 1971); (b) caring is an ethical orientation (Gilligan, 1982); (c) caring is a relational process involving engrossment, action, and reciprocity (Noddings, 1984); and (d) caring leaders make a difference (p. 11). The fourth perspective is informed by *how* leaders make a difference in the lives of students and their families. Thus, it is multifaceted, including the following elements: Caring leaders who protect and nurture are critical to maintaining schools that are good (Lightfoot, 1983); leaders grounded in an ethic of caring transform schools by embracing complexity and making an emotional investment (Beck, 1994a, 1994b); and caring leaders who advocate for the needs of individual students are critical to students' success, particularly in culturally diverse schools (Dillard, 1995; Lyman, 2000, p. 11).

As the new principal and director of the recently built early childhood education center, Hinton had supervised much of the construction of the new building, developed the instructional program, hired a new staff, established rapport in the community, and welcomed new students and their families. The school had a racially diverse student population; the majority of the students were African American and White, and a small percentage were Hispanic and Asian. Lyman characterized Hinton as a nonconformist. At times, he challenged the bureaucracy of his school district regarding the most appropriate methods for educating children. He developed his own methods for working with challenging students in his school and worked with his staff to develop innovative programs that would respond to the various social, emotional, and economic needs of students and their families.

Hinton was also compassionate. As a male African American, he had experienced various forms of discrimination in school and in the community. But he was also influenced by an upbringing that stressed a supportive family structure and strong spiritual values, and his experiences led him to engage in acts of compassion that emphasized caring and developing children to their fullest potential. For example, in interviews, school staff and parents used terms such as *caring, warm, nurturing,* and *loving* to describe Hinton's style of leadership as well as the school environment. As a builder, Hinton was able to build not only physical structures but relationships among key stakeholders: staff, students, parents, and the community. Staff members and members of the community praised Hinton for his ability to build bridges between the races and noted that "his caring for children is clearly not limited to children of color" (p. 31). He served as a role model for students, and his leadership and service extended beyond the walls of the school. Hinton expressed his beliefs about caring as follows:

Caring carries with it a loss of class, ethnicity, gender, and religion. If a teacher cares, then these things that separate us through ignorance and fear become unimportant. Status ceases to matter, and children are simply children. (Lyman, 2000, pp. 116–117)

Hinton's beliefs about caring were an extension of his experiences as a teacher and a learner. His caring leadership style was critical in enhancing student learning and was consistent with Hart and Bredeson's (1996, as cited in Lyman, 2000) assumption that "principals influence student learning outcomes directly and indirectly by what they do, what they believe, and how they use symbols" (p. 219). Hinton was motivated by his desire to "enhance the growth of others and give back to those who helped me" (p. 120). Hinton's decision to "give back" was similar to what Lightfoot (1994) referred to as "giving forward"—the concept that one cannot repay acts of caring but can engage in such acts in the future. Hinton's leadership style was also similar to aspects of Lomotey's (1993) ethno-humanist role identity; that is, he displayed commitment, compassion, and confidence in his interactions with students and their communities. However, unlike the principals in Lomotey's study, Hinton's ethno-humanist role identity was not solely based on same-race/cultural affiliation. Hinton focused his caring leadership on all students. Thus, while same-group racial and cultural membership has been shown to enhance principal-student relationships, Lyman's research suggests that other factors may influence these relationships. Lyman's findings also suggest that, because African Americans also lead mixed-race schools, there is an imperative to practice leadership that will meet the needs of students, teachers, and parents from all racial and ethnic groups represented.

Education of Black students as a priority, interpersonal caring, and resistance were dominant themes in the research on post-*Brown* principals. In some cases, principals were faced with making decisions about how they would continue to educate Black children after desegregation. Dillard had hoped that desegregation would dismantle the inequitable educational structures that had, in many ways, defined his leadership. Yet, many of the inequities remained until the school was closed and desegregation was officially implemented. Principals such as Hogans also placed the education of Black students as a priority but had a different vision for educating them. Drawing on the work of his predecessors, Hogans merged historical philosophies with his own vision and implemented a general, vocational, and academic curriculum that would prepare students for the world of work. Collectively, these post-*Brown* principals continued to make the education of Black students a priority and resisted Whites who attempted to undermine the *Brown* decision, teachers who held low expectations for students and who were resistant to change, and in some cases Black parents who, feeling disconnected from the newly integrated school, became less involved in their children's education.

The theme of interpersonal caring was also evident in the research. Several principals adopted Lomotey's ethno-humanist role identity and based their leadership on commitment, confidence, and compassion. Such principals were caring and loving and provided academic, social, and psychological support. In research on highly successful and loving elementary schools serving minority and low-income students, Scheurich (1998) found that while principals used the term *caring,* the term *loving* best described environments where principals exhibited extremely supportive attitudes toward students and adults. Scheurich's analysis was consistent with the types of interpersonal caring exhibited by Black principals in the research reviewed here. A tension exists in the research with respect to definitions of goodness in the education of Black students. While researchers sought to describe "good" schools, they also acknowledged that "good" did not necessarily represent a search for perfection. Both Sowell and Siddle Walker found imperfections in good schools. Schools that were once sites of educational excellence now struggled against being defined by external factors such as housing projects, crime, and poor student achievement. Fifty years after the *Brown* decision, schools face these as well as other challenges that affect the quality of schooling for Blacks and thus the leadership capacity of Black principals.

RESEARCH ON AFRICAN AMERICAN FEMALE PRINCIPALS

The research reviewed in this section focuses on African American female principals in the post-*Brown* period of schooling. There is limited evidence in the post-*Brown* educational leadership literature pointing to the leadership styles, accomplishments, and lives of Black female principals (Allen, Jacobson, & Lomotey, 1995; Benham, 1997; Bloom & Erlandson, 2003; Coursen et al., 1989; Pollard, 1997).[15] Benham (1997) identified several factors that have contributed to the paucity of research on Black women in school leadership. First, the number of Black women in pre-K–12 educational leadership positions, while increasing gradually, is still small relative to the numbers of White men and women and Black men. Thus, it is difficult to identify samples for large-scale studies. Second, a limited number of Black female and male researchers are investigating issues affecting Black school leaders. Furthermore, the absence of a body of research on Black female principals is exacerbated by the fact that theories about women in leadership often refer to women as teacher leaders. Finally, Benham noted that the absence of studies of Black women represents, to a great degree, "an educational leadership discourse and practice that has been structured to impede such treatment" (p. 282). Bloom and Erlandson (2003) concurred with Benham's argument and elaborated on this point in the following statement: "Findings from a minority insider's perspective are regarded as dubious and unlikely to be published in professional journals. Suspect conclusions are summarily ignored or dismissed, seldom becoming a part of administrative leadership theory" (p. 344).

Inclusion of the contributions of African American female principals within predominantly White feminist literature is also problematic. According to Bloom and Erlandson (2003), asking questions about the experiences of African American women from the perspective of a White woman results in two negative outcomes: (a) perpetuating the practice of intellectual and cultural exclusion by creating the appearance of acceptance in women's studies using an ethnic additive model and (b) failing to acknowledge that White women retain White privilege and that women of color do not hold a color of privilege, thereby making African American women's experiences similar in some ways to those of women in general but deviant from the White female norm (p. 344). The result is a privileging of knowledge that often devalues the leadership theory and practice of African American female principals in the educational leadership discourse.

A search of the educational leadership literature reveals an additional challenge in identifying research on Black female principals: Work on these women is often grouped under the topic "women and minorities." Researchers have used this categorization in conducting studies that have included Black female principals (see, for example, Adkison, 1981; Banks, 1995; Biklen & Brannigan, 1980; Crow & Glascock, 1995; Edson, 1987; Enomoto, Gardiner, & Grogan, 2000; Gardiner, Enomoto, & Grogan, 2000; E. Jones & Montenegro, 1985; Mertz & McNeely, 1998; Ortiz, 1982; Shakeshaft, 1999; Tonnsen & Truesdale, 1993; Young & McLeod, 2001). However, this research rarely presents detailed portraits of the lives, work, vision, and impact of these principals on the school community and student achievement or discriminatory practices that affect their work. As pointed out by Coursen et al. (1989), "what is true for blacks is not necessarily true for members of other racial minorities and may have nothing to do with women" (p. 87).

In a national survey of Black school administrators, Doughty (1980) found that Black women were most likely to be employed as consultants, supervisors, elementary school principals, and administrative assistants. Black women in the elementary principalship were more likely to lead in challenging urban districts with predominantly Black student populations. Black women in Doughty's study typically assumed their first leadership position in their middle 40s to early 50s, and they were older than Black or White men in such positions. In addition, Doughty's results showed that, after 1966, the percentage of Black women in the principalship decreased relative to the percentage of Black men. Black women were not the specific focus of Doughty's study. However, the findings on these women identified specific challenges and barriers faced by Black female principals and how they adapted to their roles—roles prescribed by their race *and* their gender. Doughty argued that roles associated with race and gender had negative consequences for Black women who aspired to principalship positions and also contributed to the myth of Black women as superhuman, capable of solving every problem and dealing with every crisis:

The black female school administrator is in a double bind, perhaps even a triple bind. She embodies two negative statuses simultaneously. One is her color, black, and the other is her sex, female, neither of which society values very highly. (p. 165)

These findings are significant because they focus on the ways in which both race and gender, rather than gender as a single factor, affect the leadership of Black female administrators. For example, at the time of Doughty's study (1972–1973), Black women were usually in supervisory or consultant roles. As principals, they were primarily found in elementary ranks in challenging, predominantly Black schools; they were rarely in the high school principalship, a position reserved for men. Thus, almost two decades after the *Brown* decision, Black women continued to be selected for positions on the basis of their gender. As pointed out by Shakeshaft (1989), women were well suited for teaching, but it was usually the case that men were more qualified to be administrators.

Dillard (1995) conducted a case study of an African American female principal and sought to explore and reinterpret traditional definitions of effective school leadership, particularly in the context of the increasing diversity of schools. A central question guided the research: How do African American women interpret their acts of leadership? As an African American woman, Dillard noted that she approached the research from a critical feminist perspective and was "particularly interested in the inclusion of African American women's realities in the shaping of policy and literature surrounding effective schools and schooling" (p. 543).

Gloria Natham, a caring African American secondary school principal, was the subject of the research. Natham's school was situated in a metropolitan city that had undergone mandatory district-wide desegregation, and Natham noted that, like many other Black principals, she had been "brought here to clean up this mess and relate to these kids" (p. 545). Natham modeled caring leadership in culturally meaningful ways. Her (re)interpretation of school leadership was a form of "talking back": practicing a style of educational leadership counter to traditional norms. Natham talked back by setting high expectations for students and by holding teachers accountable for helping students reach those expectations. She also talked back by "standing right in their faces" (p. 557), referring to White teachers who held low expectations in regard to the behavior and academic achievement of Black students. She maintained her role as teacher and taught one class each semester. While her decision to teach initially stemmed from her dissatisfaction with the teachers that were being sent to her school, she also taught as a way to reinterpret her role as principal and to be "part of the lives of our kids" (p. 550).

Natham practiced "othermothering" (Case, 1997; Irvine, 1999; Loder, 2005)[16]— consistently nurturing, protecting, and encouraging students and holding herself responsible for their success. Dillard labeled Natham's personal commitment to students as "authentic leadership": leadership grounded in nurturing and protecting children who were not her own. Her authentic leadership also involved establishing credibility with parents and gaining their support in efforts to enhance student achievement. Natham encountered several challenges to her caring style of leadership: racism, uncommitted faculty, lack of support for integration, resistance from veteran teachers, and lack of commitment to the academic success of all children. Despite these challenges, Natham remained committed to educating and caring for her students.

Natham was described as a role model for African American students: "She nurtures . . . and leads by her presence, by her example, by the way she conducts her life and work in putting herself on the line for them" (p. 557). In contrast to Hinton (Lyman, 2000), who did not interpret his caring leadership style as being connected to race, Natham's caring leadership was directly tied to her same-race affiliation with her students and their families, her cultural heritage, and her status as an African American woman. Natham's caring leadership, her talking back, and her commitment to African American students represented overt acts of resistance often viewed as risky, "particularly for African American women working within powerful White male dominated sites such as the high school principalship" (p. 548). Paraphrasing Derrick Bell (1992), Dillard wrote that Natham was an example of a caring African American female principal who served "to constantly remind the powers that be that there are persons like us who are not only on the side of [African Americans and other subjugated people] but are determined [through resistance and reinterpretation] to stand in their way" (p. 550).

Returning to a central question of her research—Are traditional "scientific" conceptualizations of principal leadership relevant in a time of increased diversity in schools?—Dillard concluded that Natham's story suggests "it is impossible to create such conceptualizations of teaching or leading—or their 'effectiveness'—without taking issues of culture and community context into account" (p. 558). Natham's caring leadership established a school culture focused on the needs of students. It also provided African American students with a nurturing and caring environment that was similar to what Blacks experienced in all-Black schools before desegregation but that is often missing in urban schools today. Natham's story is illustrative of the effects of race, gender, and culture on principal leadership. She chose to lead in purposeful ways that reflected her own values as an African American and a woman and in ways that she believed would help African American students. This research also provides evidence of the ethno-humanist role identity assumed by African American principals. Natham took ownership of and held herself accountable for the academic and social achievement of her students. Her decision to teach a class, her direct work with parents, and her ritual of making notes on every report card reflected her personal form of cultural management: interpreting, representing, and authenticating the school culture and her relationships with students.

Debbie Pressley, a Black female middle school principal, was the subject of research conducted by Reitzug and Patterson (1998). These researchers describe the caring and empowering practice of Pressley primarily as she interacted with students. Data were collected through interviews, observations, and "shadowing" Pressley as she went about her daily work. Pressley's school was located in an economically depressed area of a large urban city and had a predominantly African American student population. Pressley was selected for the study because of her reputation as an outstanding leader. Her community nomination (M. Foster, 1997) came from several principals, and her reputation was verified by teachers as well as other educators. Several key themes related to Pressley's leadership practice were identified: her focus on interactions with students, the caring nature of her interactions with students, and the ways in which she empowered students through her interactions with them. Pressley described her role as principal as facilitating learning, empowering others, and developing the healthy child. Using a narrative approach, the researchers told Pressley's story over the course of 2 days, documenting the typical plans, activities, interruptions, and challenges of her workday as well as her interactions with students. Pressley practiced empowerment through caring interactions with students: (a) establishing and developing a personal connection, (b) honoring their voice,

(c) showing concern for the individual well-being of students by setting standards, (d) connecting students to their communities, and (e) helping students consider alternatives to actions and decisions that could jeopardize their social and academic future.

Reitzug and Patterson observed that Pressley's roles and responsibilities did not differ significantly from those described in the principalship literature. However, Pressley's style of leadership was distinctly different with respect to "*how* she chose to engage in this responsibility and the *amount of time* she chose to devote to it" (p. 178). The "how" of Pressley's caring leadership included *receiving* the perspectives of others through an open-door policy, *responding* to students by caring for them and comforting them, and *remaining* by keeping students with the same teacher for 3 years to build positive relationships. Her focus on the healthy child, academic excellence, and merging individual needs of students and community concerns shaped her caring and empowering style of leadership.

Bloom and Erlandson (2003) conducted in-depth interviews with three middle-aged African American female principals working in urban schools. Each principal "recounted the realities (successes, failures, and limitations) of her actual work, the reconstruction of deeply held leadership belief systems, and the personal resolutions evolving from her leadership experiences within schools" (p. 340). Similar to Dillard (1995), the researchers sought to listen to the voices of Black female principals as a way to begin to "change minds and social constructs about the 'Others' in America's public school districts" (p. 352).

Educated in the segregated schooling of the Midwest and deep South, the principals drew on their "cultural consciousness" (p. 359) to guide their leadership decisions. Each woman revealed her experiences with racism, sexism, stereotypes, and assigned identities and her decision to succeed in spite of the barriers she encountered. Each worked in a school where she was challenged with implementing and maintaining policies and programs that were inequitable and impeded student achievement. Despite such challenges, these principals exhibited a personal commitment, based on their cultural affiliation, to educating African American children from low-income backgrounds, many of whom had been subjected to low teacher expectations. Seeking to build schools with a culture of caring, they implemented alternative forms of decision making that not only would benefit students but would also offer alternative definitions of organizational effectiveness in schools.

Claire, one of the principals in the study, was charged with turning around a failing school. In interviews, she discussed the "hopelessness and helplessness" at the school, the poor graduation rates (only 2%–5%), and other internal and external factors that placed the school in the "failing" category. At the end of Claire's second year as principal, student attendance and test scores had improved, and Claire had increased parental involvement by instituting family partnership nights and had improved relationships with teachers by forming teaching teams. The second principal in the study believed in the power of staff development and devoted a considerable amount of time to planning activities that would "raise the level of consciousness about racist teaching practices" (p. 353). The third principal modeled servant leadership as a way to show teachers how to serve every student. Collectively, the stories of these principals speak to a desire to make a difference in the lives of African American children. Bloom and Erlandson noted that the women's stories reject theories of inferior capabilities based on race or gender. They also acknowledged, however, that the stories do not suggest that "only African American principals know how to effectively operate urban schools" (p. 351). Rather, these stories are illustrative of leadership that is counter to what is generally described in the literature.

According to Loder (2005), "Recent work on African American women principals suggests that motherhood and its associated values of nurturing, caretaking, and helping develop children are salient to how they understand and interpret their roles" (p. 304). This was particularly the case with the principals included in the research conducted by Dillard and by Reitzug and Patterson. Gloria Natham and Debbie Pressley purposely included "othermothering" (interpersonal caring) in their leadership. Both wanted to relate to their students and treated students like their own children or members of their family. They viewed "othermothering" as consistent with the leadership roles of Black female principals, and their "othermothering"/interpersonal caring was linked to their identity: Black and female.

The Black female principals in these studies promoted student achievement in both direct and indirect ways. Gloria Natham was the exception among the cases. By choosing to teach a class each semester, she held herself personally accountable for the academic achievement of students in her school. While Dillard did not indicate whether her direct involvement helped to raise test scores, Natham choose to model how principal leadership can lead to improved student achievement. Natham is also an exception because in large urban high schools, principals rarely have time to directly participate in teaching, instructional supervision, or curriculum coordination (Mertz & McNeely, 1998). Rather, they typically fulfill bureaucrat/administrator roles focusing on more indirect goals of schooling. Natham's decisions reflected her conscious effort to merge her ethno-humanist and bureaucratic/administrator roles. The cultural perspectives of Black female principals were also a consistent theme in the studies reviewed here. These principals relied on their cultural heritage and their knowledge of the cultural norms of the Black community to motivate students and parents. In addition, their cultural perspectives also included knowing the most appropriate forms of communication, having the ability to talk to students in ways that drew upon same-race affiliation, and being part of students' lives. These principals also acknowledged that, in the post-*Brown* era, it was their responsibility to address some of the cultural norms that negatively affected students' opportunities for success.

DISCUSSION

The 1954 *Brown v. Board of Education* decision provides a context for the examination of the leadership of Black principals in the periods both before and after the decision. Ideally, the decision would have remedied inequitable educational structures and provided a racially and socially just context for educating Black children. Black principals would have continued to make significant contributions to Black children, their communities, and leadership theory and practice. However, these ideals were not always a reality. The research reviewed here indicates that Black principals often led under extremely adverse circumstances. These Black principal-leaders worked in both segregated and integrated contexts, and in many instances their leadership was defined by oppressed community and educational settings. Yet, they were resilient, resourceful, and dedicated, and they remained diligent in their commitment to the education of Black children. They were more than managers—they were also visionaries who adopted a philosophy of agency and prevailed in spite of strong opposition to their efforts.

Evidence suggests that many of these principals embodied the characteristics of Lomotey's (1993) ethno-humanist role identity: commitment to Black students, compassion for these students and their families, and confidence in the intellectual ability of these students. This was particularly evident in the stories of Black principal-leaders in the post-*Brown* era, who were typically assigned to the worst schools in the worst neighborhoods with the lowest-performing students. For example, principals such as Gloria Natham were hired to clean up messes and relate to Black students. Post-*Brown* African American principals also led in the changed contexts of schooling, particularly in urban areas. Urban schools had more racially, ethnically, and economically diverse student bodies, and they underwent complex changes in technological needs, increases in the number and kinds of social support services needed, and decreases in funding (Loder, 2005). Crosby (1999), an African American male principal at a large urban high school, lamented the decline of the urban school context:

For those of us who work in schools, it is . . . the best of times and the worst of times. Our urban schools, once the pride of our nation, are now a source of controversy and inequity. We have watched with dismay their descent into confusion and failure. (p. 298)

Clearly, 50 years after *Brown*, Black principal-leaders face different challenges in their efforts to educate Black students.

Collectively, the research reviewed here yielded four consistent themes: (a) the academic and social development of Black students as a priority, (b) resistance to ideologies and individuals opposed to the education of Black students, (c) the importance of the cultural perspectives of Black principals, and (d) leadership based on interpersonal caring. The academic and social development of Black students was a priority for the Black principal-leaders described in this review. They were committed to the academic achievement of Black students, and they fought vigorously for chairs, desks, books, money, well-equipped buildings, and qualified teachers as a way to give Black students every opportunity to experience success. They also believed that schools should be transformational institutions that provide students with various forms of support and that Black students should be given opportunities for their total development. Black students were not "other people's children" (Delpit, 1995); they belonged to their parents and to the school and the community as well. Principals accepted responsibility and held themselves accountable for the well-being of every Black student. Students were nurtured and encouraged in a manner often absent in many urban schools today. Urban schools, which today have primarily Black populations, often do not provide an atmosphere that is conducive to an ethno-humanist role identity.

Black principal-leaders engaged in both passive and overt acts of resistance in their struggles to educate Black children. They fought against theories of inferiority, funding structures that disadvantaged Black students, an emphasis on vocational over academic preparation, and the displacement of massive numbers of Black teachers and principals. They risked their professional careers and their economic livelihood and stood in the way of opposition to equitable systems of education. Lacking any real power to implement policy, they worked with Black parents who went before White school boards to secure needed resources for schools. In the face of these challenges, they continued to educate Black children, doing more with less.

The importance of the cultural perspectives of Black principal leaders is directly related to the absence of *race* in the discourse on school leadership. Mertz and McNeely (1998) argued that "school administration has been male dominated and male defined (largely White male); that is, explained, conceptualized and seen through the eyes of males" (p. 196). These authors' emphasis on the continuing focus on White males indicates that there is a privileging of one voice over another and a single lens and single authority representing the whole of educational leadership (see also Fenwick, 2001). This privileging of voice also suggests that even though Black principals possess an insider's perspective, their voices have not been considered in debates about the most effective ways to educate Black children. Culture was a constant within this theme. The work of Lomotey (1989a, 1993), Siddle Walker (1993), Dillard (1995), and Bloom and Erlandson (2003) strongly suggests the presence of a distinctly Black perspective in school leadership, a perspective based largely on culture. In the segregated schooling of the South and in many single-race urban schools today, Black principals practice leadership based on their insider status and their membership in the distinct Black culture. Same-race/cultural affiliation appears to influence decision making at the school site, as well as selection of teachers and interactions with parents.

Because the achievement gap between Black students and their White peers continues to be an important topic in education,[17] it is also important that the perspectives of Black principal-leaders be recognized and included in efforts to close this gap. Siddle Walker's research highlighting the work of Black principal-leaders provides a critical context for such debates. Her results regarding the work of successful Black principals in segregated schools raise questions about the applicability of many of the findings in the literature to today's Black principal-leaders, particularly in regard to their impact on Black student achievement. Morris (2004) concurred with Siddle Walker, asking "In what ways might the kind of agency that was evident among Black educators and institutions in the segregation era become manifest in predominantly African American schools in the post-Civil Rights era?" (p. 72).

Several of the Black principal-leaders in the studies reviewed incorporated interpersonal caring into their leadership. Leadership based on interpersonal caring includes the principal's direct and purposeful attention to meeting the psychological, sociological, and academic needs of students. Purposeful adoption of a leadership style intended to address the needs of Black students is contrary to myths of Black educators as uncaring and as unable or unwilling to relate to Black students, particularly those from low socioeconomic backgrounds (M. Foster, 1997). Interpersonal caring may be a necessary component of leadership in schools with predominantly Black student populations, given that many of these students have been subjected to external (poverty, racism, violence) and internal (underfunded schools, disproportionate placement in special education, low teacher expectations, below-grade-level achievement) factors that can contribute to low self-esteem and underachievement. As noted by Lomotey, it is important to encourage students not only to excel academically but to take pride in themselves and their culture. Evidence suggests that interpersonal caring in educational leadership is effective in creating school cultures that consider the needs of teachers, students, and parents and are conducive to promoting students' success.

The findings from the studies reviewed suggest that Black principal leaders rewrote history, redefined theory and practice, and rejected deficit theories about school leadership and the education of Black children. In the spirit in which *Brown* was intended, Black principal-leaders were *transformers, translators,* and *cultivators.* These individuals transformed education for Black children from a dream hoped for to a dream realized. They saw the possibilities for enhancing the life chances of Black students and transformed their schools into institutions that promoted Black student achievement, recognized Black culture, and promoted racial pride and self-esteem. They accepted their roles as leaders and held themselves accountable for the uplifting of a race through education, leading schools that were cultural symbols of the development of the whole child. As Black principal-leaders, they transformed the impossible into the possible for many Black children and translated the Black agenda for education to students, parents, teachers, and the White power structure. Through their models of servant leadership, they used the power of education to change lives. Also, they offered teachers and other staff members a vision, provided them with goals and objectives, and showed them the importance of continued professional development. Black principal-leaders cultivated the skills and talents of Black students and teachers. They cultivated the highest ideals of academic achievement and sought to lead "good schools."

The themes articulated in this review are not identified as such in the traditional literature on school leadership, specifically the principalship literature. Contemporary frameworks of school administration/leadership focus on the various administrative/leadership styles (Bolman & Deal, 1997; Leithwood & Duke, 1999), administrative/leadership functions (Farkas, Johnson, & Duffett, 2003; Leithwood

& Riehl, 2003), alternative perspectives on school leadership such as leadership for social justice (Dantley & Tillman, 2005; Marshall, 2004), and diversity in educational administration/leadership (González, 2002; Tillman, 2003).[18] Principals are viewed as instructional leaders who coordinate the curriculum; monitor student progress by assessing and using test data; facilitate teacher competence by providing staff development, resources, and other forms of support; and establish a climate conducive to student success.

Hallinger and Heck (1996), in their review of studies on principals' role in school effectiveness, found that personal characteristics such as gender, previous teaching experience, and values and beliefs, "influence how principals enact their role" (p. 21). There is no evidence to suggest that the race or the cultural perspectives of the principal were factors in these studies. Leithwood and Duke (1999) articulated six models of leadership: instructional, transformational, moral, participative, managerial/strategic, and contingency. Culture as a factor in principal leadership was discussed in only one of the models: transformational leadership. With respect to culture, the authors cited Reitzug and Reeves (1992), who noted that cultural leadership includes "defining, strengthening, and articulating values" but cautioned that "leaders may manipulate culture to further their own ends" (p. 50). Deal and Peterson (2000) discussed culture in educational leadership in the context of the school setting: "Culture arises in response to persisting conditions, novel changes, challenging losses, and enduring ambiguous or paradoxical puzzles" (p. 202). These conceptualizations of culture involve a different emphasis than those articulated by Lomotey (1989a, 1993), Dillard (1995), Siddle Walker (1993a, 1996), and others.

The descriptions in the contemporary literature do not differ significantly from the descriptions of African American principals who assumed both bureaucrat/administrator and ethno-humanist role identities. As Reitzug and Patterson (1998) found in their study of a Black female principal, differences in leadership philosophy, style, and effectiveness were directly related to "how" the principal practiced leadership and the amount of "time" she invested in her work. The research reviewed here also points to the "why" of principal leadership as an important factor. That is, African American principals, to a great degree, led on the basis of their same-race/cultural affiliation and their desire to positively affect the lives of Black students. In most cases, their "why" was closely linked to their identities: Black and male and Black and female.

Witziers et al. (2003) noted that literature on school leadership suggests that principals who are effective instructional leaders positively affect the school climate and student achievement (see, for example, Bredeson, 1996; Brookover, Beady, Flood, Schweitzer, & Wisenbaker, 1979; Leithwood & Montgomery, 1982). However, other scholars have questioned the effects of educational leadership on student achievement (e.g., Hallinger & Heck, 1996; Murphy, 1988). According to Hallinger and Heck, "despite the traditional rhetoric concerning principal effects, the actual results of empirical studies in the U.S. and U.K. are not altogether consistent in size or direction" (p. 1). Among the reasons given for these opposing viewpoints were the absence of an extensive body of research on the relationship between school leadership and student achievement, the difficulty in measuring the direct effects of such relationships, and the varying ways in which educational leadership is conceptualized and operationalized (Bloom & Erlandson, 2003; Pounder, Ogawa, & Adams, 1995; Witziers et al., 2003).

The research reviewed here suggests that there is a strong relationship between African American principal leadership and African American student achievement. In the pre-*Brown* era of segregated schooling, this relationship was often more subtle; that is, because schools were not driven by state testing mandates and because Black principals worked in a closed system, student achievement was promoted through encouraging students to excel, encouraging them to pursue postsecondary education, and motivating them to become productive citizens. In the immediate post-*Brown* era of schooling, Black principal-leaders (even after they had lost their positions) continued to encourage students to excel in the face of resistance to integration. Later, these principal-leaders established environments, policies, and procedures that would lead to academic success. They hired competent teachers, coordinated curricula, instituted innovative support programs, and began to use test data to assess student achievement.

While the literature provides evidence of a positive relationship between Black principal leadership and Black student achievement, the literature is less clear on the relationship between White principals and African American student achievement (as well as the achievement of other minority and low-income students). Because often the race of principals is not revealed in research studies (e.g., Kimball & Sirotnik, 2000; Portin, 2000), there is little conclusive evidence regarding the ways in which this factor affects student achievement. Thus, it may be difficult to determine in what direct and indirect ways cross-race relationships are a factor in improved student achievement. Several studies have examined the role of White principals in the academic achievement of African American students. Tillman (in press-c) found that the White male high school principal in her study attempted to affect student achievement in indirect rather than direct ways. For example, he felt his personal connection to the Black students in his school allowed him to use informal conversations with students and their parents as one way to encourage students to excel. He did not use more direct approaches such as empowering teachers to implement practices that would lead to student achievement, nor did he use standardized test data to make decisions about improving test scores.

Mertz and McNeely (1998) studied a White female principal of a high school with a student population that was mixed along racial, ethnic, and class lines. The principal wanted her school to be "an academic giant" (p. 207) and expressed her commitment to "academic excellence, curriculum improvement, and student learning" (p. 212). However, the researchers found that she spent more of her time on managerial tasks than on instructional tasks. While she visited classrooms to evaluate teachers or to check on students, the majority of her time was spent on discipline matters, patrolling the halls, and responding to requests from parents and the central office. Similar to the principal in Tillman's study, her work was consistent with literature describing the high school principalship; that is, instructional leadership and curriculum are not among the top five tasks that dominate the work of high school principals. Thus, while this principal professed her commitment to academics, she was constrained by the culture of the traditional high school setting.

Riester, Pursch, and Skrla (2002) examined the roles of six principals in highly successful elementary schools that primarily served minority and low-income students. Each of the schools had achieved "recognized" or "exemplary" status in the state accountability system. Three of the principals were White, and one, a White woman, was placed at her school to raise low test scores. Collectively, these principals shared a common belief system that included (a) promoting a democratic culture, (b) adopting a prescriptive approach to literacy and academic success, and (c) demonstrating a stubborn persistence in "getting there" (p. 292). They believed that it was teachers who did the real work in schools and that principals must empower them to "enact specific practices that lead to learning for all" (p. 283). As noted by a White male principal, "If the children can't learn the way we teach, then we need to learn how to teach to how the children learn" (p. 293). White principals believed that students should not be blamed for poor achievement; rather, after assessing student test scores, they used specific prescriptive approaches to developing literacy skills. According to the authors, all of the principals used tools such as benchmarks and assessment of prior performance to guide placement of students. In addition, all held themselves accountable to every student, a characteristic the authors suggested is typically absent in schools. The principals' beliefs that all students could and would be academically successful and a culture of persistence in each school were instrumental in facilitating academic achievement. A key in the students' academic achievement appeared to be the principal's willingness to allow teachers to make decisions about the most effective curriculum and instructional techniques that would lead to student success. Riester et al.'s findings suggest that White, African American, and Hispanic principals shared similar leadership philosophies and practices with respect to enhancing the academic achievement of minority and low-income students.

RECOMMENDATIONS FOR FUTURE RESEARCH

The majority of the research reviewed here involved the use of qualitative methods. This suggests that qualitative methods represent an effective approach to conducting research with Black principals. These methods allowed researchers to conduct in-depth interviews, observations, and document analyses that yielded thick, rich descriptions of Black principal-leaders. As Tillman (2002) has argued, when research is approached from a cultural perspective, "the individual and collective knowledge of African Americans is placed at the center of the inquiry" (p. 3). However, there is also a need for more research about Blacks in the principalship in which quantitative methods are employed. Survey research based on national samples can yield results that are generalizable to the broader population of Black principals. Such studies are important given that recent large-scale principalship surveys have grouped Black principals in the category of women and minorities (e.g., Farkas et al., 2003; Gates, Ringel, Santibañez, Ross, & Chung, 2003) and have failed to illuminate the specific circumstances that affect the leadership of these principals.

Several questions warrant further research. First, what factors affect the leadership of Black principals in urban school contexts in the post-*Brown* era of schooling? Most Black principals are employed in urban school districts; however, the research on urban schools is diffused, and no specific themes are evident in the research that has been conducted on Black principals in these schools. The research described here suggests that post-*Brown* Black principals typically lead schools that are underfunded, have shortages of qualified teachers, and have low standardized test scores. There is a need for research investigating how these factors, as well as others, affect the leadership capacity of Black principals.

Second, what specific leadership styles are exhibited by Black principals? The research reviewed here suggests that culture is an important factor in the leadership styles of African American principals, and some principals adopted both bureaucrat/administrator and ethno-humanist role identities. While the studies reviewed indicate that Black principals may employ more than one leadership style, little is known about the specific styles (as articulated in the traditional educational leadership literature) adopted (i.e., transformational, contingency, managerial, participative).

Third, what is the relationship between African American school leadership and African American student achievement? Findings from the studies reviewed here suggest that this relationship is positive. However, there is only limited evidence suggesting the specific ways in which same-race/cultural affiliation is directly linked to African American student achievement, particularly with respect to achievement gaps. While much has been written about the achievement gap between African American students and their White counterparts, there is a shortage of research on the specific ways in which African American leaders directly contribute to African American student achievement.

What are the links between White school leadership and African American student achievement, particularly in urban schools? Fifty years after *Brown*, urban schools are now resegregated. Yet, 65% of principals in urban schools with predominantly African American and other minority student populations are White (National Center for Education Statistics, 1998). These principals are responsible for facilitating the academic achievement of large numbers of African American students. More research is needed to determine the direct ways in which White principals promote student achievement through their leadership practices.

Research on these as well as other questions regarding the leadership of African American principals in pre-K–12 education would enhance our knowledge of important issues in the field of educational leadership. Moreover, such research is needed to continue the hope, promises, and legacy of *Brown*.

ACKNOWLEDGMENTS

I would like to thank my editorial consultants, Kofi Lomotey and Rodney Ogawa, for their helpful comments. I would also like to thank Veronica Bielat, Paula Hinton, Michelle Norris, and Jane Gorey for their assistance in preparing this chapter.

NOTES

[1] See, for example, Anderson (2004), Tillman (2004b), L. Foster (2004), a special issue of the *Journal of Negro Education* on *Brown* at 50 edited by Frank Brown (2004), Ogletree (2004), Orfield and Lee (2004), and a special issue of the *History of Education Quarterly* edited by Michael Fultz (2004b).

[2] The terms *Black* and *African American* are used interchangeably in this chapter.

[3] The terms *educational leadership* and *educational administration* are used interchangeably here. While it is not within the scope of this chapter to enter into a complete discussion of the similarities and differences between the two terms, much of the focus in the field is on school leadership versus school administration. For a more extensive discussion of the evolution of and increased use of the term *leadership,* see Leithwood and Duke (1999).

[4] Leithwood and Duke (1999) reviewed feature-length articles about various types of educational leadership in "four representative English-language educational administration journals" (p. 46). The review included articles published as early as 1988, the year the first edition of the *Handbook of Research on Educational Administration* (Boyan, 1988) was published. According to Leithwood and Duke, two of the journals, *Educational Administration Quarterly* and the *Journal of School Leadership,* publish empirical and theoretical work primarily from North America. The *Journal of Educational Administration* and *Educational Management and Administration* publish work from countries such as Australia, New Zealand, and the United Kingdom as well as from North America. Another journal, not reviewed in Leithwood and Duke's work, is the *International Journal of Leadership in Education,* which also publishes research on educational leadership/administration from other countries as well as those of North America.

[5] There is an emerging body of research on the urban school principalship (see, for example, Bryant, 1998; Carter & Fenwick, 2001; Chapman, 1973; Cistone & Stevenson, 2000; Edmonds, 1979; Gooden, in press; Lightfoot, 1983; Mukuria, 2002; Osterman, Crow, & Rosen, 1997; Polite, 1997). In addition, articles published in educational journals such as the *Journal of Negro Education, Urban Review, Urban Education,* and *Education and Urban Society* typically focus on urban schooling. However, no specific lines of research on Blacks in the principalship are evident in the general category of urban school leadership.

[6] A forthcoming publication, the *Sage Encyclopedia of Educational Leadership and Administration* (English, in press), will include a greater diversity of perspectives in the field of educational leadership/administration. This work is intended to be a reference for graduate students, practitioners, and scholars in the field.

[7] Servant leadership is a term that has been used to describe the leadership of Blacks in leadership positions such as ministers, civil rights activists, and educators. Greenleaf (1977) defined a servant leader as one who is "committed to serving others through a cause, a crusade, a movement, a campaign with humanitarian[,] not materialistic, goals" (p. 13). For more extensive discussions of the concept of African Americans and servant leadership, see Alston and Jones (2002) and Williams (1998).

[8] Most of the research conducted on the displacement of Black educators after *Brown* has focused on the massive firing of Black teachers (see, for example, Ethridge, 1979; M. Foster, 1997; Fultz, 2004a; Hooker, 1971; Hudson & Holmes, 1994; Lewis, Garrison-Wade, Scott, Douglas, & Middleton, 2004; Milner & Howard, 2004; Orfield, 1969; Tillman, 2004a).

[9] For a more extensive discussion about the ways in which Black principals lost their jobs, see Franklin and Collier (1999).

[10] For other work on the education of Blacks that also examines the role of the principal, see Jones (1981), Morris (1999, 2004), Savage (2001), and Ward Randolph (1997).

[11] Sowell conducted his research at five public schools (Booker T. Washington High School in Atlanta, Georgia; Frederick Douglass High School in Baltimore, Maryland; McDonough 35 High School in New Orleans, Louisiana; P.S. 91 in Brooklyn, New York; and Dunbar High School in Washington, D.C.) and three private Catholic schools (St. Paul of the Cross in Atlanta and St. Augustine and Xavier Prep in New Orleans).

[12] Lightfoot conducted her study in two urban high schools (George Washington Carver High School in Atlanta and John F. Kennedy High School in New York City), two suburban high schools (Highland Park High School in Highland Park, Illinois, and Brookline High School in Brookline, Massachusetts), and two elite, private high schools (St. Paul's School in Concord, New Hampshire, and Milton Academy in Boston).

[13] Although the participants in this study were female African Americans, their gender was not the focus of the study. Thus, the study is not included in the research on African American female principals.

[14] For more extensive discussions on this point, see Dempsey and Noblit (1996) and Edwards (1996).

[15] The topic of women in school leadership has also been discussed by Jones (2003), Ortiz and Marshall (1988), and Shakeshaft (1988, 1989, 1999).

[16] Loder drew on Collins's (1991) definition of "othermothers" as women "who work on behalf of the Black community by expressing ethics of caring and personal accountability, which embrace conceptions of transformative power and mutuality" (p. 132).

[17] See, for example, Anderson (2003); Barton (2004); Caldas and Bankston (1998); Hale (2004); Klein (2002); Kozol (1991); Lomotey (1987, 1989b); Ogbu (2003); Perry (2003); Perry, Steele, and Hilliard (2003); Resnick (2004); and Sizemore (2003).

[18] Lomotey, Allen, Canada, Mark, and Rivers (2003) conducted a comprehensive review of the theoretical and empirical literature on African American school leaders. The review covered the years 1972 through 2002 and included dissertations, journal articles, conference papers, books, and bulletins. The authors identified six categories that included work on assistant principals, principals, and superintendents: (a) African American female educational leaders, (b) mobility opportunities for African American educational leaders, (c) roles and role expectations of African American leaders, (d) job satisfaction of African American educational leaders, (e) factors affecting the performance of African American leaders, and (f) management styles of African American leaders.

REFERENCES

Abney, E. E. (1980). A comparison of the status of Florida's Black public school principals, 1964–65/1975–76. *Journal of Negro Education, 69,* 398–406.

Adkison, J. A. (1981). Women in school administration: A review of the research. *Review of Educational Research, 51,* 311–343.

Allen, K., Jacobson, S., & Lomotey, K. (1995). African American women in educational administration: The importance of mentors and sponsors. *Journal of Negro Education, 64,* 409–420.

Alston, J. A., & Jones, S. N. (2002). Carrying the torch of the Jeanes Supervisors: 21st-century African American female superintendents and servant leadership. In B. Cooper & L. Fusarelli (Eds.), *The promises and perils facing today's school superintendent* (pp. 65–75). Lanham, MD: Scarecrow Press.

Anderson, J. D. (1988). *The education of Blacks in the South, 1860–1935.* Chapel Hill: University of North Carolina Press.

Anderson, J. D. (2003). *The historical context for understanding the test score gap.* Unpublished manuscript.

Anderson, J. D. (2004). Crosses to bear and promises to keep: The jubilee anniversary of *Brown v. Board of Education. Urban Education, 39,* 359–373.

Banks, C. M. (1995). Gender and race as factors in educational leadership and administration. In J. A. Banks & C. M. Banks (Eds.), *Handbook of research on multicultural education* (pp. 65–80). New York: Macmillan.

Barton, P. E. (2004). Why does the gap persist? *Educational Leadership, 62*(3), 8–14.

Beck, L. G. (1994a). Cultivating a caring school community: One principal's story. In J. Murphy & K. S. Louis (Eds.), *Reshaping the principalship* (pp. 177–202). Thousand Oaks, CA: Corwin Press.

Beck, L. G. (1994b). *Reclaiming educational administration as a caring profession.* New York: Teachers College Press.

Bell, D. (1992). *Faces at the bottom of the well: The permanence of racism.* New York: Basic Books.

Benham, M. K. P. (1997). Silences and serenades: The journeys of three ethnic minority women school leaders. *Anthropology and Education Quarterly, 28,* 280–307.

Biklen, S. N., & Brannigan, M. B. (1980). *Women and educational leadership.* Lexington, MA: Lexington Books.

Bloom, C. M., & Erlandson, D. A. (2003). African American women principals in urban schools: Realities, (re)constructions, and resolutions. *Educational Administration Quarterly, 39,* 339–369.

Bolman, L. G., & Deal, T. E. (1997). *Reframing organizations: Artistry, choice, and leadership* (2nd ed.). San Francisco: Jossey-Bass.

Boyan, N. (Ed.). (1988). *Handbook of research on educational administration: A project of the American Educational Research Association.* New York: Longman.

Bredeson, P. V. (1996). New directions in the preparation of educational leaders. In K. Leithwood, J. Chapman, D. Corson, P. Hallinger, & A. Hart (Eds.), *International handbook of educational leadership and administration* (pp. 251–277). Dordrecht, the Netherlands: Kluwer Academic.

Brookover, W. B., Beady, C., Flood, P., Schweitzer, J., & Wisenbaker, J. (1979). *School social systems and student achievement: Schools can make a difference.* New York: Praeger.

Brown, F. (Ed.). (2004). *Brown v. Board of Education* at 50 [special issue]. *Journal of Negro Education, 73*(3).

Brown, H. V. (1960). *The education of Blacks in the South.* Chapel Hill: University of North Carolina Press.

Brown v. Board of Education, 347 U.S. 483 (1954).

Bryant, N. (1998). Reducing the relational distance between actors: A case study in school reform. *Urban Education, 33,* 34–49.

Bullock, H. (1967). *A history of Negro education in the South from 1619 to the present.* Cambridge, MA: Harvard University Press.

Butchart, R. E. (1988). "Outthinking and outflanking the owners of the world": A historiography of the African American struggle for education. *History of Education Quarterly, 28,* 333–366.

Caldas, S. J., & Bankston, C., III. (1998). The inequality of separation: Racial composition of schools and academic achievement. *Educational Administration Quarterly, 34,* 533–557.

Carter, M., & Fenwick, L. (2001). Keeping a close watch: A cultural philosophy of school change. *National Association of Secondary School Principals Bulletin, 85,* 15–21.

Case, K. I. (1997). African American othermothering in the urban elementary school. *Urban Review, 29,* 25–39.

Cecelski, D. S. (1994). *Along freedom road: Hyde County, North Carolina, and the fate of Black schools in the South.* Chapel Hill: University of North Carolina Press.

Chapman, R. L. (1973, February). *The role expectation of the Black urban principal as perceived by himself, administrators, influentials, and other active community persons.* Paper presented at the annual meeting of the American Educational Research Association, New Orleans, LA.

Cistone, P. J., & Stevenson, J. M. (Eds.). (2000). Perspectives on the urban principalship [special issue]. *Education and Urban Society, 32*(4).

Clark, K. B. (1963). *Prejudice and your child.* Boston: Beacon Press.

Coffin, G. C. (1972). The Black school administrator and how he's being pushed to extinction. *American School Board Journal, 159,* 33–36.

Collins, P. H. (1991). *Black feminist thought: Knowledge, consciousness, and the politics of empowerment.* New York: Routledge.

Cooper, A. J. (1988). *A voice from the South.* New York: Oxford University Press. (Original work published 1892)

Coursen, D., Mazzarella, J., Jeffress, L., & Hadderman, M. (1989). Two special cases: Women and Blacks. In S. C. Smith & P. K. Piele (Eds.), *School leadership: Handbook for excellence* (pp. 85–106). Eugene, OR: ERIC Clearinghouse on Educational Management.

Crosby, E. A. (1999). Urban schools: Forced to fail. *Phi Delta Kappan, 81,* 298–303.

Crow, G. M., & Glascock, C. (1995). Transformational leadership: Attractions of women and minority recruits to the principalship. *Journal of School Leadership, 5,* 356–378.

Dantley, M. E. (1990). The ineffectiveness of effective schools leadership: An analysis of the effective schools movement from a critical perspective. *Journal of Negro Education, 59,* 585–598.

Dantley, M. E., & Tillman, L. C. (2005). Social justice and moral/transformative leadership. In C. Marshall & M. Oliva (Eds.), *Leadership for social justice: Making revolutions in education* (pp. 16–30). Boston: Allyn & Bacon.

Deal, T. E., & Peterson, K. D. (2000). Eight roles of symbolic leaders. In *Jossey-Bass reader on educational leadership* (pp. 202–214). San Francisco: Jossey-Bass.

Delpit, L. (1995). *Other people's children: Cultural conflict in the classroom.* New York: New Press.

Dempsey, V., & Noblit, G. (1996). Cultural ignorance and school desegregation: A community narrative. In M. Shujaa (Ed.), *Beyond desegregation: The politics of quality in African American schooling* (pp. 115–137). Thousand Oaks, CA: Corwin Press.

Dillard, C. (1995). Leading with her life: An African American feminist (re)interpretation of leadership for an urban high school principal. *Educational Administration Quarterly, 31,* 539–563.

Doughty, R. (1980). The Black female administrator: Woman in a double bind. In S. K. Biklen & M. B. Brannigan (Eds.), *Women and educational leadership* (pp. 165–174). Lexington, MA: Lexington Books.

Edmonds, R. (1979). Effective schools for the urban poor. *Educational Leadership, 37,* 15–24.

Edson, S. K. (1987). Voices from the present: Tracking the female administrative aspirant. *Journal of Educational Equity and Leadership, 7,* 261–277.

Edwards, P. (1996). Before and after school desegregation: African American parents' involvement in schools. In M. Shujaa (Ed.), *Beyond desegregation: The politics of quality in African American schooling* (pp. 138–161). Thousand Oaks, CA: Corwin Press.

English, F. (Ed.). (in press). *Sage encyclopedia of educational leadership and administration.* Newbury Park, CA: Sage.

Enomoto, E., Gardiner, M., & Grogan, M. (2000). Notes to Athene: Mentoring relationships for women of color. *Urban Education, 35,* 567–583.

Ethridge, S. (1979). Impact of the 1954 *Brown vs. Topeka Board of Education* decision on Black educators. *Negro Educational Review, 30,* 217–232.

Farkas, S., Johnson, J., & Duffett, A. (2003). *Rolling up their sleeves: Superintendents and principals talk about what's needed to fix public schools.* New York: Wallace Foundation.

Fenwick, L. (2001). *Patterns of excellence: Policy perspectives on diversity in teaching and school leadership.* Atlanta, GA: Southern Education Foundation.

Foster, L. (2004). Administrator and teacher recruitment and selection post-*Brown*: Issues, challenges, and strategies. *Journal of School Public Relations, 25,* 220–232.

Foster, M. (1997). *Black teachers on teaching.* New York: New Press.

Franklin, V. P. (1984). *Black self-determination: A cultural history of the faith of our fathers.* Westport, CT: Lawrence Hill.

Franklin, V. P. (1990). "They rose and fell together": African American educators and community leadership, 1795–1954. *Journal of Education, 172*(3), 39–64.

Franklin, V. P., & Collier, B. T. (1999). *My soul is a witness: A chronology of the civil rights era, 1954–1965.* New York: Henry Holt.

Fultz, M. (2004a). The displacement of Black educators post-*Brown:* An overview and analysis. *History of Education Quarterly, 44,* 11–45.

Fultz, M. (Ed.). (2004b). Fiftieth anniversary of the *Brown v. Board of Education* decision [special issue]. *History of Education Quarterly, 44*(1).

Gardiner, M. E., Enomoto, E., & Grogan, M. (2000). *Coloring outside lines: Mentoring women in school leadership.* Albany: State University of New York Press.

Gates, S. M., Ringel, J. S., Santibañez, L., Ross, K. E., & Chung, C. H. (2003). *Who is leading our schools?: An overview of school administrators and their careers.* Arlington, VA: RAND Education.

Georgia Teacher and Education Association. (1970). *Guide to developing an inclusive integration plan.* Atlanta, GA: Author.

Gilligan, C. (1982). *In a different voice: Psychological theory and women's development.* Cambridge, MA: Harvard University Press.

González, M. L. (2002). Professors of educational administration: Learning and leading for the success of ALL children. *University Council for Educational Administration Review, 64,* 4–9.

Gooden, M. A. (in press). The role of an African American principal in an urban information technology high school. *Educational Administration Quarterly.*

Gordon, E. W. (2004, October). *Education, excellence and equity: Toward equitable access to excellence in education.* First Annual Brown Lecture in Educational Research, Washington, DC.

Greenleaf, R. K. (1977). *Servant leadership: A journey into the nature of legitimate power and greatness.* New York: Paulist Press.

Hale, J. (2004). How schools shortchange African American children. *Educational Leadership, 62*(3), 34–39.

Hallinger, P., & Heck, R. H. (1996). Reassessing the principal's role in school effectiveness: A review of empirical research, 1980–1995. *Educational Administration Quarterly, 32,* 5–44.

Hart, A. W., & Bredeson, P. V. (1996). *The principalship.* New York: McGraw-Hill.

Henig, J. R., Hula, R. C., Orr, M., & Pedescleaux, D. S. (1999). *The color of school reform: Race, politics, and the challenge of urban education.* Princeton, NJ: Princeton University Press.

Hine, D. C., & Thompson, K. (1998). *A shining thread of hope: The history of Black women in America.* New York: Broadway Books.

Hobson-Horton, L. D. (2000). *African American women principals: Examples of urban educational leadership.* Unpublished doctoral dissertation, University of Wisconsin.

Hooker, R. (1971). Displacement of Black teachers in the eleven southern states. *Afro-American Studies, 2,* 165–180.

Hudson, M. J., & Holmes, B. J. (1994). Missing teachers, impaired communities: The unanticipated consequences of *Brown v. Board of Education* on the African American teaching force at the precollegiate level. *Journal of Negro Education, 63,* 388–393.

Irvine, J. J. (1999). The education of children whose nightmares come both day and night. *Journal of Negro Education, 68,* 224–253.

James, J. C. (1970, September). Another vanishing American: The Black principal. *New Republic,* pp. 17–20.

Jones, E., & Montenegro, X. (1985). *Women and minorities in school administration.* Washington, DC: Office of Minority Affairs, American Association of School Administrators.

Jones, F. (1981). *A traditional model of educational excellence.* Washington, DC: Howard University Press.

Jones, S. N. (2003). *The praxis of Black female educational leadership from a systems perspective.* Unpublished doctoral dissertation, Bowling Green State University.

Karpinski, C. (2004, April). *Faculty diversity: Brown and the demise of the Black principal.* Paper presented at the annual meeting of the American Educational Research Association, San Diego, CA.

Kimball, K., & Sirotnik, K. (2000). The urban school principalship: Take this job and . . .! *Education and Urban Society, 32,* 536–543.

Klein, D. W. (2002). Beyond *Brown v. Board of Education:* The need to remedy the achievement gap. *Journal of Law and Education, 31,* 431–457.

Kluger, R. (1977). *Simple justice.* New York: Random House.

Kozol, J. (1991). *Savage inequalities: Children in America's schools.* New York: HarperCollins.

Ladson-Billings, G. (2004). Landing on the wrong note: The price we paid for *Brown. Educational Researcher, 33*(7), 3–13.

Leithwood, K., & Duke, L. (1999). A century's quest to understand school leadership. In J. Murphy & K. Seashore Louis (Eds.), *The handbook of research on educational administration* (2nd ed., pp. 45–72). San Francisco: Jossey-Bass.

Leithwood, K., & Montgomery, D. (1982). Forms and effects of school-based management: A review. *Educational Policy, 12,* 325–346.

Leithwood, K. A., & Riehl, C. (2003). *What we know about successful school leadership.* Philadelphia: Laboratory for Student Success, Temple University.

Lewis, C., Garrison-Wade, D., Scott, M., Douglas, B, & Middleton, V. (2004). A synthesis of evidence-based research on the status of African American teachers 50 years after *Brown* and its impact on African American student achievement: Implications for teachers and administrators. *E-Journal of Teaching & Learning in Diverse Settings, 2*(1). Retrieved February 10, 2005, from http://subr.edu/coeducation/ejournal

Lightfoot, S. L. (1983). *The good high school: Portraits of character and culture.* New York: Basic Books.

Lightfoot, S. L. (1994). *I've known rivers: Lives of loss and liberation.* New York: Penguin.

Loder, T. L. (2002). On women becoming and being principals: Pathways, patterns, and personal accounts. *Dissertation Abstracts International, 63,* 3804.

Loder, T. L. (2005). African American women principals' reflections on social change, community othermothering, and Chicago public school reform. *Urban Education, 40,* 298–320.

Lomotey, K. (1987). Black principals for Black students: Some preliminary observations. *Urban Education, 22,* 173–181.

Lomotey, K. (1989a). *African-American principals: School leadership and success.* Westport, CT: Greenwood Press.

Lomotey, K. (1989b). Cultural diversity in the school: Implications for principals. *NASSP Bulletin,* pp. 81–88.

Lomotey, K. (1993). African-American principals: Bureaucrat/administrators and ethnohumanists. *Urban Education, 27,* 394–412.

Lomotey, K., Allen, K. L., Canada, T. J., Mark, D. L. H., & Rivers, S. (2003). *Research on African American educational leaders: The state of the art.* Unpublished manuscript.

Lyman, L. (2000). *How do they know you care? The principal's challenge.* New York: Teachers College Press.

Mann, H. B. (1970). *The Negro school and professional in America.* Englewood Cliffs, NJ: Prentice Hall.

Marshall, C. (2004). Social justice challenges to educational administration: Introduction to a special issue. *Educational Administration Quarterly, 40,* 3–13.

Mayeroff, M. (1971). *On caring.* New York: Harper & Row.

Mertz, N. T., & McNeely, S. R. (1998). Women on the job: A study of female high school principals. *Educational Administration Quarterly, 34,* 196–222.

Milner, H. R., & Howard, T. C. (2004). Black teachers, Black students, Black communities and *Brown:* Perspectives and insights from experts. *Journal of Negro Education, 73,* 285–297.

Mitchell, D. E., Ortiz, F. I., & Mitchell, T. K. (1987). *Work orientation and job performance: The cultural basis of teaching rewards and incentives.* New York: State University of New York Press.

Morris, J. E. (1999). A pillar of strength: An African American school's communal bonds with families and community since *Brown. Urban Education, 35,* 584–605.

Morris, J. E. (2004). Can anything good come from Nazareth? Race, class, and African American schooling and community in the urban South and Midwest. *American Educational Research Journal, 41,* 69–112.

Mukuria, G. (2002). Disciplinary challenges: How do principals address this dilemma? *Urban Education, 37,* 432–452.

Murphy, J. (1988). Methodological, measurement and conceptual problems in the study of instructional leadership. *Educational Evaluation and Policy Analysis, 4,* 290–310.

National Center for Education Statistics. (1998). *Digest of educational statistics.* Washington, DC: U.S. Government Printing Office.

National Center for Education Statistics. (2004). *Contexts of elementary and secondary education.* Retrieved May 31, 2005, from http://nces.ed.gov/programs/coe/2004

Noddings, N. (1984). *Caring: A feminine approach to ethics and moral education.* Berkeley: University of California Press.

Ogbu, J. (2003). *Black American students in an affluent suburb: A study of academic disengagement.* Mahwah, NJ: Erlbaum.

Ogletree, C. J., Jr. (2004). *All deliberate speed: Reflections on the first half century of Brown v. Board of Education.* New York: Norton.

Orfield, G. (1969). *The reconstruction of southern education: The schools and the 1964 Civil Rights Act.* New York: Wiley.

Orfield, G., & Lee, C. (2004). *Brown at 50: King's dream or Plessy's nightmare?* Retrieved January 26, 2004, from www.civilrightsproject.harvard.edu

Ortiz, F. I. (1982). *Career patterns in education: Women, men and minorities in public school administration.* South Hadley, MA: Bergin.

Ortiz, F. I., & Marshall, C. (1988). Women in educational administration. In N. Boyan (Ed.), *Handbook of research on educational administration* (pp. 123–141). New York: Longman.

Osterman, K. F., Crow, G. M., & Rosen, J. L. (1997). New urban principals: Role conceptions at the entry level. *Urban Education, 32,* 373–393.

Perkins, L. (1987). *Fannie Jackson Coppin and the Institute for Colored Youth, 1865–1902.* New York: Garland.

Perry, T. (2003, January 10). Tackling the myth of Black students' intellectual inferiority. *Chronicle of Higher Education,* p. B10.

Perry, T., Steele, C., & Hilliard, A. (2003). *Young, gifted, and Black: Promoting high achievement among African-American students.* Boston: Beacon Press.

Polite, V. C. (Ed.). (1997). Professional development focused on the exigencies of urban principals [special issue]. *Urban Education, 31*(5).

Pollard, D. (1997). Race, gender, and educational leadership: Perspectives from African American principals. *Educational Policy, 11,* 353–374.

Portin, B. S. (2000). The changing urban principalship. *Education and Urban Society, 32,* 492–505.

Pounder, D. G., Ogawa, R. T., & Adams, E. A. (1995). Leadership as an organization-wide phenomenon: Its impact on school performance. *Educational Administration Quarterly, 31,* 564–588.

Reitzug, U. C., & Patterson, J. (1998). "I'm not going to lose you!" Empowerment through caring in an urban principal's practice with students. *Urban Education, 33,* 150–181.

Reitzug, U. C., & Reeves, J. E. (1992). Miss Lincoln doesn't teach here: A descriptive narrative and conceptual analysis of a principal's symbolic leadership behavior. *Educational Administration Quarterly, 28,* 185–219.

Resnick, L. (2004). Closing the gap: High achievement for students of color. *Research Points, 2,* 1–4.

Riester, A. F., Pursch, V., & Skrla, L. (2002). Principals for social justice: Leaders for school success for children from low-income homes. *Journal of School Leadership, 12,* 281–302.

Rodgers, F. A. (1967). *The Black high school and its community.* Lexington, MA: Lexington Books.

Savage, C. G. (2001). "Because we did more with less": The agency of African American teachers in Franklin, Tennessee: 1890–1967. *Peabody Journal of Education, 76,* 170–203.

Scheurich, J. J. (1998). Highly successful and loving, public elementary schools populated mainly by low-SES children of color: Core beliefs and cultural characteristics. *Urban Education, 33,* 451–491.

Shakeshaft, C. (1988). Women in educational administration: Implications for training. In D. E. Griffiths, R. T. Stout, & P. B. Forsyth (Eds.), *Leaders for America's schools: The report and papers of the National Commission on Excellence in Educational Administration* (pp. 403–416). Berkeley, CA: McCutchan.

Shakeshaft, C. (1989). *Women in educational administration.* Newbury Park, CA: Sage.

Shakeshaft, C. (1999). The struggle to create a more gender-inclusive profession. In J. Murphy & K. Seashore Louis (Eds.), *The handbook of research on educational administration* (2nd ed., pp. 99–118). San Francisco: Jossey-Bass.

Shotwell, R. H. (1999). *Leadership theory and context: Black and White principals during desegregation.* Unpublished doctoral dissertation, University of North Carolina at Greensboro.

Siddle Walker, E. V. (1993a). Caswell County Training School, 1933–1969: Relationships between community and school. *Harvard Educational Review, 63,* 161–182.

Siddle Walker, E. V. (1993b). Interpersonal caring in the "good" segregated schooling of African-American children: Evidence from the case of the Caswell County Training School. *Urban Review, 25,* 63–77.

Siddle Walker, E. V. (1996). *Their highest potential: An African American school community in the segregated South.* Chapel Hill: University of North Carolina Press.

Siddle Walker, V. (2000). Value of segregated schools for African American children in the South, 1935–1969: A review of common themes and characteristics. *Review of Educational Research, 70,* 253–285.

Siddle Walker, V. (2001). African American teaching in the South: 1940–1960. *American Educational Research Journal, 38,* 751–779.

Siddle Walker, V. (2003). The architects of Black schooling in the segregated South: The case of one principal leader. *Journal of Curriculum and Supervision, 19,* 54–72.

Siddle Walker, V., & Archung, K. N. (2003). The segregated schooling of Blacks in the southern United States and South Africa. *Comparative Education Review, 47,* 21–40.

Sizemore, B. A. (2003). The imputation of Black inferiority: Does it contribute to the achievement gap? In C. Camp-Yeakey & R. D. Henderson (Eds.), *Surmounting all odds: Education, opportunity and society in the new millennium* (pp. 273–304). Greenwich, CT: Information Age.

Sowell, T. (1976). Patterns of Black excellence. *Public Interest, 43,* 6–58.

Starratt, R. J. (1991). Building an ethical school: A theory for practice in educational leadership. *Educational Administration Quarterly, 27,* 185–202.

Tillman, L. C. (2002). Culturally sensitive research approaches: An African American perspective. *Educational Researcher, 31*(9), 3–12.

Tillman, L. C. (2003). From rhetoric to reality? Educational administration and the lack of racial and ethnic diversity within the profession. *University Council for Educational Administration Review, 45*(3), 1–4.

Tillman, L. C. (2004a). (Un)intended consequences?: The impact of the *Brown v. Board of Education* decision on the employment status of Black educators. *Education and Urban Society, 36,* 280–303.

Tillman, L. C. (2004b). African American parental involvement in a post-*Brown* era: Facilitating the academic achievement of African American students. *Journal of School Public Relations, 25,* 161–176.

Tillman, L. C. (in press-a). Bringing the gifts that our ancestors gave: Continuing the legacy of excellence in African American school leadership. In J. Jackson (Ed.), *Strengthening the educational pipeline for African Americans: Informing policy and practice.* Albany: State University of New York Press.

Tillman, L.C. (Ed.). (in press-b). Pushing back resistance: African American discourses on school leadership [special issue]. *Educational Administration Quarterly.*

Tillman, L. C. (in press-c). Mentoring new teachers: Implications for leadership practice in an urban school. *Educational Administration Quarterly.*

Tonnsen, S., & Truesdale, V. (1993). Women and minorities in educational administration: Programs and processes that work. *Journal of School Leadership, 3,* 679–687.

Valverde, L., & Brown, F. (1988). Influences on leadership development of racial and ethnic minorities. In N. Boyan (Ed.), *The handbook on educational administration* (pp. 143–158). New York: Longman.

Ward Randolph, A. (1997, March). *Champion Avenue School: A historical analysis.* Paper presented at the annual meeting of the American Educational Research Association, Chicago.

Washington, B. T. (1993). *Up from slavery.* New York: Gramercy Books. (Original work published 1901)

Washington, M. H. (1988). *A voice from the South.* New York: Oxford University Press.

Watkins, W. (2001). *The White architects of Black education: Ideology and power in America, 1865–1954.* New York: Teachers College Press.

Wells, G. F. (1991). *A comparison of the role perceptions of Black high school principals.* Unpublished doctoral dissertation, University of North Carolina at Chapel Hill.

White, A. L. (1995). *Factors that affect the professional experiences of African American female principals in the state of Arizona: A case study.* Unpublished doctoral dissertation, Arizona State University.

Williams, L. S. (1998). *Servants of the people: The 1960s legacy of African American leadership.* New York: St. Martin's Griffin.

Witziers, B., Bosker, R. J., & Krüger, M. L. (2003). Educational leadership and student achievement: The elusive search for an association. *Educational Administration Quarterly, 39,* 398–425.

Yeakey, C. C., Johnston, G. S., & Adkison, J. A. (1986). In pursuit of equity: A review of research on minorities and women in educational administration. *Educational Administration Quarterly, 22,* 110–149.

Young, M., & McLeod, S. (2001). Flukes, opportunities, and planned interventions: Factors affecting women's decisions to become school administrators. *Educational Administration Quarterly, 37,* 462–502.

Chapter 5

Brown, Political Economy, and the Scientific Education of African Americans

WILLIAM F. TATE IV
Washington University

Comparing them [Blacks] by their faculties of memory, reason, and imagination, it appears to me, that in memory they are equal to the whites; in reason much inferior, as I think one could scarcely be found capable of tracing and comprehending the investigations of Euclid; and that in imagination they are dull, tasteless, and anomalous. It would be unfair to follow them to Africa for this investigation. We will consider them here, on the same stage with the whites, and where the facts are not apocryphal on which a judgment is to be formed. It will be right to make great allowances for the difference of condition, of education, of conversation, of the sphere in which they move. (Thomas Jefferson, *Notes on the State of Virginia*)

  I am happy to be able to inform you that we have now in the United States a Negro, the son of a black man born in Africa, and a black woman born in the United States, who is a very respectable mathematician [Benjamin Banneker]. I procured him to be employed under one of our chief directors in laying out the new federal city on the Potowmac, & in the intervals of his leisure, while on that work, he made an Almanac for the next year . . . I have seen very elegant solutions of Geometrical problems by him. Add to this that he is a very worthy & respectable member of society. He is a free man. I shall be delighted to see these instances of moral eminence so multiplied as to prove that the want of talents observed in them is merely the effect of their degraded condition, and not proceeding from any difference in the structure of the parts on which intellect depends.

(Thomas Jefferson, cited in Bedini, 1972, p. 159)

The history of African American life in the United States is inextricably linked to ideological debates of intellect, economy, and humanity.[1] Perhaps nowhere is this more apparent than in the remarks of Thomas Jefferson recorded in *Notes on the State of Virginia*. Jefferson's argument about the African's blackness was moral in nature (Peters, 1982). Furthermore, Peters argued that the Jeffersonian perspective on African people was foundational for segregation in the United States. While Jefferson's thinking about the scientific capabilities of the Negro was informed by his interactions with Benjamin Banneker, the ideology expressed in *Notes on State of Virginia* was consistent with the prevailing cultural ethos of the time. African Americans were seen as devoid of humanity and its byproducts: reason, intellect, scientific thought, and mathematical ability.

Yet, Jefferson's personal struggle to understand the "African American intellect" is worthy of further discussion. Jefferson remarks reflect a kind of sociological thought

147

experiment wherein he attempts to compare various constructs associated with humanity across demographic groups—Whites, Blacks, and Indians. Interestingly in the face of evidence, Jefferson tempered his remarks and outlook related to the scientific ability of African Americans. Benjamin Banneker served as an existence proof in the mind of Jefferson: The African American could reason quantitatively! Initially, he questioned the Negro's ability to reason scientifically and mathematically with some caveats related to environmental constraints, presumably slavery and its associated conditions. However, it appears that Jefferson was not sure of the rationale behind his initial thinking. Was this perceived inability to reason due to Negroes' social condition, economic state, or mental deficiencies inherent in their genetic composition? This question and associated debates continue to this very day in both academic literature and public discourse (e.g., Black, 2003; Hernnstein & Murray, 1994; Lemann, 2000; Yeakey & Henderson, 2003).

The goals of this chapter are threefold. The first goal is to examine the scientific attainment of African Americans in the post-*Brown* era. The term *scientific attainment* is used here to describe more broadly mathematics and scientific achievement as measured in trend studies, academic coursework, and degrees. A second, related goal is to provide a brief overview of the role of scientific education in the United States, with a particular focus on the African American experience. Scientific education, as described here, includes the mathematical sciences and the natural and physical sciences. A third and final goal is to examine the role of science as a tool used to both open and close opportunity structures in educational settings, with *Brown* as the specific context for this examination. Arguably, the *Brown* case and subsequent related legal cases associated with tracking best capture how science is situated in the midst of important matters of justice in education. In keeping with the *Brown* theme of this volume, a particular focus will be on environmental factors associated with segregated conditions and their influence on the scientific achievement of African Americans.[2] On face value, it may appear to be a bit of an intellectual stretch to link the *Brown* case, a matter of civil rights, and scientific education. Scholar and social activist Robert Moses, in his book *radical equations: Math Literacy and Civil Rights,* examined the question "Is school mathematics and science a civil right?" In his response to this question, Moses stated:

In those days [1950s and 1960s], of course, the issue was the right to vote, and the question was political access. Voter registration was by no means the only issue one could have fought for, but it was crucial and urgent: Black people had no real control over their political lives, and the time was right to organize a movement to change this. There existed a powerful consensus on the issue of gaining the political franchise, and the drive for voter registration—especially where it took place deep in the Black belt of the South—captured the imaginations of Americans, particularly African Americans. So, for a period of time, because there was agreement among all of the people acting to change Mississippi, we were able to get resources and people from around the country to come and work. . . . Today I want to argue, the most urgent social issue affecting poor people is economic access. In today's world, economic access and full citizenship depend crucially on math and science literacy. I believe that the absence of math literacy in urban and rural communities throughout this country is as urgent as the lack of registered Black voters in Mississippi was in 1961. (Moses & Cobb, 2001, pp. 4–5)

Moses's argument is relatively straightforward. Many of the vestiges of segregation are less prominent or of a different form than in 1961. Furthermore, while the political process is more open now, economic access—in particular, professional and entrepreneurial opportunities in the information economy—is restricted according to individual knowledge, skills, and understandings associated with science and technology. This knowledge base is closely linked to the mathematical sciences. Wright and Chorin (1999) argued that science and engineering problems are so complex that they can be solved only through the guidance and participation of mathematical scientists. All three approaches to science—theory, modeling, and observation/experiment—are required to understand the complex phenomena investigated today by scientists and engineers, and each approach is informed by the mathematical sciences. The interaction among scientific disciplines represents a paradigmatic shift in knowledge production.

Historically, technological shifts have been positive in regard to the broader economic good but have had a significant negative impact on demographic groups displaced by newer technologies and lacking the skills to take advantage of the economic opportunities created by these technologies (Thurow, 1999). In what ways are African Americans prepared to contribute to the science that undergirds the shifts in the economic order? This question frames the teaching and learning of mathematics and science as largely a human resource development challenge for emerging commercial interests. A more complete vision of scientific education would reflect the rapid advancements of science, the implications of this growth for school mathematics and science, and the increasing role of science and mathematics in social decision making. As scientific discoveries change the fabric of American society, it is imperative that all citizens have the opportunity to learn science in a manner sufficient to engage the ethical challenges associated with new technologies. Mathematics and science taught strictly to improve the economic opportunities and status of an entity, either individual or corporate, fail to capture the complete role of a scientific education (Ernest, 1991; Hurd, 1997). The next section provides an outline of the goals and organization of this chapter.

CHAPTER GOALS AND ORGANIZATION

The goals of this chapter are threefold. The first goal is to describe relevant trends related to African American scientific attainment. The next section provides a brief review of the state of such attainment, including a review of longitudinal trend studies of mathematics and science achievement, student course-taking patterns, and college majors. More specifically, the section focuses, where possible, on within-group trends among African Americans. These trends suggest that African American scientific attainment has improved in the post-*Brown* era. However, certain school-related factors are limiting progress. Any limiting factors related to scientific attainment have grave consequences given that science—and, thus, knowledge of science—has had a special role in the political and economic development of the United States.

The second section is linked conceptually to the first in that it reviews the role of science in political thought and political economy and the influence of science in the broader American culture and society. This section provides insights into the historical importance of science knowledge and why social conditions, including segregation laws and related folkways, were vitally important in regard to the nature and extent of student advancement in scientific education. The relationships among scientific attainment, political thought, and democracy are critical in terms of the advancement of African Americans. Science can influence and inform debates about legal rights (as argued in the fourth section). However, legal debates about civil rights can be influenced by a wide range of factors. What led to the shift in political thinking related to segregation policy in the United States?

The third section of the chapter addresses this question. In building on arguments of political economy described in the second section, three theories are provided to explain how *Brown* and related policies designed to dismantle segregation were influenced by the national interests of the United States, the desire for technological superiority, and related economic factors. These three theories complement the role that science played in the litigation strategy leading to *Brown* and the expansion of African Americans' civil rights in that, at the macro level, the desire for scientific advancement and related economic expansion supported the rationale for *Brown*. Furthermore, if viewed at the micro level, science informed the litigation strategy in *Brown*.

The co-action of science and African American rights is exemplified in the *Brown* litigation. The fourth section provides a selected historical review of the evolving role of social science in legal debates associated with segregation policies along with insights into the relationship between segregation and opportunity to learn in the sciences. The *Brown* case embodies how scientific knowledge has had a special role in a litigation strategy organized to eliminate segregation in schools. In addition, science has played a key role in post-*Brown* litigation involving African American students' learning conditions, in particular tracking litigation. Thus, *Brown* is a useful example of the power of science in the political and legal debates taking place in the United States. Moreover, the *Brown* litigation and related tracking litigation that followed serve as a model of how science can be used to influence the scientific learning opportunities of African Americans. This history provides a more contemporary context for situating Jefferson's "Genetics vs. Environment" thought experiment. The fifth and final section looks to the future in light of the past.

AFRICAN AMERICAN SCIENTIFIC ATTAINMENT

This section briefly reviews the state of African American scientific attainment. Here the term *scientific* refers to the mathematical sciences, the natural sciences, and the physical sciences. Numerous indicators are used to gauge scientific accomplishment. The indicators used in this section include achievement trends, transcript data, and college majors. Each indicator provides a different perspective of the scientific pipeline.

It is a generally accepted practice in the social sciences to examine differences among racial groups on indicators measuring education, health, employment, and other areas of interest to policymakers and citizens. The focus in this section, where possible, is on the nature and extent of African American attainment. This strategy is intentional. A focus on achievement and attainment differences often results in discussions of solutions that draw from the educational strategies employed with the highest-performing groups. Often ignored are strategies used within a demographic group that may involve greater possibilities for implementation and traction. The way in which the problem is framed influences the types of solution strategies offered.

Although racial comparisons are not prominent in this review, comparative information incorporating socioeconomic status (SES) is used. Regardless of U.S. region of residence, African American children experience the highest rates of poverty (U.S. General Accounting Office, 1993). While the poverty rate in 2000 among Blacks was the lowest since 1959, poverty among Black children is pronounced (National Center for Education Statistics [NCES], 2003). Thirty-one percent of Black children lived in poverty in 2000, a rate higher than that among White children (9%) and Hispanic children (28%). Thus, it is important to have insights into scientific attainment according to social class. Most notions of social class are derived from the economic roots of class and, with some variation, link class to political and cultural indicators. The traditional practice in school mathematics and science is to organize a hierarchy of classes that objectifies high, middle, and low positions on a particular metric such as SES, where "parental education level" or "family income" serves as a proxy for class. The limitations of this practice have been discussed in detail elsewhere (Grant & Sleeter, 1986; Knapp & Woolverton, 1995; Secada, 1992). For the purposes of better understanding African American scientific attainment, limitations not withstanding, SES information is incorporated into this review.

The goal of examining Black scientific attainment and achievement is not trivial. Finding relevant literature is difficult. For example, in a survey of more than 3,000 mathematics education research articles, Lubienski and Bowen (2000) found 52 pertaining to social class, 47 pertaining to Black students, and 13 considering race and class together. With this limitation noted, the next section presents a selective review of African American student performance in mathematics and science.

Student Performance in Mathematics and Science

The rapid growth of the school-aged population and changing discourses regarding racial categories have made it more difficult to classify Black or African American, immigrant, and language groups of African descent. Numerous subgroups have formed, and many have sought unique demographic labels. Most national trend studies of mathematics and science performance are not conducted at this level of detail.

Different NAEP programs are associated with mathematics. The two major programs are the long-term trend study and the main NAEP study. The trend study was initiated in 1973 and has remained constant over the ensuing time period. The main study is subject to design changes in response to standards-based efforts. Only the trend study, which provides a longitudinal view of African American performance, is incorporated into the present review. The NAEP mathematics trend assessment is largely a basic skills examination. To allow measurement of performance trends, subsets of the same items have been a part of successive assessments. Some of the items have been included in each examination. As a result of this practice, the findings from nine NAEP trend assessments provide insight into how African American students' mathematics proficiency has changed between 1973 and 1999. NAEP mathematics proficiency scores are available for 1973, 1978, 1982, 1986, 1990, 1992, 1994, 1996, 1999, and 2003. (Because, at the time of the writing of this chapter, 2003 NAEP scores were not included in the trend study, they are not incorporated into this discussion.) Tests are administered to samples of students across the United States at the ages of 9, 13, and 17 years. Scale scores, which range from 0 to 500, provide a common metric for determining levels of proficiency across assessments and demographic characteristics. NAEP scores reflect student performance at five scale levels:

- Level 150: Basic Arithmetic Facts
- Level 200: Beginning Skills and Understanding
- Level 250: Basic Operations and Beginning Problem Solving
- Level 300: Moderately Complex Procedures and Reasoning
- Level 350: Multistep Problem Solving and Algebra

The performance-level categories were developed for the 1973 assessment and remained in use through the 1999 assessment. However, the language associated with these categories evolved and changed over this period. Thus, it is important for school administrators and teachers charged with making decisions about curriculum, teaching, and other relevant educational inputs to be aware that although this trend analysis may use language consistent with today's standards-based discourse (National Council of Teachers of Mathematics, 2000; Tate, 2004), the test items may not reflect the problem-solving and reasoning descriptions found in more recent standards documents and state content and performance assessment documents. With this limitation noted, NAEP trend analysis is a valuable gauge of student performance progress over time. Table 1 provides a summary of NAEP African American trends in mathematics from 1973 to 1999.

Mathematics performance among Blacks was higher at 9, 13, and 17 ages of age in 1999 than in 1973–1982. However, there has been no statistically significant change at any age level since the 1980s. The trend suggests that African American progress has slowed and that the gains achieved since 1973 have been more consis-

TABLE 1   NAEP Trends in Black Students' Average
Mathematics Scale Scores

Year	Age 9	Age 13	Age 17
1999	210.9 (1.6)	251.0 (2.6)	283.3 (1.5)
1996	211.6 (1.4)	252.1 (1.3)	286.4 (1.7)
1994	212.1 (1.6)	251.5 (3.5)	285.5 (1.8)
1992	208.0 (2.0)	250.2 (1.9)	285.8 (2.2)
1990	208.4 (2.2)	249.1 (2.3)	288.5 (2.8)
1986	201.6 (1.6)[a]	249.2 (2.3)	278.6 (2.1)
1982	194.9 (1.6)[a]	240.4 (1.6)[a]	271.8 (1.2)[a]
1978	192.4 (1.1)[a]	229.6 (1.9)[a]	268.4 (1.3)[a]
1973	190.0 (1.8)[a]	228.0 (1.9)[a]	270.0 (1.3)[a]

Note. Standard errors appear in parentheses. Data were derived from National Center for Education Statistics (2000).
[a]Significantly different from 1999.

tent on items that reflect low-level and basic skills mastery. Use of NAEP trend data to make school-level decisions is not recommended, since scores are based on samples of students and thus are considered estimates of all students' average performance. This uncertainty is reflected in the NAEP standard errors. This limitation noted, the NAEP mathematics performance trends suggest that Black students, in the aggregate, require additional opportunities to learn moderately complex procedures, algebra, reasoning, and multiple-step problem solving. Beyond the labels associated with NAEP performance levels, what does the NAEP trend study reveal about the scientific advancement of Black children? Clearly, the study indicates that algebraic understanding is underdeveloped (see also Kilpatrick, Swafford, & Findell, 2001; Rand Corporation, 2003). Other research in mathematics education suggests that concepts such as rational number, ratio, and proportions are serious obstacles to the mathematical development of children (Behr, Harel, Post, & Lesh, 1992). These concepts are foundational to algebra and some types of problem-solving tasks associated with the mathematics curriculum. It is reasonable to speculate that an increased focus in these areas of the curriculum is worth further investigation by researchers interested in the scientific attainment of Black students.

L. S. Miller (1995) examined the intersection of race and SES using data from the NAEP trend mathematics-testing program. Lubienski (2002) provided insights from the main NAEP mathematics assessment of race-SES intersections. The discussion here is limited to the NAEP trend analysis. Miller presented a secondary analysis of an unpublished Educational Testing Service report authored by Bernice Taylor Anderson. In this analysis, "did not finish high school," "graduated from high school," and "some post–high school education" were used as proxies for SES. The discussion included NAEP mathematics performance data from 1978, 1982, 1986, and 1990 by race and SES for 9- and 13-year-olds. Miller calculated that within-social-class gains for Blacks in both age groups were moderate to large between 1978 and 1990. Each SES group's gain estimates were positive in this comparison. The largest gain, of 23 points, was achieved by students classified as "9-year-old/parent did not complete high school." The Miller analysis indicates that the overall gains reflected in the Black trend data at 9 and 13 years of age were produced across all three SES groups. Unfortunately, because of the sample size limitations of the NAEP mathematics tests, it is difficult to determine the magnitude of the improvements in the scores of Black students at each parent education level.

The NAEP science trend study includes content and cognitive dimensions (NCES, 2000). The content dimension assesses students' knowledge of life science, physical science, and earth and space science. The cognitive dimension assesses students' ability to solve problems and conduct inquiries and their knowledge of science. There also is an assessment of students' understanding of the nature of science within the context of both the content and cognitive dimensions. A multiple-choice format is used to assess students' knowledge of science. As with the mathematics trend study, the knowledge and skills demonstrated by students are classified into five performance levels. At Level 150, students demonstrate knowledge of the kinds of scientific facts present in everyday experiences. Students performing at Level 200 have some degree of understanding of simple scientific principles. By Level 250, students demonstrate they can apply general scientific knowledge and understanding of life science and basic knowledge of the physical sciences. Level 300 performance is characterized by the ability to analyze scientific principles and data and a growing understanding of physical science concepts. At Level 350, the highest performance level, students can integrate specialized scientific information, including genetics and chemistry. Table 2 provides a summary of NAEP African American trends in science performance from 1973 to 1999.

In the 9-year age group, there has been slow growth since the inception of the NAEP science trend study, with performance nearing the point at which some understanding of simple scientific principles is occurring. Similarly, the 13-year group has exhibited a slow rate of growth; there is evidence of understanding of some simple scientific principles, but performance has failed to reach Level 250. In the 17-year age group, the attainment level has been just over Level 250 since 1986; at this level, students demonstrate consistent application of scientific information and understanding of life sciences and some basic knowledge of physical sciences. Reaching Level 300 is the next major challenge for Black high school students. Demonstrating the performance associated with this level, including analysis of scientific principles, analysis of data, and understanding of physical sciences, would reflect the skills and insights aligned with the science requirements of a college preparatory school experience.

**TABLE 2 NAEP Trends in Black Students' Average
Science Scale Scores**

Year	Age 9	Age 13	Age 17
1999	198.9 (2.5)	226.9 (2.4)	254.4 (2.9)
1996	201.9 (3.0)	225.7 (2.1)	260.3 (2.4)
1994	201.4 (1.7)	223.9 (4.2)	256.8 (3.1)
1992	200.3 (2.7)	224.4 (2.7)	256.2 (3.2)
1990	196.4 (2.0)	225.7 (3.1)	253.0 (4.5)
1986	196.2 (1.9)	221.6 (2.5)	252.8 (2.9)
1982	187.0 (3.0)[a]	217.1 (1.3)[a]	234.7 (1.7)[a]
1977	174.8 (1.8)[a]	208.1 (2.4)[a]	240.2 (1.5)[a]
1973	177.0 (1.9)[a]	205.0 (2.4)[a]	250.0 (1.5)

Note. Standard errors appear in parentheses. Data were derived from National Center for Education Statistics (2000).
[a]Significantly different from 1999.

Perkins, Kleiner, Roey, and Brown (2004) reported a positive relationship between secondary science and mathematics coursework and NAEP scores. The next section examines the scientific attainment of Black students using the secondary curriculum as a measure of advancement.

College Preparatory Opportunities in Mathematics and Science

Two correlates of student mathematics and science achievement that have been used in numerous studies of achievement are (a) increased time on task in cognitively demanding curriculums and (b) number of advanced courses taken in mathematics and science. Research indicates that African Americans and low-SES students are less likely to be enrolled in higher-level mathematics and science courses than middle-class White students (Oakes, 1990; Secada, 1992). Furthermore, African American students, as a demographic group, are consistently outperformed by White students on national assessments of mathematics and science achievement (Doran, Lawrenz, & Helgeson, 1994; Rodriguez, 2004; Tate, 2005). Again, the intention here is not to engage in a comparative discussion; rather, the goal is to highlight that a positive relationship between mathematics and science achievement and course taking exists across multiple data sets: NAEP, National Education Longitudinal Study (NELS), SAT, and ACT (Perkins et al., 2004; "Stubborn Racial Scoring Gap," 2004; Tate, 1997). However, in the context of discussing scientific attainment and coursework patterns, some comparative analysis is useful.

For example, Hoffer, Rasinski, and Moore (1995) examined the relationship between number of mathematics courses completed by high school students of different racial and socioeconomic backgrounds and their achievement gain from the end of Grade 8 to Grade 12. The findings indicated that when African

American and White students who completed the same courses were compared, the differences in average achievement gains were small in magnitude, and none were statistically significant. Moreover, none of the SES comparisons showed significant differences among students taking the same number of courses. These findings suggest that some of the racial and SES differences in mathematics achievement in Grades 9–12 are a product of the quality and number of mathematics courses that African American and high- and low-SES students complete during secondary school. A similar argument can be made in secondary science (Perkins et al., 2004).

In an extensive analysis of data gathered in the 1982 High School and Beyond study, data gathered in three High School Transcript Studies (1987, 1990, 1994), and additional data gathered in 1998, Roey and colleagues (2001) provided insight into scientific course-taking trends among Black students. Arguably, the most relevant data related to scientific attainment and course taking are those associated with advancement in the college preparatory track, which is an indicator of students' readiness for additional study in the sciences. Tables 3 and 4 summarize relevant

TABLE 3   **Percentages of Black Graduates Earning Credits in Mathematics Courses: Selected Years**

Course	Year of graduation			
	1998	1994	1990	1982
Algebra	63.56 (2.45)	64.99(2.63)	64.69 (2.43)	43.06 (1.77)
Geometry	72.46 (2.16)	58.13 (2.93)	55.78 (2.60)	29.26 (1.77)
Algebra II	52.36 (2.43)	43.90 (2.38)	40.61 (2.80)	24.18 (2.03)
Analysis/precalculus	12.73 (1.77)	9.72 (1.18)	6.11 (0.95)	2.27 (0.45)
Calculus	5.46 (1.64)	3.77 (0.60)	2.73 (0.54)	1.34 (0.38)

Note. Standard errors are in parentheses. Data were derived from Roey et al. (2001).

TABLE 4   **Percentages of Black Graduates Earning Credits in Science Courses: Selected Years**

Course	Year of graduation			
	1998	1994	1990	1982
Biology	93.22 (0.76)	91.78 (1.52)	91.05 (2.18)	72.93 (1.93)
Biology/chemistry	52.03 (2.10)	42.32 (2.63)	39.23 (2.24)	20.01 (1.45)
Biology/chemistry/ physics	15.64 (1.77)	13.34 (1.20)	11.97 (1.22)	4.89 (0.72)

Note. Standard errors are in parentheses. Data were derived from Roey et al. (2001).

mathematics and science course-taking patterns among Black students in the college preparatory track.

The most striking differences in the data occur between 1982 and 1990. Across the spectrum of college preparatory mathematics and sciences courses, the percentage of Black students earning credits increased dramatically. These increases reflect changes in state policies. In many states across the country, new standards and graduation requirements called for more mathematics and science credits (Massell, 1994; M. S. Smith & O'Day, 1991). While there was marked growth in higher-level mathematics and sciences (i.e., precalculus, calculus, and the biology/chemistry/physics combination) course credit generation, this end of the college preparatory track did not exhibit the same magnitude of change as the lower end of the college preparatory track in the period from 1982 to 1998. Completing precalculus or calculus and the biology/chemistry/physics combination provides a sound foundation for a wide variety of college majors. The next section reviews college majors as part of this discussion on scientific attainment.

College Student Majors

Trends related to college majors in the sciences and engineering provide another indicator of scientific attainment. During the decade of the 1990s, the number of Black students earning bachelor's degrees in science and engineering slowly increased each year. Table 5 provides data summarizing the period from 1991 to 2000, excluding 1999.

Since 1991, Black students have earned a larger percentage of science and engineering degrees at the undergraduate level. This positive trend is also present in the number of earned master's degrees in science and engineering. Hill's (2002) data can be used to calculate percentage distributions of earned master's degrees; these data indicate that, in 1991, Blacks earned 2.8% of the degrees in science and engineering and that slow, yet steady, growth continued through the year 2000, when the percentage distribution was nearly 4.7%. Overall, production of Black undergraduate- and master's-level science and engineering majors can be characterized as positive but incremental.

TABLE 5   Numbers of Bachelor's Degrees in Science and Engineering Earned by Blacks: 1991–2000 (Excluding 1999)

Field	1991	1992	1993	1994	1995	1996	1997	1998	2000
Science	17,758	20,069	21,884	23,630	24,683	26,005	27,368	28,380	30,400
Engineering	2,229	2,362	2,577	2,659	2,845	3,000	3,076	3,018	3,062
Total	19,987	22,431	24,421	26,289	27,528	29,055	30,444	31,398	33,462
	(5.6)	(6.0)	(6.3)	(6.6)	(6.9)	(7.2)	(7.4)	(7.6)	(8.0)

Note. Percentage distributions of earned bachelor's degrees in science and engineering appear in parentheses. Data were derived from Hill (2002).

158

Summary

The indicators examined in this section all reflect slow and steady progress during the decades of the 1980s and 1990s. The NAEP mathematics and science trend studies suggest that Black students are making progress in regard to basic mathematical and scientific concepts. However, the challenging concepts associated with the trend studies represent significant opportunities for student growth. Course-taking patterns suggest that significant progress has been made at the beginning stages of the college preparation curriculum in mathematics and science. Changes in state policy have resulted in many more Black students enrolling in algebra and, to a lesser extent, biology. As the cognitive demands of the curriculum increase toward calculus and completion of the biology/chemistry/physics combination, the percentage of Black students declines dramatically. However, the percentage of students completing this more rigorous sequence of mathematics and science gateway courses increased between 1982 and 1998.

Increases in state course requirements and the steady growth of Black students taking higher-level scientific courses have overlapped with a steady trend of Black students earning a larger percentage of undergraduate and master's degrees in science and engineering. Some may argue that these increases are small and not particularly significant in terms of the larger production of scientific infrastructure. However, this growth must be understood in light of the past. Before the 1954 *Brown* decision and many years after, the United States largely involved a segregated and transparent caste system wherein race greatly influenced all opportunity structures, including scientific attainment and advancement. The next section provides insight into this history.

POLITICAL ECONOMY, SCIENTIFIC EDUCATION, AND *BROWN*

Scientific knowledge has played a special role in the political and economic advancement of the United States. Trends associated with African American scientific attainment can be understood in light of the historical importance of science— and thus knowledge of science—in the United States. Separating African American scientific attainment trends from the history and politics of the scientific enterprise in America does a disservice to the progress that has been made to date. With some insights into the history of science in the United States and the politics of science and scientific opportunity to learn as a backdrop, post-*Brown* trends related to the scientific attainment of African Americans are decidedly more useful. The goal of this section is to briefly describe the role of scientific education in the political economy of the United States. Discussion also focuses on who has had access to scientific education in the United States and to what extent.

Scientific education has been central to the political economy of the United States since its inception. For more than two centuries, economists and public officials have argued that advancement of the country's business and commercial interests rests on a scientifically literate and capable citizenry. Thomas Jefferson (1954), in his *Notes on the State of Virginia,* argued for a limited public system of education. He proposed creating small districts of 5 or 6 square miles each that would have their own school and would teach reading, writing, and arithmetic. All residents of the district would be entitled to send their children 3 years at no cost, with additional years paid for by the parents.

Under Jefferson's proposed system, the highest-ranked boy whose parents lacked the fiscal means to pay for his education would be sent forward to one of 20 grammar schools for instruction in Greek, Latin, geography, and the higher branches of numerical arithmetic. The boys sent to grammar school were to take a trial or test, and the "best genius" was to be selected for 6 years of additional study and the "residue dismissed." In this manner, 20 of the best thinkers would "be raked from the rubbish annually" and educated at the public's expense. After 6 years of grammar school instruction, half of the students were to be dismissed and the other half, because of their superior intellect, were to be sent for an additional 3 years of study in the sciences at William and Mary, a college Jefferson envisioned as having a strong scientific focus in contrast to the theological curriculum dominant in this era. The point here is that Jefferson articulated an elitist scheme to support the educational advancement of great minds capable of contributing to the economic advancement of the state of Virginia and the country. Furthermore, science education was central to this plan.

In Jefferson's scheme, all of the great minds afforded an education were White men—most wealthy and a few from limited means. This vision of education would provide only a few individuals real opportunities to learn mathematics and science. Yet, in fairness to Jefferson, his plan was more open and democratic than the tradition of the time. According to Jefferson (1954), the objective was to provide an education adapted to the years, the capacity, and the condition of the individual. Jefferson was not the only thinker of his time with this particular outlook on education. Similarly, Adam Smith (1937) argued that commoners in a civilized society cannot obtain the same level of instruction as those of high social standing and fortune. Yet, essential aspects of education such as reading, writing, and arithmetic should be afforded to those of lesser economic standing before they begin their vocation.

Adam Smith (1937) called not only for the establishment of education "essentials" or academic standards but also for the implementation of a system of examinations for the purpose of economic efficiency. These examinations would provide the information required to assign or approve workers for appropriate vocations. Smith's view would prove prophetic in the history of American education. Testing has served as a vehicle to sort and control limited resources in a country fixated on scientific advancement linked to industrial goals (Heubert & Hauser, 1999; Lemann, 2000).

School Mathematics

School subject matter, in particular mathematics, has been central to discussions of industrial advancement in the United States. According to P. C. Cohen (1982), early on in American history mathematics was viewed as vitally important to commercial endeavors and the economic advancement of the nation. Moreover, mathematics was part of a political and economic worldview that gripped the nation and its leadership. In her history of the spread of mathematics in the United States, Cohen (1982) provided some insight into the political nature of mathematics:

> What people chose to count and measure reveals not only what was important to them but what they wanted to understand and, often, what they wanted to control. Further, how people counted and measured reveals underlying assumptions ranging from plain old bias—the historian's easy target, when it is detected—to ideas about the structure of society. In some cases, the activity of counting and measuring itself altered the way people thought about what they were quantifying: numeracy would be an agent of change. (p. 206)

Since this country's beginnings, mathematics has been viewed as a powerful tool for understanding the worlds of business, employment, housing, and other public goods and services. According to Kamens and Benavot (1991), arithmetic was introduced as a compulsory subject in the primary school curricula of the United States in 1790. Two themes are important in accounting for the initial adoption of arithmetic in the U.S. curriculum: first, its link with a progress-oriented worldview and, second, the political value of the analytical citizen as the dominant actor in the newly formed country. While interest in rudimentary statistics or "political arithmetic" as census-taking tools began in 17th-century England, the United States was the first country to embrace the subject of arithmetic as part of the school curriculum. Numeracy and literacy were linked to the process of political modernization and the development of citizens. According to Kamens and Benavot (1991):

> Numeracy became intertwined with the notion of societal progress in the early nineteenth century. Since the purpose of the republican institutions was to foster political and religious freedom and the pursuit of individual happiness in the aggregate, it was argued the effectiveness of existing social relationships in achieving these ends could and should be periodically assessed. Hence, institutionalizing progress as the goal of society also meant an ideological commitment to continuous societal evaluation and reform. (p. 147)

As a result of the ideological commitment to continuous societal evaluation and reform, counting and measuring were vital components of the republic for several reasons. First, numeracy proponents argued that political arithmetic was objective and opinion free. Thus, numbers could be used to measure social gains and to illustrate the need for community problem solving in arenas where progress and freedom were being impeded. Difficult social problems—from the spread of disease to alcohol consumption—could be analyzed in statistical terms. Second, because numbers were viewed as objective and value free, early advocates of political arithmetic believed they would be more powerful in political debates than rhetorical arguments or personal thoughts. Third, and directly related to the first two points, numeracy was vital because of the role of individual agency in the American political vision. Individual citizens were viewed as the source of action and problem solving in the community. Progress rested on this view of individual actors seeking to optimize self interest, properly understood (Kamens & Benavot, 1991).

However, there were limits. Most certainly, Negro slaves were excluded from the world of learning about numbers, yet they were objectified mathematically in numerous ways. Perhaps the most notable example of the intersection of mathematics, race, and political economy is found in Article I, Section 2, of the Constitution, better known as the three-fifths compromise. The proposal to count slaves as three fifths of a person predated the Constitutional Convention; it emerged as a response to the problem of taxation under the Articles of Confederation (Meyerson, 2002). Southerners did not want to pay taxes on the nearly 40% of the population who were enslaved, so they argued that slaves should be counted as one half or one fourth of "one freeman." A group of northerners urged that, at least for the purpose of taxation, a slave should be counted as the equivalent of a freeman. Ultimately, the 3 to 5 ratio was approved. The political, economic, and educational products of this decision and other practices and customs related to maintaining social inequality, such as post–Civil War segregation policies, remain in various forms to this day (Margo, 1990). The point here is that academic performance, family wealth, long-term health, and other indicators of social welfare, including scientific achievement, are intergenerational (e.g., Gadsden, 1994; L. S. Miller, 1995; Shapiro, 2004).

What should not be lost in a chapter of this nature is that access to mathematical literacy is vitally important to an active citizenry and the ability to understand debates related to political rights.[3] The Constitution still contains provisions that illustrate how numbers communicate political perspective and advance ideological goals. Mathematics is embedded in the very fabric of American political philosophy. Failure to understand mathematics and the role of mathematics in this democracy is a limiting condition with real consequences for individuals and underrepresented demographic groups (P. C. Cohen, 1982; Robinson, 1996; Tate, 1995). Clearly, mathematics, particularly school mathematics in the form of arithmetic, was linked to early notions of citizenship and modern political thought.

During the late 18th and early 19th centuries, knowledge in more advanced forms of mathematics such as algebra, geometry, trigonometry, and calculus was foundational to those seeking careers as surveyors, navigators, and military leaders (Tolley, 2003). Advanced mathematical topics conferred a collegiate status on institutions offering this academic course of study. Moreover, this course of study was linked to vocational and economic opportunity and was part of the Jeffersonian view of "nation": selecting a few White men capable of contributing to society's advancement and then providing them a strong academic preparation in mathematics. This approach to mathematics education is closely associated with Eurocentric philosophies of elitism and social stratification (Joseph, 1987). Specifically, if mathematics were in any way associated with non-Europeans, this would imply that these individuals were capable of creating and leading their own technology-based economies or able to contribute to political thought and governance. The notion of African American contributions to business leadership and political advancement was clearly counter to the prevailing cultural ethos of Jefferson's era and the subsequent post–Civil War Jim Crow ideology (Woodward, 1974).

School Science

Science as a school subject shared similarities with mathematics, but there were some distinct differences. Both mathematics and science had broad support from Thomas Jefferson for the same reason: enhancing the progress of a developing nation (Hurd, 1997). During his tenure as vice president, Jefferson noticed that science was not part of the schooling experience. He sought congressional support to fund the writing of textbooks that reflected natural history and mechanics, but his request was denied on the grounds that school curricula were the domain of local communities. However, Jefferson was not alone in his support of science. In 1743, Benjamin Franklin founded the American Philosophical Society with the goal of advancing the development of new knowledge and improving the scientific experience; if well executed, this might result in discoveries benefiting the nation's agrarian economy and humankind in general.

Yet, unlike the case with mathematics, science teaching and learning for the masses faced three major objections (Kamens & Benavot, 1991). First, educators, political officials, and their allies perceived science as an applied, narrow subject not capable of developing loyal and morally upright citizens. Unlike instruction in the classics, science was thought to be devoid of the attributes required to produce reasoning facilities and moral character. Second, science was linked to secular movements and was viewed as undermining religious beliefs and authority. Third, political leaders and the dominant elite saw science instruction as capable of subverting the established political and social order. Those in positions of leadership claimed authority in part because of their insights into the natural and physical worlds. Thus, extending literacy and scientific knowledge to the masses would accelerate their desire for political power and social opportunity.

According to Tolley (2003), in the years immediately following the Civil War, White middle- and upper-class girls and boys had access to scientific texts and laboratory equipment; however, the picture for students in other ethnic groups and social classes was less certain. Tolley's historical perspective of girls in science also provides insight into the experiences of African American children of both sexes. For example, the postwar years afforded emancipated African Americans the opportunity to study science for their benefit; however, in spite of political rhetoric describing the benefits of scientific education for African Americans, the documentary evidence suggests that the distribution of educational resources was uneven in public school systems, thus contributing to differences in opportunities to learn science between White and African American students. In addition, in the South, just after the turn of the century, African American students studied the sciences in segregated public secondary schools; evidence for some areas indicates that students usually learned scientific concepts without the benefit of laboratory work (e.g., Memphis, Nashville, and Chattanooga, Tennessee, and Lynchburg, Virginia). In contrast, students preparing to be teachers may have had laboratory equipment and experiences as part of their teacher training institutions. Photographs of African American teacher candidates at Hampton Institute show them conducting experiments in chemistry and physics classes at the turn of the century.

While the 19th century witnessed significant conflict over science instruction and its role in public schooling, opposition to science education weakened in the 20th century as industrialists and policymakers viewed a growing international consensus on the importance of learning both science and arithmetic in schools as a key factor undergirding economic development. The intensity of this line of thinking grew throughout the century. Perhaps nowhere is this more evident than in the 1950s with the launch of Sputnik.

BROWN, THE NATIONAL INTEREST, AND ECONOMICS

The purpose of this section is to discuss three theories that potentially explain the changes in political philosophy in many parts of the United States from Jim Crow norms to notions of a society devoid of legal segregation. Some background information on the period under consideration is instructive. In 1957, two years after *Brown II,* the Soviet Union launched Sputnik, the world's first earth-orbiting satellite. *Brown* and Sputnik extend beyond a mere overlap of historical space. According to D. K. Cohen (1970), *Brown* and Sputnik share a common faith. Cohen argued that the Sputnik debates related to schooling were part of a long-standing belief that, in advanced industrial societies, occupational status is a function of intellect. He posited that this belief permeated both the *Brown* and Sputnik education-related debates. Both events evoked a deeply American concept (discussed in the previous section): that knowledge is power and is key to individual economic well-being and collective political advancement.

The general consensus among the U.S. mass media was that the Soviets' technological advancement was attributable to their education system. In stark contrast, the 1950s brought criticism of the American system of education, specifically scientific and mathematics education, from industry, university, and military officials. According to Kliebard (1987):

Just as Prussian schools were widely believed to be the basis for the victory of the Prussians over the Austrians in the Battle of Konigratz in 1866, so, implausibly, did the Soviet technological feat become a victory of the Soviet educational system over the American. (p. 265)

The media reported that Soviet children were exposed to the hard sciences and mathematics required for the global competition that was at the heart of the Cold War. The embarrassment and shock of Sputnik ignited an effort to advance scientific education in the United States, because it was thought that science was the primary means through which the American dream could be realized and preserved.

Moreover, this mathematics and scientific reform effort was seemingly connected to the political climate of the time. Devault and Weaver (1970) speculated that the post-Sputnik scientific reform effort benefited from the political climate associated with McCarthyism. Though unhealthy, McCarthyism, combined with an extensive pre-Sputnik scientific education lobby, made arguments for educational funding more attractive to legislators.

The political and economic interests associated with the Cold War would have a significant influence on investments in and the direction of scientific education broadly defined. According to Kliebard (1987), many influential figures in the United States sought to ensure a reform strategy that linked the best and brightest students to the opportunity structures created in science education. Such an argument was consistent with Jefferson's view of scientific education. For example, Vice Admiral Hyman G. Rickover, who is credited with the development of the atomic submarine, argued that American education had gone soft and that a misconceived notion of equality had led schools astray. Rickover argued that the gifted and talented of the country were neglected. Why is Rickover's position important to this discussion of political economy and African American scientific attainment? Admiral Rickover and officials from the College Entrance Examination Board and the National Council of Teachers of Mathematics sought to restrict mathematics reform to "college-capable" students (Devault & Weaver, 1970; Kliebard, 1987; National Council of Teachers of Mathematics, 1959). The appeal to constrain scientific reforms in education to gifted and talented students was built in part on a political philosophy that sought to protect the national interest.

While sharing a common American perspective about the importance of education, the timing of *Brown* and Sputnik put matters of social justice and global competition into the same political sphere. The political rationale for Sputnik education-related investment appears to straightforward: global competition, technological superiority, and the national interest. Some scholars have argued that the *Brown* decision was principled on a similar rationale.

Theory 1: *Brown* and the National Interest

Bell (1980) argued the interests of Blacks seeking racial equality would be accommodated only when they converged with the interests of Whites. In addition, he noted that the matter of school segregation and the harm segregation inflicted on African American students had been part of legal writing for more than over a century at the time of the *Brown* decision. Yet, prior to *Brown*, claims related to the harm of segregated schools were met with orders to equalize facilities or other educational inputs, orders that rarely met with compliance. "What accounted, then, for the sudden shift in 1954 away from the separate but equal doctrine and towards a commitment to desegregation?" (Bell, 1980, p. 96). Bell's hypothesis was that the break from the long-held segregationist doctrine had to be understood in light of not only growing concern among many Whites regarding racial injustice and immorality but also concern among White policymakers about the national interest.

Bell (1980) theorized that the *Brown* decision produced an important public relations victory in the struggle to minimize the spread of communist philosophy to third-world countries. In many nations, the credibility of the United States was damaged by the racial structures associated with Jim Crow doctrines and practices. Both the National Association for the Advancement of Colored People (NAACP) and government lawyers argued in the *Brown* case that eliminating segregation would bring credibility to the political and economic philosophies of the United States in the view of developing nations. Bell's theoretical position has been examined in various legal and political histories.

For example, Dudziak (1988, 2000) provided a comprehensive review of federal policy and public relations efforts related to civil rights issues during the Truman administration. Both policy and public relations efforts were framed at critical junctures with the international implications of U.S. race relations in mind. Moreover, amicus briefs prepared by the administration describing the potential negative impact of racial segregation on U.S. foreign policy interests impressed upon the Supreme Court the connections among national security, economic expansion, and upholding civil rights at home. Of particular concern was the need to align United States policy with democratic symbols of freedom, liberty, and justice. Failure to secure appropriate policy in the area of race relations and civil rights resulted in numerous public relations embarrassments for the administration and represented a challenge to the spread of democratic ideals worldwide. Ironically, many southern politicians and community leaders argued that the civil rights agenda was part of a communist effort to upset the way of life in the South. Yet, federal administrators sought in many ways to advance the civil rights agenda in order to minimize communist attacks on democratic ideals and to create an offensive strategy in support of democracy by advocating for the desegregation of schools and other accommodations.

Dudziak (2004) argued that the connections between *Brown* and the Cold War are so ubiquitous that it takes greater skill to explain them away than to place them in the historical narrative. She noted that legal scholars might object to a viewpoint in which *Brown* is seen as a Cold War case, because legal analysis is generally organized into doctrinal categories (e.g., equal protection clause or First Amendment). This is an excellent strategy for building a line of cases that inform a legal argument and writing briefs. However, Dudziak remarked that it is important for legal historians to think and analyze differently when traditional legal analyses construct barriers that potentially prohibit making connections across categories. In the case of *Brown*, she remarked that this was the long way of saying that *Brown* belongs in the Cold War chapter of American legal history. Dudziak's (1988, 2000, 2004) legal histories provide an empirical basis supporting Bell's argument that the *Brown* decision converged with the national interest at the time. Bell also offered a second theory to explain the shift in political support in favor of *Brown*.

Theory 2: *Brown* and the Political Economy of the South

Bell (1980) theorized that support for *Brown* was in part a logical response to a rapidly changing economy. He asserted that it was reasonable to assume those in control of America's capitalist enterprise understood that the South could not be transformed from a largely agrarian society to a more industrialized "Sunbelt" in the context of divisive conflicts over state-supported segregation. Since World War II, the Sunbelt (which includes the states of Florida, Texas, Arizona, and California and extends as far north as Virginia) has grown in economic and political influence in the United States as the shift in population to the South and West has increased from the 1960s to the present. Economic growth in numerous Sunbelt cities since the 1950s has stimulated interregional migration from the North; by 2000, Dallas, Houston, San Antonio, Phoenix, and San Diego were among the largest cities in the United States. Aerospace firms, oil companies, defense contractors, and other high-technology ventures were attracted to the Sunbelt by the prospect of cheaper labor costs and fewer labor unions. Labor costs aside, political stability is a necessary condition for consistent economic advancement. This is part of Bell's argument. Many industrialists in the South championed peaceful resolutions to desegregation orders. Norfolk, Dallas, Atlanta, and other cities demonstrate the point (Abbott, 1981; Bayor, 1989; Linden, 1995). A closer examination of Norfolk illustrates the role of commercial interests in the southern model of politics and race relations in the post-war era.

According to Abbott (1981), in the period surrounding the end of World War II, Norfolk's slow-moving municipal government had done a poor job in managing the city's resources. The city was described in local newspapers as dilapidated, with crowded ghettos, inferior public transportation, a dated airport, and deteriorating streets. The city council, whose majority had close political ties to the organization of Senator Harry Byrd, a key figure in the history of the Virginia battle over school desegregation, was viewed as second rate.

Senator Byrd's reaction to the 1954 *Brown* decision was to engineer the passage of a set of laws that moved Virginia to a course of massive resistance to the Supreme Court decision. In Norfolk, this resistance gained traction in the fall of 1958, when the U.S. District Court ordered the admission of 17 Black students to three junior and three senior high schools. The governor assumed control of the affected schools on September 27, locking the doors on 9,950 White and 17 Black students. Although a total of 36,000 Black and White students continued their education in segregated schools, attention focused on the students restricted from educational access as a result of the resistance strategy. The Norfolk City Council offered outspoken support for massive resistance and assigned the city's problems to ungrateful Blacks.

The crisis peaked in the middle of January, when the city council voted to spread the burden of the massive resistance by cutting off funding for segregated Black junior and senior high schools. On January 26, two local newspapers published a position statement signed by 100 leading business and professional men offering support for the preservation of public schools and legal compliance with the deseg-regation order. Analysis of this "Committee of 100" provides insight into the back-grounds of people involved in municipal reform movements in Sunbelt cities (Abbott, 1981). The men who joined as signatories were respected citizens of means and position but not of extraordinary wealth. Most of the businesses represented on the Committee of 100 shared a chamber-of-commerce perspective toward Norfolk markets and the health of Norfolk real estate. This orientation toward commerce proved successful. Seven days later, the schools reopened and the 17 Black students were admitted. The Committee of 100 is given major credit for resolving the deseg-regation crisis and, more important, redirecting Norfolk toward its primary goal of economic advancement.

The behavior and actions of the Committee of 100 reflect a major paradigmatic shift in political philosophy toward resolving racial issues in the South. According to Bayor (1989), the history of the urban South until well into the 20th century was more consistent with the pattern of the southern model—Jim Crow politics (see also Woodward, 1974). With few exceptions, Whites did not attempt to address or acknowledge Blacks' concerns or in any fashion legitimize them as a political enter-prise. Yet, the cities of the postwar urban South, with significant population growth and expanding economies, were led by coalitions of business and civic leaders work-ing to adopt a northern model of race relations that fostered stability and improved the possibility of cooperation among various racial/ethnic communities.

The northern strategy of intergroup relations appears to have informed numerous post-*Brown* desegregation implementation efforts in the Sunbelt. R. M. Miller (1989) posited that, after World War II, the most striking changes in the South's political economy were the decreasing preoccupation with White supremacy and a trend toward investment in and migration to this region. In addition, he argued that this shift made it possible for a successful civil rights movement. The shift in politi-cal philosophy was designed for the dual purposes of public image and fairness. Low-ering racial tensions made it easier to attract outside capital and to minimize outside agitators in local matters. This shift in philosophy should not be confused with a willingness to share power or spare Black neighborhoods from demolition. While the direct influence of industrialists on matters of equality of educational opportunity in the form of desegregation support is clear, it should not be lost that, on purely aca-demic terms, the South was not prepared for full-scale technological advancement.

In part, Bell's theory retrospectively suggests that capitalists understood the need for political stability and improved human capital in order to advance the Sunbelt. There appears to be sufficient evidence to suggest that Bell's theory is plausible. The human resource development component of the South was not sufficient from a capacity perspective for rapid technological advancement. It is doubtful that many business leaders in the South viewed the *Brown* decision as a mechanism to produce more educated Blacks who could serve as captains of industry in the Sunbelt. Yet, the benefits of political stability and good weather and the promise of expanding economic opportunities resulted in a great in-migration to the Sunbelt on the part of both Blacks and Whites, and reductions in out-migration were seen (Weinstein & Firestine, 1978). During 1955–1960 and 1965–1970, younger, more educated Blacks and Whites migrated to the Sunbelt, counterbalancing the region's older and less educated indigenous (largely rural and poor) population. As a result of these reductions in out-migration, it is instructive to briefly examine the academic state of affairs among Blacks and the relationship of education to economic well-being in the South in the years leading up to the *Brown* decision.

This examination is part of a third theory, one that represents a shift in that the first two theories attempted to explain why the government and capitalists may have supported *Brown*. The third theory offers an explanation of why it was imperative for African Americans to support a desegregation policy.

Theory 3: *Brown* and the Economics of Discrimination

Support for desegregation policy in education was not universal among African Americans in the postwar era (Bell, 2004; Edwards, 1996). However, most African Americans in the South had seen or experienced the discriminatory practices of Jim Crow segregation and its related influence on economic opportunities. In many respects, *Brown* was linked to economic advancement in that American cultural norms associate educational preparation with occupational potential (D. K. Cohen, 1970). However, discrimination can negatively influence this association. Margo's (1990) economic history of the South demonstrates the importance for African Americans to combat discrimination.

Prior to 1950 in the South, quantifiable indicators of schooling, measured by literacy rates, school attendance, and educational attainment, reflected significant racial differences (Margo, 1990). These differences extended to quality factors, as measured by educational inputs such as school funding expenditures, class sizes, and length of the academic year. While the racial gap in illiteracy and school attendance decreased steadily over time, racial differences in educational attainment remained large, declining only toward the end of this period. Margo (1990) estimated that the Black illiteracy rate continued to decrease during the first half of the 20th century, falling to about 25% in 1920. By 1950, he calculated that between 88% and 91% of southern Blacks were literate, as measured by the census.

With this information as a backdrop, Margo (1990) employed econometric techniques in an attempt to examine two frameworks for interpreting long-term trends in racial income differences: a supply-side, human-capital model and a demand-side, institutionalist model. The human-capital model focused on racial differences in the quantity and quality of schooling, theorizing that once these differences narrowed after World War II, relative Black status would improve. In the institutionalist model, by contrast, positive growth in the relative economic status of Blacks depended on changes in the economy that increased non-agrarian demands for Black labor. Margo concluded that strict enforcement of the "equal" portion of the separate-but-equal doctrine would have narrowed racial differences in school attendance rates, literacy rates, and test scores. Thus, violation of the separate-but-equal doctrine in education contributed to the relatively slower long-term economic progress of Black Americans.

In addition, implementing the separate-but-equal doctrine in education would not have been enough to fully equalize educational outcomes. Only a major redistribution of school finances in favor of Black children might have compensated for the intergenerational effects associated with family background that kept Black children out of school, impeded the spread of literacy, and negatively influenced the test scores of Black children. Margo's analysis of employment in the South during the first half of the 20th century, which involved the use of census samples, suggested that differences in quantity and quality of education limited Blacks' participation in the nonagricultural southern economy. Consistent with the human-capital model, a reduction in the racial gap in the quantity and quality of schooling would have improved the employment opportunities of southern Blacks, leading to higher earnings ratios prior to World War II.

However, the quantitative impact of racial differences in schooling was modest, and it was concentrated in certain industries. More and improved schooling would have increased the number of self-employed Blacks in white-collar professions. A major finding was that employment segregation increased after control for racial differences in schooling and other factors. Thus, employment segregation was not centrally a function of racial differences in human capital. Instead, the economic evidence strongly suggests that Black participation in the southern economy was constrained by discrimination and social norms. The state of discrimination led the NAACP to embark on the ambiguous litigation strategy associated with *Brown* (Bell, 2004).

The three theories just discussed each shed light on why certain groups may have joined the desegregation battle. These theories are plausible and not mutually exclusive. Each describes a shortcoming of discriminatory practices. The next section outlines how science played an important role in making discriminatory practices transparent in the legal struggle to desegregate schools.

BROWN AND THE SCIENCE OF PSYCHOLOGY

In this chapter, science and mathematics are described as being part of a vision of modern political thought. Both subjects have been viewed as central to the economic advancement and democratic progress of the United States. Thus, it should come as no surprise that the science of psychology and applied statistics played a role in the evidentiary base of *Brown*. The purpose of this section is to review the role of social science in *Brown* and related cases, with a particular focus on the evolution of educational opportunities in the post-*Brown* era.

Today, studies from the social science discipline, particularly studies focusing on student achievement and related information about student advancement, are commonplace in policy considerations and matters of law pertaining to education (Elliott, 1987). This fact is partly a product of advances in the social sciences and the ability of some social scientists to organize programs of study related to questions of policy and law. Arguably, the most important exemplars of this statement in the field of education are found in the litigation leading to *Brown*, *Brown* itself, and subsequent cases related to matters of segregation.

Before a direct discussion of this issue, some background related to legal thought and social science is useful. Faigman (2004), in his historical review of the integration of science and law, argued that the *Brown* decision paralleled a golden age of social science. Prior to the decision, legal theorists and scholars vigorously debated the merits of classical legal thought. According to Unger (1983): "Classical legal thought which flourished between approximately 1885 and 1940 . . . conceived of a law as a network of boundaries that marked off distinct spheres of individual and governmental power. Judicial authorities were thought to arbitrate conflict though impartial elaboration of a mechanical legal analytic" (p. 1670).

The legal realist movement developed out of dissatisfaction with principles of classical legal analysis according to which judicial decision making was viewed primarily as the product of reasoning produced through a finite set of determined rules (White, 1972). In contrast, many legal realists asserted that legal rules were too narrow and could not provide guidance or definitive answers to courts in specific cases (Llwellyn, 1931). Legal realism was closely aligned with the philosophical traditions of pragmatism, instrumentalism, and progressivism. With their links to New Deal politics, the realists advocated for identifying a coherent public interest and aligning political strategies to advance it (Lasswell & McDougal, 1943). To support the design of a political strategy, the legal realists advocated removing dogmas of classical legal theory they believed prevented legal reform and substituting a rational scientific method of legal scholarship (Livingston, 1982). Specifically, they contended that a more prominent role for statistical method and applications of the behavioral sciences in legal analysis would result in improved and more innovative forms of legal thought and, consequently, social policy.

By the late 1920s, legal realists were situated at three major higher education institutions: the law schools of Columbia and Yale and the Institute of Legal Study at Johns Hopkins. These scholars did not seek "truth" through the paradigmatic view of legal formalism; rather, they found truth by way of experience, using statistics as a vehicle. This movement was not without problems. The legal realists were enthusiastic converts to the growing field of statistical analysis; however, they had little understanding of it and little desire to collect data or conduct the analyses required to make sense of the complex situations in which they were interested (Faigman, 2004). According to Faigman (2004), there was a more severe problem:

The realists saw social science as a tool in the Progressives' political battles and as a tool for promoting their reform agenda. Past reform efforts failed, they believed, because of an absence of data. Therefore, data were needed to support reform efforts already in the works. Ordinarily, data collection reveals the need of reform. The realists already knew what needed reforming. The data merely filled the details and confirmed the need for action. . . . The basic premise of their work was that if facts were known about extant social conditions, reform would naturally follow. Therefore, if research did not support immediate reform, it was not worth doing. The realists thought that data that did not conform to their view of society were little more than an "irrelevant jumble of figures." (p. 119)

While the political and statistical reasoning of legal realists involved clear flaws, their orientation toward pragmatic policy reform, iconoclastic historiography, and rigorous analytic jurisprudence appears in mature forms of social and political theory (Livingston, 1982). Moreover, the social science orientation of the legal realists proved useful to NAACP lawyers battling to overturn the 1896 *Plessy v. Ferguson* decision. The "separate-but-equal" doctrine of *Plessy* reflected the prevailing social temperament, a belief in the inherent inferiority of African Americans, and directly related to this belief the appropriateness of limited access to valuable social goods— education, accommodations, and economic marketplace and political participation. The NAACP lawyers, under the leadership of Charles Hamilton Houston, former dean of the Howard University Law School, sought to overturn *Plessy* using a meta-strategy of social engineering vis-à-vis litigation. During his tenure as chief counsel of the NAACP, Houston hired Thurgood Marshall, his former student at Howard, to assist in the implementation of the social engineering strategy. Ultimately, Marshall replaced his mentor as chief counsel, but he continued on the course charted by Houston and the Margold plan.

The Margold strategy was clear and to the point. The NAACP would attack *Plessy* by seeking specific enforcement of its doctrine. Instead of seeking integration, they demanded that the law be fulfilled. This strategy required expert testimony and evidence drawn from economics and sociology. In *Sweat v. Painter* and *McLaurin v. Oklahoma State Regents for Higher Education* (1950), Marshall relied on systemic attacks on segregation; such arguments were focused on broad-based incriminations best supported by combinations of sociological and economic evidence.

For example, in *Sweat v. Painter*, the NAACP legal team represented Herman Sweat. Sweat applied for admission to the law school at the University of Texas at Austin. He was denied admission to the state-supported school solely because of his race and the associated state law that restricted Negroes from attending. He was offered, but refused, admission to a separate law school created by the state legislature while the case proceeded to trial. The state had established this new school for Negroes. It is here that the research methods and techniques of economics and sociology proved useful in the trial. The data on the two law schools reflected clear inequalities. The University of Texas Law School had 16 full-time and 3 part-time professors, 850 students, a library of 65,000 volumes, a law review, moot court facilities, scholarship funds, an Order of the Coif honor society, many influential and recognized alumni, a significant tradition, and public acclaim. The separate law school for Negroes had 5 full-time professors, 23 students, a library of 16,500 volumes, a practice court, a legal aid association, and one alumnus admitted to the Texas Bar. Furthermore, it excluded from its student body members of racial groups that totaled 85% of the population of Texas, including most of the attorneys, witnesses, jurors, judges, and other public officials with whom Sweat would interact as a member of the Texas Bar.

During the trial, the state objected to Marshall's use of scientific evidence to illustrate that segregation was scientifically unjustified and socially harmful (Faigman, 2004). The state attempted to limit the discussion to the educational offerings. The judge permitted the use of scientific evidence. Despite victory in this case and in *McLaurin v. Oklahoma*, the NAACP legal team recognized the limitations of the Margold plan and the type of scientific evidence undergirding their attacks on *Plessy*. Continuation of the Margold plan would require significant fiscal resources and a tremendous investment of human capital. The effort to equalize resources related to public education—a good associated with the massive segregation machinery in the United States—was not realistic. The Margold plan, fully implemented, would have required a continuous state of litigation.

Instead, *Plessy* would have to be attacked on principle as harmful to individuals. A change in the legal strategy to focus on individual harm differed from the broader social effects arguments but was deemed timely and appropriate by the NAACP legal team. The evidence drawn from sociology and economics provided information related to the macro-level effects of segregation, but these disciplines lacked the epistemological tenets to make transparent the pain and suffering experienced by individual men, women, and children who were the victims of segregation. It was time for a paradigmatic shift from sociology and economics to social psychology.

Typically, legislative bodies examine models and evidence from sociology and economics. In contrast, courts are structured to evaluate evidence regarding a specific event or occurrence. Malpractice and accident cases, for example, involve proving that a defendant caused an injury, along with the fact and degree of the injury. Marshall stated that "if your car ran over my client, you'd have to pay up, and my function as an attorney would be to put experts on the stand to testify to how much damage was done. We need exactly that kind of evidence in the school cases" (cited in Faigman, 2004, p. 176).

On the recommendation of Robert Carter, a member of the NAACP legal team, the psychological research of Professor Kenneth Clark and his colleague and wife Mamie became part of the new litigation strategy. The Clarks used projective testing to evaluate segregation's effect. A commonly used projective psychological test is the Rorschach, or inkblot, test. Examinees are told to look at a series of inkblots and to indicate what each looks like or what it could be. Because the stimulus is ambiguous, examinees must envision their own structures. Therefore, thoughts, emotions, and habits of mind, some of which are unconscious, are projected into the descriptions of the inkblots. Rather than inkblots, the Clarks used dolls.

The procedures and results of the doll tests were reported by Clark and Clark (1952) as part of a larger scope of work focused on investigating the development of racial identification and preferences of Negro children. The participants in this study were presented with four dolls identical in every respect other than skin color. Two of these dolls were brown with black hair, and two were white with yellow hair. The dolls were presented in order—white, colored, white, colored—to half of the participants. For the remaining participants, the order of presentation was reversed. Participants were asked to respond to the following requests by choosing one of the dolls and giving it to the experimenter:

1. Give me the doll that you like to play with— (a) like best.
2. Give me the doll that is a nice doll.
3. Give me the doll that looks bad.
4. Give me the doll that is a nice color.
5. Give me the doll that looks like a white child.
6. Give me the doll that looks like a colored child.
7. Give me the doll that looks like a Negro child.
8. Give me the doll that looks like you.

According to the Clarks, Requests 1 through 4 were designed to reveal preferences; Requests 5 through 7 indicated knowledge of "racial differences"; and Request 8 provided self-identity information. Two hundred fifty-three Negro children took part in this experiment. One hundred thirty-four of the children tested formed the southern group. These children were drawn from segregated nursery schools and public schools in Hot Springs, Pine Bluff, and Little Rock, Arkansas. The children had no experience in racially mixed school settings. The northern group of examinees was composed of 119 children from racially mixed nursery schools and public schools in Springfield, Massachusetts. The children in the study ranged from 3 to 7 years of age. The ratio of female to male students was 137:116. The Negro students also were divided into three skin color categories: light (practically white), medium (light brown to dark brown), and dark (dark brown to black). The ratio of students categorized as light to medium to dark was 46:128:79.

A key finding of the study was that the majority of the Negro children preferred the white doll and rejected the colored doll. Slightly more than two thirds of participants asked to play with the white doll. Fifty-nine percent of the children selected the white doll as a "nice doll," and the same percentage indicated that the colored doll looked "bad." Only 17% of the children labeled the white doll as looking bad. Sixty percent of the children thought that the white doll was a "nice color," as compared with 38% for the colored doll. Many other results were derived from the experiment; however, these findings and some of the qualitative data in the form of unsolicited verbalizations were relevant to the type of individual harm argument Marshall and his colleagues sought to make in the *Brown* case. According to Clark and Clark (1952):

On the whole, the rejection of the brown doll and the preference for the white doll, when explained at all, were explained in rather simple, concrete terms: for white-doll preference—"'cause he's pretty" or "'cause he's white"; for rejection of the brown doll—"'cause he's ugly" or "'cause it don't look pretty" or "'cause him black" or "got black on him." (p. 560)

The findings in the Clarks' study and the research of other social psychologists provided Marshall an evidentiary base to argue the injurious effect of segregation on individual students' racial formation and identity. The NAACP brief to the Supreme Court included a lengthy appendix signed by 35 social scientists arguing that enforced segregation has negative psychological effects on members of the segregated group. Legal scholars have debated for decades the influence of this program of social science research on the outcome of *Brown*. Cahn (1955) warned:

In the months since the utterance of the Brown and Bolling opinions, the impression has grown that the outcome, either entirely or in major part, was caused by the testimony and opinions of the scientists, and a genuine danger has arisen that even lawyers and judges may begin to entertain this belief. The word "danger" is used advisedly, because I would not have the constitutional rights of Negroes—or of other Americans—rest on any such flimsy foundation as some of the scientific demonstrations in these records. . . . [S]ince the behavioral sciences are so young, imprecise, and changeable, their findings have an uncertain expectancy of life. Today's sanguine assertion may be cancelled by tomorrow's new revelation—or new technical fad. It is one thing to use the current scientific findings, however ephemeral they may be, in order to ascertain whether the legislature has acted reasonably in adopting some scheme of social or economic regulation; deference here is not so much to the findings as to the legislature. It would be quite another thing to have our fundamental rights rise, fall, or change along with the latest fashion of psychological literature. Today the social psychologists—at least the leaders of discipline—are liberal and egalitarian in basic approach. Suppose, a generation hence, some of their successors were to revert to the ethnic mysticism of the very recent past; suppose they were to present us with a collection of racist notions and label them "science." What then would be the state of our constitutional rights? (pp. 157–158, 167)

The debate regarding the importance of social science evidence in the *Brown I* decision is complex and probably irresolvable. Robert Carter and Thurgood Marshall argued that social science evidence was central to their case. Other legal scholars have argued that *Brown I* is, at its essence, a straightforward legal interpretation of the equal protection clause acknowledging that state-sanctioned segregation is an invidious policy and for that reason is unconstitutional. Thus, *Brown I* is supportable without the evidentiary base offered by the research of social scientists. What is not debatable is that social science evidence provided a context for understanding in part the conditions of segregated education and some of the associated effects. Moreover, psychological research and related techniques remained a central part of post-*Brown* litigation in the field of education. However, as Cahn warned, the science of psychology could prove harmful to Negro rights. The next section of this chapter explores the relationship between IQ testing and school segregation in the post-*Brown* era.

IQ TESTING, TRACKING, AND THE POLITICS OF KNOWLEDGE

IQ tests, developed by psychologists, have been used in a wide variety of settings to inform and guide social decisions. The histories of science and school desegregation are linked in that IQ testing was central in the decision-making strategies of school districts across the country in the post-*Brown* era. Unfortunately, the warning by Cahn (1955) proved prophetic as school district leaders used IQ tests to segregate Black and White students. Heubert and Hauser (1999) argued that history provides many striking examples of the misuse of IQ tests to make decisions regarding individuals. The post-*Brown* era has seen numerous examples of this kind of misuse. In the period immediately following the *Brown* decision, school districts around the country struggled with how to interpret the law and how to implement policies complying with desegregation mandates (Shujaa, 1996).

Problems involving interpretation can be at least partially attributed to *Brown II*. In handing down this decision, the Supreme Court failed to indicate its intended outcome. Instead, the court transferred authority for elucidating, assessing, and solving the desegregation challenge to school authorities. The role of the courts was relegated in many cities to a monitoring function. Numerous educational programs devised to appear as "good-faith" implementation efforts were instead clever strategies to resegregate within school districts. For example, the Miami and Houston school systems classified Hispanic Americans as White and bused low-income Black children to low-income Hispanic schools, and vice versa (Orfield, 1988). Other forms of segregation emerged as well, including disproportionate placement of Blacks into special education, "zero-tolerance" suspensions, and juvenile justice placements (Losen & Orfield, 2002; Verdugo & Henderson, 2003; Yeakey, 2003). It is not the intent here to review all of the maladies associated with the U.S. educational system. Rather, the goal is to review one form of segregation directly linked to the teaching and learning of mathematics and science: tracking.

The literature on tracking is extensive and complex. Ferguson's (1998) examination of the effect of schools on the Black-White test score gap included a review of the tracking literature. He concluded that the fundamental problem is not tracking per se. Instead, among critics and proponents alike, the problem with tracking is the expected quality of instruction for the students in question. If teacher assignments were fairly distributed, student placements were flexibly based on student growth, and teaching practices were student centered, then criticism might cease. In addition, if tracking advocates felt confident that the quality of instruction for high-achieving and gifted students would not decline under more heterogeneous placements, they might cease their protests. These remarks are based on the reasonable assumption that consumers of schooling desire to optimize all students' learning opportunities. Moreover, they reflect a belief that important human resources such as teachers can be distributed fairly. Both assumptions are questionable in the context of American schooling, where capital, tax structures, local control, neighborhood differences, and other factors influence educational inputs.

Interestingly, Ferguson's research in another study captures the realities of the distribution challenge. Ferguson's (1991) study of 900 Texas school districts demonstrated the importance of quality teachers and the unfairness of teacher distribution along racial lines. He found that teacher expertise, as measured by years of experience and level of training, accounted for about 40% of the variance in students' mathematics achievement during Grades 1 through 11. This amount was more than that accounted for by any other factor. In addition, the effects were so strong and the variations in teacher expertise so wide that, after control for SES, the achievement differences between Black and White students were almost singularly accounted for by differences in teacher expertise. Thus, discussions of the pros and cons of tracking must be coupled with concerns about teacher quality. However, there is another factor that must be considered in the tracking debate.

Ferguson's initial argument did not account for at least one socializing factor. For example, J. B. Smith (1996) examined the effects of early eighth-grade access to algebra on students' access to advanced mathematics courses and subsequent high school mathematics achievement. Her findings suggested that early access to algebra has an effect beyond increased achievement and that it may, in fact, socialize students into taking more mathematics. Thus, possession of the algebra credit in eighth grade is a credential that regulates access to more advanced coursework in mathematics. This credential increases both students' and educators' expectations about how the amount of mathematics students will take in high school. The process helps keep students in the college track longer and produces higher achievement as a result. What is clear from discussions of tracking is that tracking is important and that it represents a type of segregation with a legal history linked to *Brown*.

Tracking is a form of segregation. Green (1999) noted the 1960s and 1970s were a period of reduced broad-based support for equal access and equal educational opportunities, including school desegregation. One artifact of this era was a series of legal challenges opposing tracking on the basis that this practice helped to produce intraschool segregation.[4] A major legal challenge to tracking was initiated by the plaintiffs in *Hobson v. Hansen* (1967), who alleged that tracking in the Washington, D.C., school system fostered racial segregation of students because African Americans were disproportionately placed into vocational and lower academic tracks. Similar to numerous other school districts in the country, Washington, D.C., used a combination of standardized tests and teacher recommendations to organize students into academic tracks. The school superintendent argued that students were sorted on the basis of ability and educational need, not on the basis of race (*Hobson v. Hansen*, 1967). This argument is strikingly similar to Jefferson's desire to provide an education adapted to the years, the capacity, and the condition of an individual.

The court did not concur with the superintendent, and it ordered that the tracking policy be abandoned in the school district. Building on the legal precedent of *Brown*, the court argued that the tracking system was unconstitutional and denied African American and poor children their right to the opportunities afforded to White and more affluent children. In his written opinion, Judge J. Skelly Wright stated that, "even in concept, the track system is undemocratic and discriminatory. Its creator [the superintendent of schools] admits it is designed to prepare some children for white-collar, and other children for blue-collar jobs" (p. 407). The ruling was built on two major findings. First, African American students were disproportionately relegated to the lower track, thus segregating the student body. Second, the lower track was determined to be inferior to the academic track in terms of educational quality. The judge argued that students needed stimulating, enriching, and challenging instruction rather than instruction designed to serve perceived levels of ability.

Moses v. Washington Parish School Board (1972) was another major legal challenge to tracking. The schools of Washington Parish, in Louisiana, were segregated until 1965. In response to court desegregation orders, the school board created and put into place a plan to group students by ability. Similar to *Hobson*, the plaintiffs argued that ability grouping produced segregation within the district. Specifically, the plaintiffs alleged that the use of IQ tests to place students into tracks positioned African American students at a distinct disadvantage to Whites, a demographic group historically afforded an education superior to that afforded to African Americans. The Fifth Circuit Court concurred, arguing that the use of standardized achievement tests for classification purposes deprived African American students of their constitutional rights. As in *Hobson*, the court stated that homogeneous grouping was educationally detrimental to students placed into lower tracks, and African Americans constituted a disproportionate number of students in these tracks.

Another case heard by the Fifth Circuit Court, *McNeal v. Tate County School District* (1975), signaled a narrowing of the grounds to litigate questions about tracking. In *McNeal*, the court ruled that testing could not serve as the instrument to sort students into track placements in a desegregated system until the district had resolved the products of de jure segregation. The court argued that this provision was needed to ensure that the track assignment methodology, in this case IQ testing, was not based on the present results of past discrimination. This decision left open the possibility that curricular and ability segregation in public education might be constitutional. Schools could legally assign students to tracks that resulted in segregated racial groups as long as the segregation was a de facto outcome rather than an explicit goal of district policy (Green, 1999).

Between 1980 and 1992, the federal courts often deferred to school districts' policy guidelines allowing for organizational strategies and instructional policies such as tracking and ability grouping (see, e.g., *Montgomery v. Starkville Municipal Separate School District*, 1987; *Quarles v. Oxford Municipal Separate School District*, 1989). Green (1999) argued that judicial retreat from equal access and equal educational opportunity ended with the election of President Bill Clinton in 1992. He noted that the Justice Department position during the Clinton administration concerning tracking was that it represented the segregation tool of the 1990s. During this period, several cases, including *People Who Care v. Rockford Board of Education* (1994), *Vasquez v. San Jose Unified School District* (1994), *Simmons v. Hooks* (1994), and *Coalition to Save Our Children v. State Board of Education* (1995), produced rulings that called for the elimination of tracking practices in school districts. The first of these cases, commonly referred to as *Rockford*, is particularly important in regard to the work of educational researchers.

Rockford represented a shift from past tracking litigation—for example, *Hobson, Moses*, and *McNeal*—with respect to supporting evidence. Prior to *Rockford*, litigators largely concentrated on the discriminatory intent of school district tracking systems and the disproportionate assignment of African American students to lower tracks. While this strategy resulted in victories for opponents of tracking, the rationale produced by the courts was not consistent. Once a "biased" scientific instrument was eliminated (e.g., IQ testing), the practice of tracking could be resumed.

In *Rockford,* social scientist Jeannie Oakes accumulated a set of evidence from the district such as curriculum guides, district reports, enrollment figures (disaggregated by grade, race, track, and school), standardized test scores, teacher recommendations for course enrollment, discovery responses, and deposition testimony. This wealth of quantitative and qualitative evidence convinced the court that tracking practices skewed enrollments in favor of White students over and above what could be reasonably attributed to measured achievement. One example of compelling evidence produced by Oakes was an analysis of the student body by deciles of achievement as measured via test scores. Her analysis focused on student records rather than students themselves. A student record represented one student enrolled into one course. One student who enrolls in four courses will produce four student records. This method allows the analysis to account for students who take courses at different levels in numerous subjects of study. By way of example, consider the data in Table 6: There are not 2,271 majority students scoring in the ninth decile; rather, majority students scoring in the second highest decile enrolled into a total of 2,271 courses, 74% of which were advanced. Similarly, there were not 227 minority students scoring in the ninth decile, instead, minority students scoring at the second highest decile enrolled in a total of 227 courses, 70% of which were advanced.

The enrollment patterns of high-scoring and low-scoring students were very similar. Students at these ends of the spectrum were enrolled in advanced classes at similar rates. The greatest racial disparities occurred at the fifth, sixth, and seventh

TABLE 6   Course Enrollment Evidence From the *Rockford* Desegregation Case: Numbers of Student Records by Decile

Decile	Majority	Minority
Tenth (highest)	2,124 (86)	9 (81)
Ninth	2,271 (74)	227 (70)
Eighth	2,346 (61)	377 (59)
Seventh	1,788 (46)	446 (37)
Sixth	1,819 (31)	650 (24)
Fifth	1,367 (20)	667 (15)
Fourth	1,492 (15)	1,109 (13)
Third	1,166 (7)	1,103 (7)
Second	941 (5)	1,207 (4)
First (lowest)	633 (3)	1,212 (2)

Note. Percentages of students enrolled in advanced courses appear in parentheses. Data were derived from *People Who Care v. Rockford Board of Education* (2001).

deciles, where students were perceived as borderline with respect to advanced classes. Oakes's use of disaggregated test data to help create opportunity to learn in more advanced coursework represented a shift from the *Hobson, Moses,* and *McNeal* cases, in which IQ testing served as a tool to limit African Americans' access to more rigorous coursework. In each instance, the science of testing played a role in the legal and political debates related to the academic preparation of African American students. Thus, ironically, science as defined by psychology—and, more particularly, by psychometrics—has been vitally important in the legal battles and political challenges associated with opening the scientific pipeline more broadly to include African Americans at all levels. This irony is consistent with the modern view of political thought according to which scientific knowledge is part of the foundation for democratic debate, evaluation, and social decision making.

SOME THOUGHTS ON THE FUTURE

This final section offers a few thoughts about the future of African Americans and scientific education. Before this discussion, a brief review of the chapter's four central themes is useful:

1. African Americans' knowledge of science has improved over the past few decades (especially since *Brown*), but tracking practices in schools continue to limit their opportunities to learn more demanding forms of science and mathematics.
2. Science—and, thus, knowledge of science—has been central to political thought in the United States, including the country's political economy, strategies for economic expansion, and discussions of culture and humanity. Hence, knowledge of science is tremendously important for all groups and individuals in the United States, and it is vitally important to understand the nature and extent of African American scientific attainment (see Theme 1).
3. The rationale to support a *Brown*-like decision extended beyond notions of discrimination to include matters of national interest, technological advancement, and the economic expansion of the Sunbelt. In combination, these factors are strongly linked to the political logic associated with scientific preparation and advancement of the country's economic interests (see Theme 2).
4. Scientific knowledge, in particular knowledge in the areas of psychology and psychometrics, has had a special role in legal decisions about education, especially in the *Brown* decision and subsequent cases. Thus, *Brown* represents an example of the role of science in political and legal debates in the United States (see Theme 2).

The history of African American scientific education is closely aligned with the segregation narrative of the United States. Early in the history of this country, mathematics and science were positioned as key disciplines in the preparation of leaders. This leadership preparation was based on elite education schemes. Slowly, opportunities to learn science and mathematics were extended and encouraged. However, resources and investments in scientific education have varied significantly, and historically African Americans have not experienced the full array of advanced course-taking opportunities in science and mathematics, nor has the distribution of teachers been uniformly fair within or across school districts. However, policy changes appear to have had important consequences for scientific attainment in the past two decades. More African American students are engaging the challenge of higher-level mathematics and science courses. Similarly, African Americans are earning a greater percentage of science and mathematics undergraduate and graduate degrees.

Yet, significant future challenges must be faced if the promise of *Brown* is to be realized. Too many African American students fail to matriculate toward more rigorous and cognitively challenging coursework, and too many fail to perform at the highest levels of scientific achievement as measured by the NAEP. However, those African American students experiencing more rigorous scientific curricula and completing majors in mathematics and science represent modern-day Benjamin Bannekers. Their existence suggests that the nature/nurture thought experiment of Thomas Jefferson can be put to rest. Nurturing the scientific advancement of African Americans has borne fruit. Future discussions should build on the body of evidence suggesting that opportunity structures matter.

ACKNOWLEDGMENTS

This chapter was supported by funding from the St. Louis Center for Inquiry in Science Teaching and Learning (National Science Foundation Grant ESI-0227619). I would like to thank Robert Floden (editor), Frances Lawrenz (advisory editor), and William Clune (advisory editor) for their insightful comments.

NOTES

[1] The terms *Black*, *Negro*, and *African American* are used interchangeably throughout this chapter. The term *Negro* is used to accurately convey the language of a historical time period. In addition, the term *colored* is used in historical context.

[2] In this chapter, scientific education includes both mathematics and science unless otherwise noted.

[3] This is not to suggest that mathematical understanding would have helped slaves. Political access was not a reality during this time period. However, today it is clear that mathematical skills can serve to advance a political agenda (e.g., Tate, 1994).

[4] Tate and Rousseau (2002) discussed this case history with a focus on research methodology and scholarship in mathematics education.

REFERENCES

Abbott, C. (1981). *The new urban America: Growth and politics in Sunbelt cities.* Chapel Hill: University of North Carolina Press.

Anderson, B. T. (1991). *Mathematics proficiency of minority students, 1978–1990: A descriptive analysis of trend data for ages nine and thirteen by background factors.* Princeton, NJ: Educational Testing Service.

Bayor, R. H. (1989). Race, ethnicity, and political change in the urban Sunbelt South. In R. M. Miller & G. E. Pozzetta (Eds.), *Essays on ethnicity, race, and the urban South* (pp. 127–142). Boca Raton: Florida Atlanta University Press.

Bedini, S. A. (1972). *The life of Benjamin Banneker: The definitive biography of the first Black man of science.* Rancho Cordova, CA: Landmark Enterprises.

Behr, M. J., Harel, G., Post, T., Lesh, R. (1992). Rational number, ratio, and proportion. In D. A. Grouws (Ed.), *Handbook of research on mathematics teaching and learning* (pp. 296–333). New York: Macmillan.

Bell, D. A. (1980). *Brown v. Board of Education* and the interest-convergence dilemma. *Harvard Law Review, 93,* 518–533.

Bell, D. (2004). *Silent covenants: Brown v. Board of Education and the unfilled hopes for racial reform.* Oxford, England: Oxford University Press.

Black, E. (2003). *War against the weak: Eugenics and America's campaign to create a master race.* New York: Four Walls Eight Windows.

Brown v. Board of Education, 347 U.S. 483 (1954).

Brown v. Board of Education, 349 U.S. 294 (1955).

Cahn, E. (1955). Jurisprudence. *New York University Law Review, 30,* 150.

Clark, K. B., & Clark, M. P. (1952). Racial identification and preferences in Negro children. In G. E. Swanson, T. M. Newcomb, & E. L. Hartley (Eds.), *Readings in social psychology* (rev. ed., pp. 551–560). New York: Henry Holt.

Coalition to Save Our Children v. State Board of Education, 901 F. Supp. 784 (D. Del., 1995).

Cohen, D. K. (1970). Immigrants and the schools. *Review of Educational Research, 40,* 13–28.

Cohen, P. C. (1982). *A calculating people: The spread of numeracy in early America.* Chicago: University of Chicago Press.

Devault, M. V., & Weaver, J. F. (1970). Forces and issues related to curriculum and instruction, K–6. In A. F. Coxford & P. S. Jones (Eds.), *A history of mathematics education in the United States and Canada* (pp. 92–152). Washington, DC: National Council of Teachers of Mathematics.

Doran, R. L, Lawrenz, F., & Helgeson, S. (1994). Research on assessment in science. In D. L. Gabel (Ed.), *Handbook of research on science teaching and learning* (pp. 388–442). New York: Macmillan.

Dudziak, M. L. (1988). Desegregation as a Cold War imperative. *Stanford Law Review, 41,* 61–120.

Dudziak, M. L. (2000). *Cold War civil rights: Race and the image of American democracy.* Princeton, NJ: Princeton University Press.

Dudziak, M. L. (2004). *Brown* as a Cold War case. *Journal of American History, 91,* 32–42.

Edwards, P. A. (1996). Before and after school desegregation: African American parents' involvement in schools. In M. J. Shujaa (Ed.), *Beyond desegregation: The politics and quality of African American schooling* (pp. 138–161). Thousand Oaks, CA: Corwin Press.

Elliott, R. (1987). *Litigating intelligence: IQ tests, special education, and social science in the courtroom.* Dover, MA: Auburn House.

Ernest, P. (1991). *The philosophy of mathematics education.* London: Falmer Press.

Faigman, D. L. (2004). *Laboratory of justice: The Supreme Court's 200-year struggle to integrate science and the law.* New York: Times Books.

Ferguson, R. F. (1991). Paying for public education: New evidence on how and why money matters. *Harvard Journal on Legislation, 28,* 465–498.

Ferguson, R. F. (1998). Teachers' perceptions and expectations and the Black-White test score gap. In C. Jencks & M. Phillips (Eds.), *The Black-White test score gap* (pp. 273–317). Washington, DC: Brookings Institution Press.

Gadsden, V. L. (1994). Understanding family literacy: Conceptual issues facing the field. *Teachers College Record, 96,* 58–86.

Grant, C. A., & Sleeter, C. E. (1986). Race, class, and gender in education research: An argument for integrative analysis. *Review of Educational Research, 56,* 195–211.

Green, P. (1999). Separate and still unequal: Legal challenges to school tracking and ability grouping in America's public schools. In L. Parker, D. Deyhle, & S. Villeras (Eds.), *Race is . . . race isn't: Critical race theory and qualitative studies in education* (pp. 231–250). Boulder, CO: Westview Press.

Hernnstein, R. J., Murray, C. (1994). *The bell curve: Intelligence and class structure in American life.* New York: Free Press.

Heubert, J. P., & Hauser, R. M. (Eds.). (1999). *High stakes: Testing for tracking, promotion, and graduation.* Washington, DC: National Academy Press.

Hill, S. T. (2002). *Science and engineering degrees by race/ethnicity of recipients: 1991–2000.* Arlington, VA: National Science Foundation.

Hobson v. Hansen, 265 F. Supp. 902 (D.D.C., 1967).

Hoffer, T. B., Rasinski, K. A., & Moore, W. (1995). *Social background differences in high school mathematics and science coursetaking and achievement.* Washington, DC: U.S. States Department of Education.

Hurd, P. D. (1997). *Inventing science education for the new millennium.* New York: Teachers College Press.

Jefferson, T. (1954). *Notes on the state of Virginia.* New York: Norton.

Joseph, G. (1987). Foundations of Eurocentrism in mathematics. *Race and Class, 28,* 13–28.

Kamens, D. H., & Benavot, A. (1991). Elite knowledge for the masses: The origins and spread of mathematics and science education in national curricula. *American Journal of Education, 99,* 137–180.

Kilpatrick, J., Swafford, J., & Findell, B. (Eds.). (2001). *Adding it up: Helping children learn mathematics.* Washington, DC: National Academy Press.

Kliebard, H. M. (1987). *The struggle for the American curriculum 1893–1958.* New York: Routledge & Kegan Paul.

Knapp, M. S., & Woolverton, S. (1995). Social class and schooling. In J. A. Banks & C. A. McGee Banks (Eds.), *Handbook of research on multicultural education* (pp. 548–569). New York: Macmillan.

Lasswell, H. D., & McDougal, M. S. (1943). Legal education and public policy: Professional training in the public interest. *Yale Law Review, 52,* 203.

Lemann, N. (2000). *The big test: The secret history of the American meritocracy.* New York: Farrar, Straus & Giroux.

Linden, G. M. (1995). *Desegregating schools in Dallas: Four decades in the federal courts.* Dallas, TX: Three Forks.

Livingston, D. (1982). Round and round the bramble bush: From legal realism to critical legal scholarship. *Harvard Law Review, 95,* 1669–1690.

Llwellyn, K. (1931). Some realism about realism: Responding to Dean Pound. *Harvard Law Review, 44,* 1222–1264.

Losen, D., & Orfield, G. (Eds.). (2002). *Racial inequity in special education.* Cambridge, MA: Harvard Educational Publishing.

Lubienski, S. T. (2002). A closer look at Black-White mathematics gaps: Intersections of race and SES in NAEP achievement and instructional practices data. *Journal of Negro Education, 71,* 269–287.

Lubienski, S. T., & Bowen, A. (2000). Who's counting? A survey of mathematics education research 1982–1998. *Journal for Research in Mathematics Education, 31,* 626–633.

Margo, R. A. (1990). *Race and schooling in the South, 1880–1950: An economic history.* Chicago: University of Chicago Press.

Massell, D. (1994). Setting standards in mathematics and social studies. *Education and Urban Society, 26,* 118–140.

McLaurin v. Oklahoma State Regents for Higher Education, 339 U.S. 637 (1950).

McNeal v. Tate County School District, 508 F.2d 1017 (Ct. App., 1975).

Meyerson, M. I. (2002). *Political numeracy: Mathematical perspectives on our chaotic constitution.* New York: Norton.

Miller, L. S. (1995). *An American imperative: Accelerating minority educational advancement.* New Haven, CT: Yale University Press.